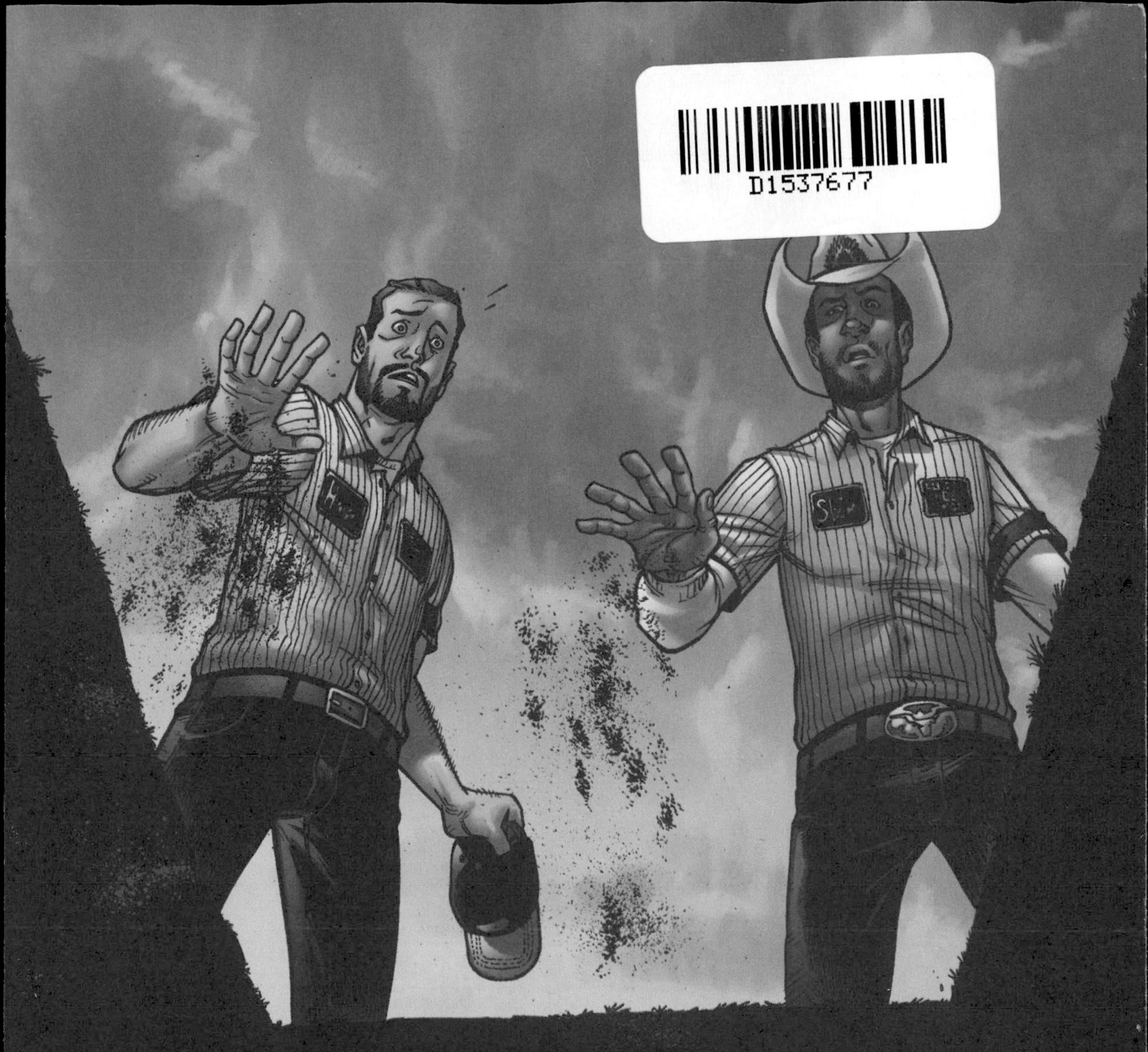

THE EXTERMINATORS
LIES OF OUR FATHERS

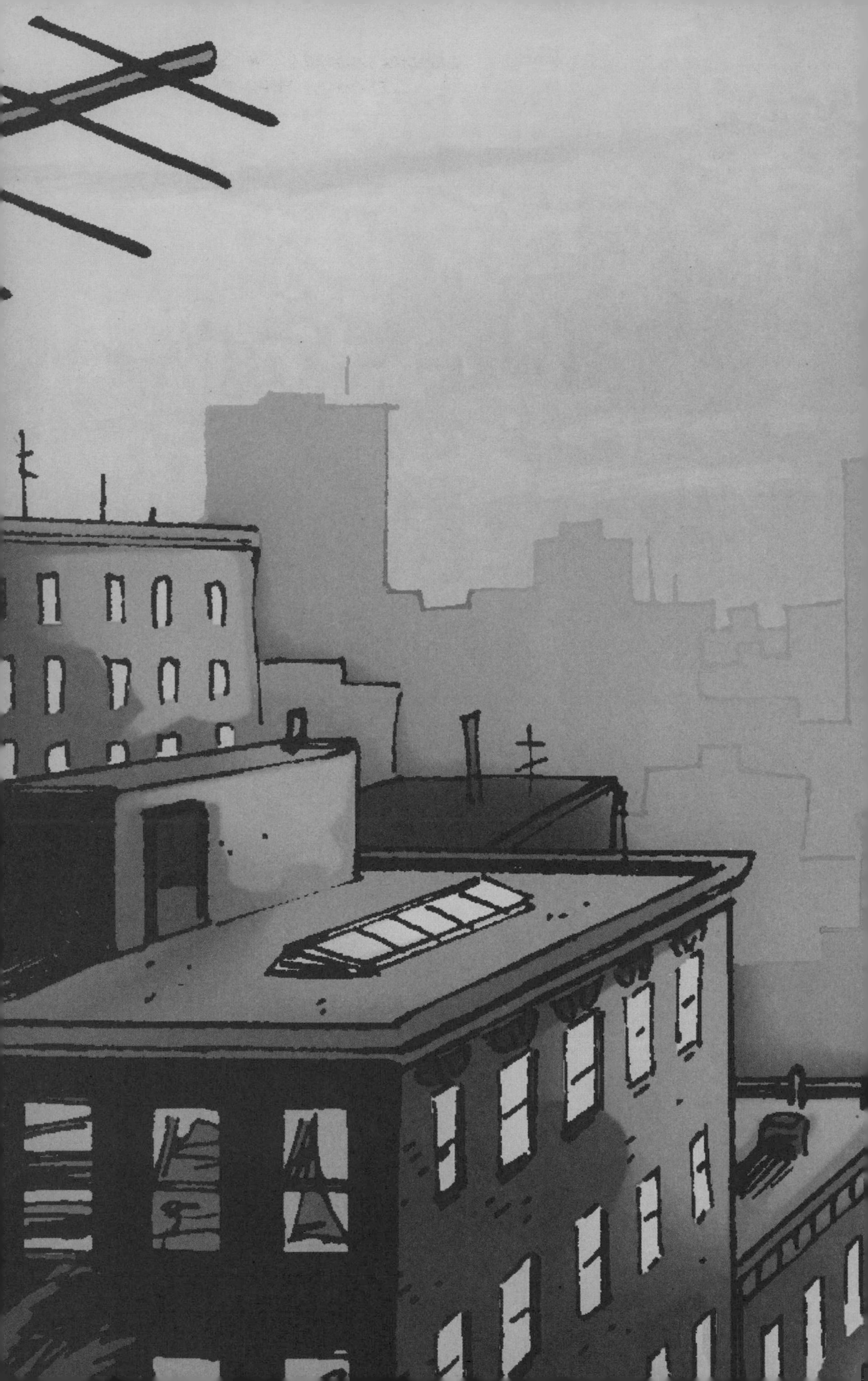

SIMON OLIVER WRITER

TONY MOORE   MIKE HAWTHORNE
JOHN LUCAS PENCILLERS

THE EXTERMINATORS
LIES OF OUR FATHERS

ANDE PARKS   DAN GREEN   MIKE HAWTHORNE   JOHN LUCAS INKERS

BRIAN BUCCELLATO   J.D. SMITH COLORISTS

PAT BROSSEAU LETTERER

PHILIP BOND   DARICK ROBERTSON ORIGINAL SERIES COVERS

INTRODUCTION BY BRIAN AZZARELLO

THE EXTERMINATORS CREATED BY
SIMON OLIVER & TONY MOORE

Karen Berger Senior VP-Executive Editor / Jonathan Vankin Editor-original series / Mark Doyle Assistant Editor-original series

Bob Harras Editor-collected edition / Robbin Brosterman Senior Art Director / Paul Levitz President & Publisher

Georg Brewer VP-Design & DC Direct Creative / Richard Bruning Senior VP-Creative Director

Patrick Caldon Executive VP-Finance & Operations / Chris Caramalis VP-Finance / John Cunningham VP-Marketing

Terri Cunningham VP-Managing Editor / Alison Gill VP-Manufacturing / Hank Kanalz VP-General Manager, WildStorm

Jim Lee Editorial Director-WildStorm / Paula Lowitt Senior VP-Business & Legal Affairs

MaryEllen McLaughlin VP-Advertising & Custom Publishing / John Nee VP-Business Development

Gregory Noveck Senior VP-Creative Affairs / Sue Pohja VP-Book Trade Sales / Cheryl Rubin Senior VP-Brand Management

Jeff Trojan VP-Business Development, DC Direct / Bob Wayne VP-Sales

Cover illustration by Philip Bond / Publication design by Amelia Grohman / Logo design by Ken Lopez

THE EXTERMINATORS: LIES OF OUR FATHERS

Published by DC Comics. Cover, introduction and compilation copyright © 2007 DC Comics.

All Rights Reserved. Originally published in single magazine form as THE EXTERMINATORS 11-16.

DC Comics, 1700 Broadway, New York, NY 10019 / A Warner Bros. Entertainment Company.

Printed in Canada.   First Printing.   ISBN: 1-4012-1475-4   ISBN 13: 978-1-4012-1475-3

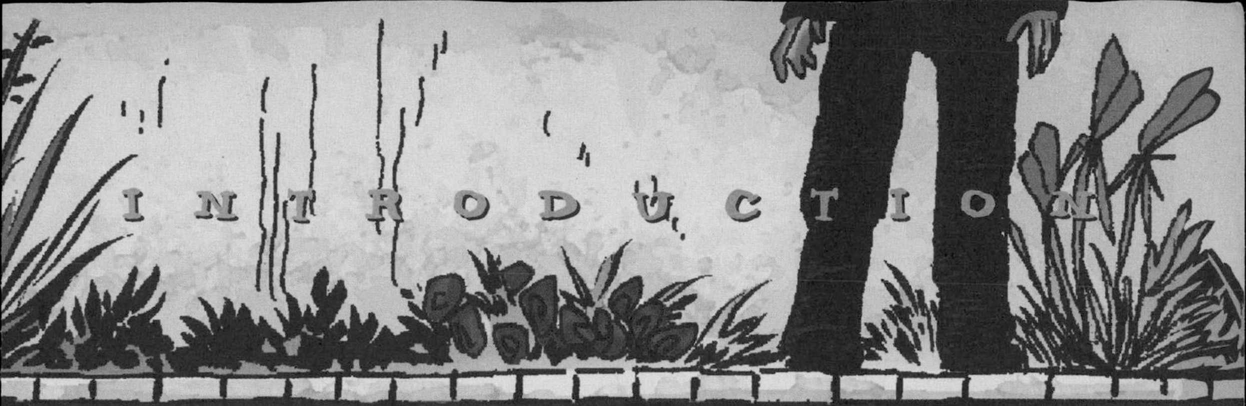
INTRODUCTION

Forty years ago, I found a dead rat in the backyard.

I remember it having dirty bright red fur (not saying it did, but that I remember it did) and an ugly, ugly frown with long, nasty teeth. I sat there staring at it for longer than I can remember because *I'd never seen anything like it before*. I mean this twice; I'd never seen a rat and I'd never seen a dead animal, so this was... I had no name for it. I was looking at something beyond my comprehension. It was one of "those moments" in life — when the world reveals itself and at the same time closes in and becomes more personal.

I remember sitting with it all afternoon. When I was done looking, I touched it. I picked it up; it was heavy and a bit stiff. Kind of damp, on the side that was on the ground. I held it. It didn't stop frowning. I didn't stick my finger in its mouth, but the nails on its clawed fingers were sharp, I can tell you that. And its tail was hard and rough, like my father's face in the morning.

My father. He came out the back door of the house, home from work, ready to light the grill. He saw me, way in the back of the yard. I held up this... I didn't know what it was, and showed him...

...The water coming out of the faucet was the hottest I'd ever felt in my life. He held my hands under it, soaping them up with a purpose. My clothes had already been stripped by my mother ("Jesus, didn't you see what he was doing?" "I thought he was playing, Frank!") and were thrown in the trash before I even came in the house. Once my hands were good, red and raw, he started the shower and scrubbed 'til the rest of me was too. And he made me understand: that was a rat. Never touch one. They live in garbage. They bite. They're dirty, and they have diseases that can kill you. *That can kill you...*

The next day he took me to the Natural History Museum. That was a special place, because that's where the dinosaurs were, and I had a thing for Thunder Lizards. This trip was different though. Rather than go straight to the giant bones, he took me down a hall we hadn't been before. It was filled with animals — not like the zoo, with animals behind bars — but behind glass, because they were stuffed. Or "Not alive anymore," as my father put it. There were lions in a painted desert, and polar bears on Styrofoam icebergs. Natural habitat stuff, very educational. But there was one window on his mind that he wanted on mine. We stopped. I stared.

It was full of rats. Not alive anymore, but stuffed in positions that made them look very, very alive. And menacing. On top of a turned-over garbage can, fighting with each other, eating rotten food. All of them with dirty bright red fur, and ugly, nasty frowns. And open, beady black eyes. This wasn't a diorama, this was real. Real, real scary. Because I now knew, they wanted to kill me.

Forty years later, I still believe that, because of my father. I doubt that was his intention. When writing this introduction to the incredible book you're about to read (believe me, THE EXTERMINATORS is a cunning, provocative slab of graphic fiction... extremely *graphic* fiction. It's not for the weak-hearted — or minded.) I called him and asked him if he remembered any of this. He didn't, but when I related the story he considered it good advice. The fact is, there is nothing in this world that scares me more. My father turned rats into nightmares that haunt me to this day.

Though for an innocent, sunny afternoon in my memory, a dead rat meant...

Azz 06.27.07

Brian Azzarello is a big fan of THE EXTERMINATORS. He is a multiple Eisner and Harvey award winner for series that include 100 BULLETS, LOVELESS, and HELLBLAZER, also published by Vertigo. He lives in Chicago with his wife, whom he desperately loves, and two cats, whom he pathologically needs.

CHAPTER ONE

COVER ART BY PHILIP BOND
INTERIOR ART BY MIKE HAWTHORNE

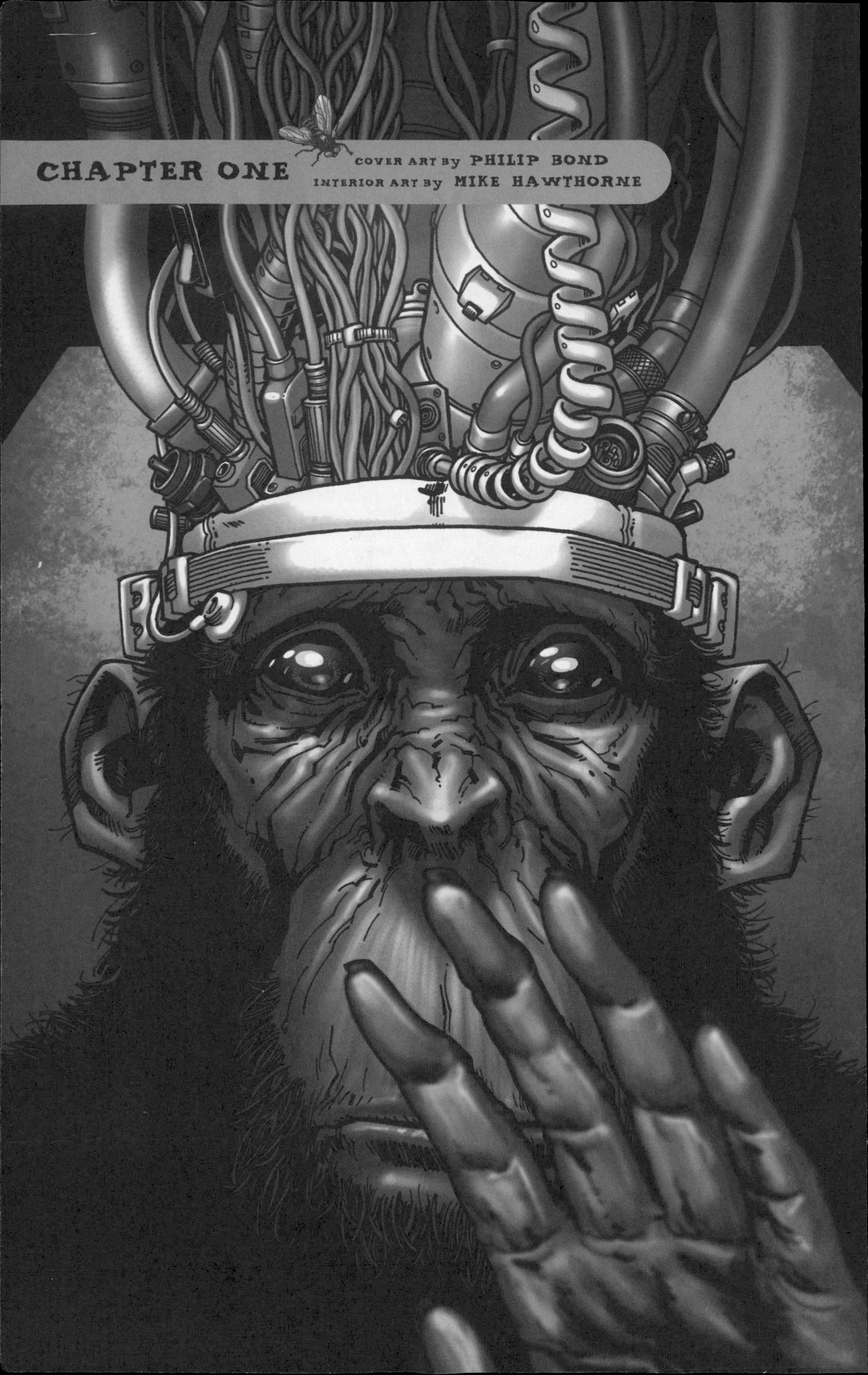

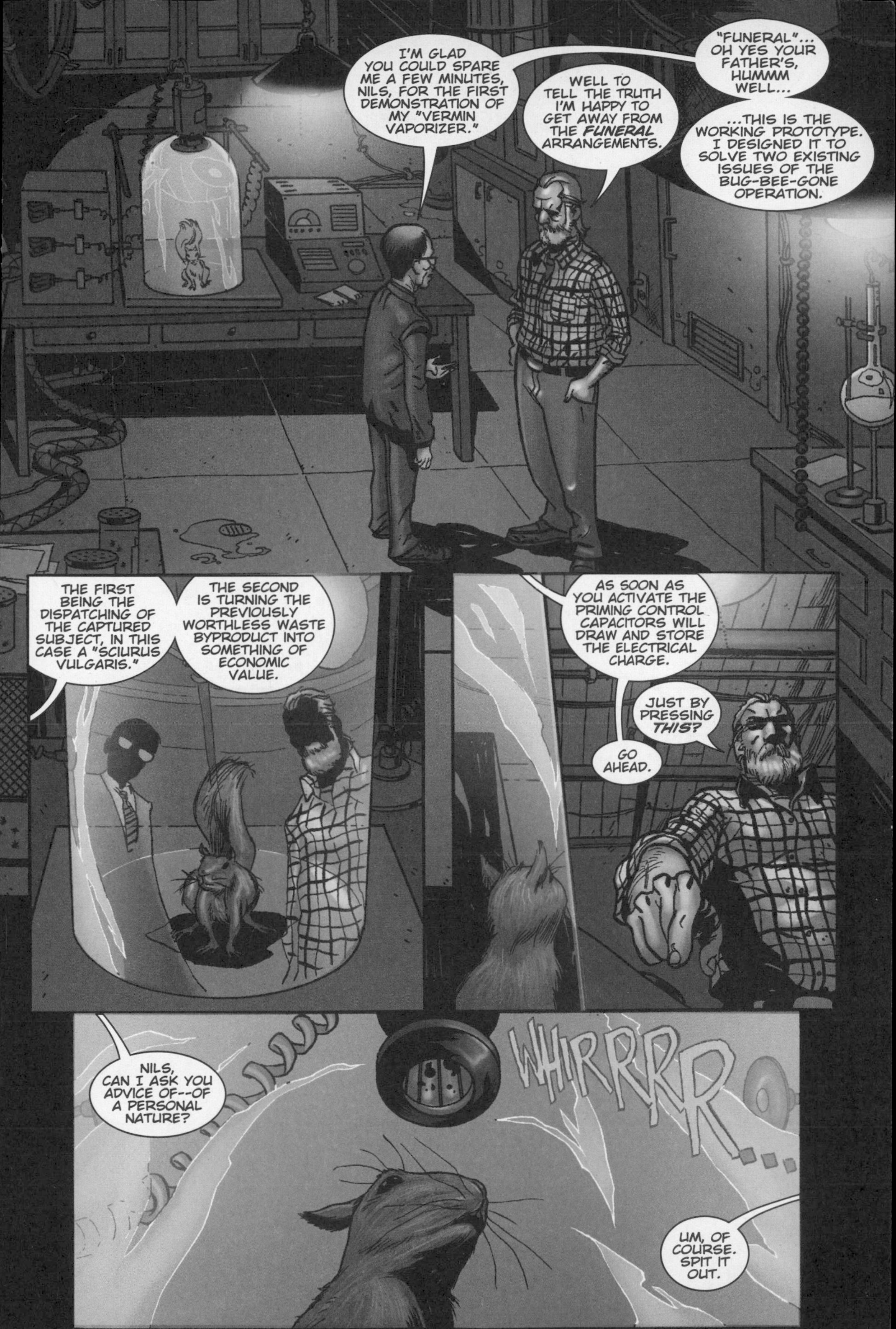
I'M GLAD YOU COULD SPARE ME A FEW MINUTES, NILS, FOR THE FIRST DEMONSTRATION OF MY "VERMIN VAPORIZER."
WELL TO TELL THE TRUTH I'M HAPPY TO GET AWAY FROM THE *FUNERAL* ARRANGEMENTS.
"FUNERAL"... OH YES YOUR FATHER'S, HUMMM WELL...
...THIS IS THE WORKING PROTOTYPE. I DESIGNED IT TO SOLVE TWO EXISTING ISSUES OF THE BUG-BEE-GONE OPERATION.
THE FIRST BEING THE DISPATCHING OF THE CAPTURED SUBJECT, IN THIS CASE A "SCIURUS VULGARIS."
THE SECOND IS TURNING THE PREVIOUSLY WORTHLESS WASTE BYPRODUCT INTO SOMETHING OF ECONOMIC VALUE.
AS SOON AS YOU ACTIVATE THE PRIMING CONTROL CAPACITORS WILL DRAW AND STORE THE ELECTRICAL CHARGE.
JUST BY PRESSING *THIS?*
GO AHEAD.
NILS, CAN I ASK YOU ADVICE OF--OF A PERSONAL NATURE?
WHIRRRR...
UM, OF COURSE. SPIT IT OUT.

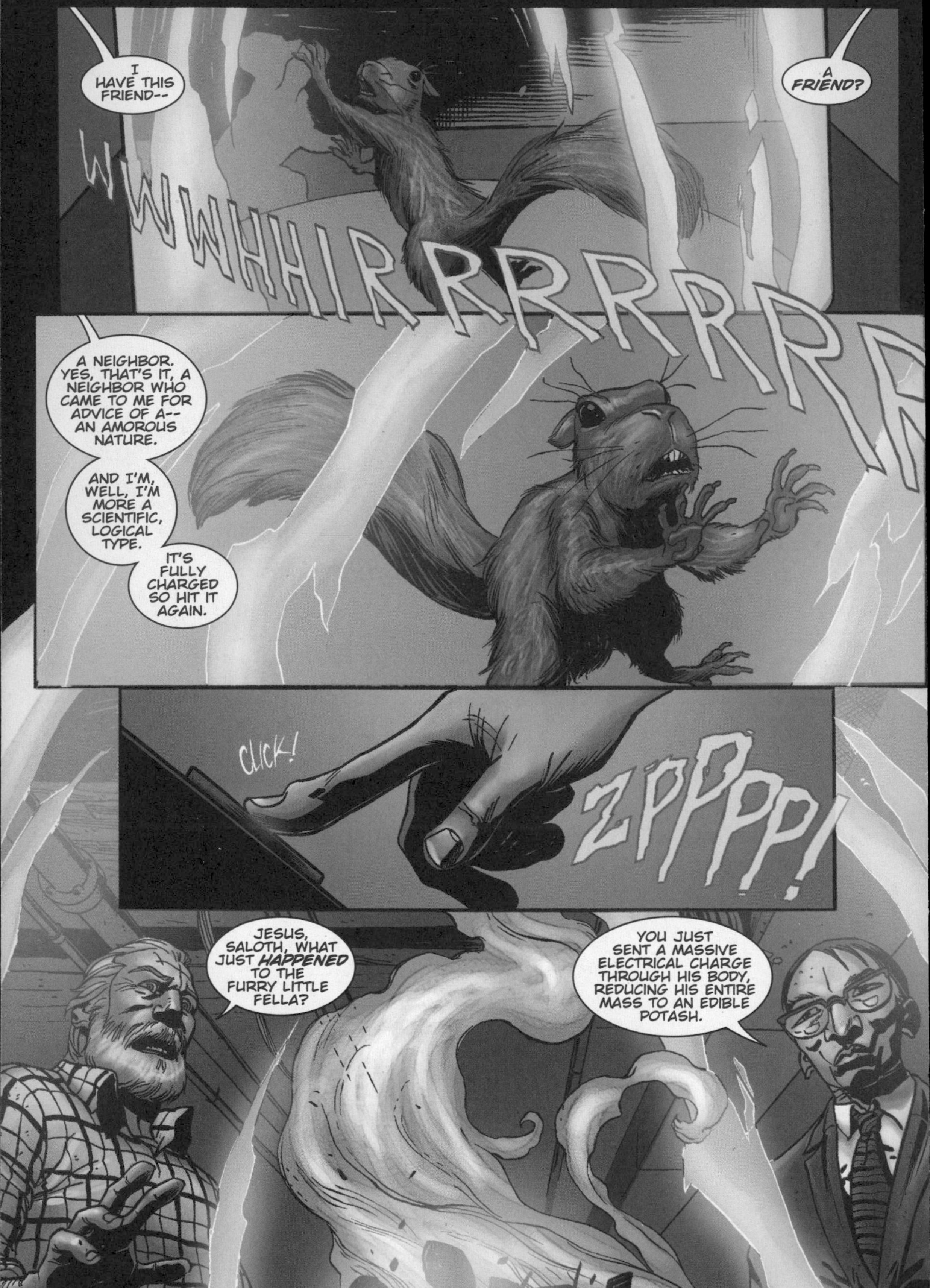
I HAVE THIS FRIEND--
A *FRIEND?*
WWWHHIRRRRRRRR
A NEIGHBOR. YES, THAT'S IT, A NEIGHBOR WHO CAME TO ME FOR ADVICE OF A-- AN AMOROUS NATURE.
AND I'M, WELL, I'M MORE A SCIENTIFIC, LOGICAL TYPE.
IT'S FULLY CHARGED SO HIT IT AGAIN.
CLICK!
ZPPPPP!
JESUS, SALOTH, WHAT JUST *HAPPENED* TO THE FURRY LITTLE FELLA?
YOU JUST SENT A MASSIVE ELECTRICAL CHARGE THROUGH HIS BODY, REDUCING HIS ENTIRE MASS TO AN EDIBLE POTASH.

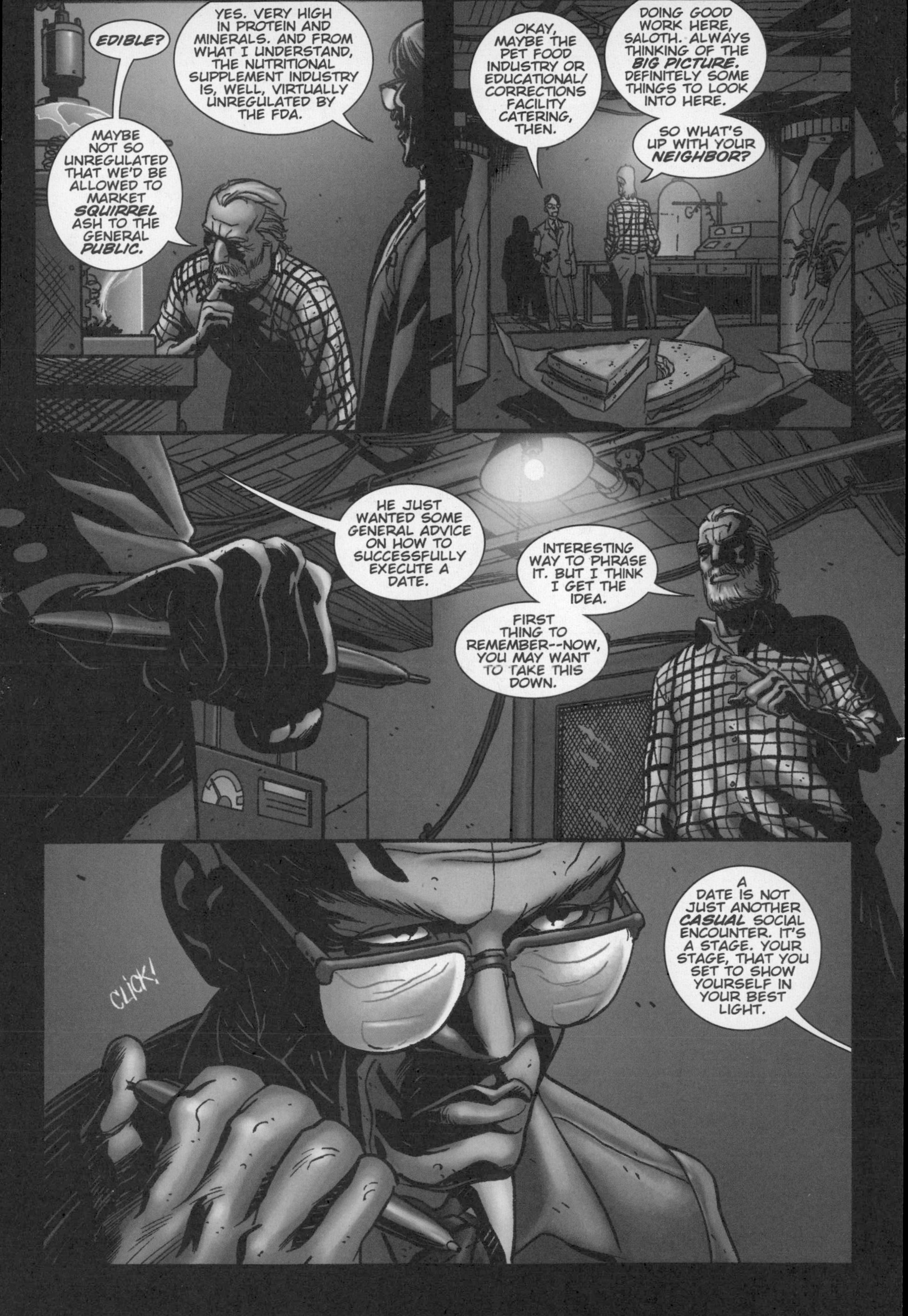
EDIBLE?
YES. VERY HIGH IN PROTEIN AND MINERALS. AND FROM WHAT I UNDERSTAND, THE NUTRITIONAL SUPPLEMENT INDUSTRY IS, WELL, VIRTUALLY UNREGULATED BY THE FDA.
MAYBE NOT SO UNREGULATED THAT WE'D BE ALLOWED TO MARKET SQUIRREL ASH TO THE GENERAL PUBLIC.
OKAY, MAYBE THE PET FOOD INDUSTRY OR EDUCATIONAL/ CORRECTIONS FACILITY CATERING, THEN.
DOING GOOD WORK HERE, SALOTH. ALWAYS THINKING OF THE BIG PICTURE. DEFINITELY SOME THINGS TO LOOK INTO HERE.
SO WHAT'S UP WITH YOUR NEIGHBOR?
HE JUST WANTED SOME GENERAL ADVICE ON HOW TO SUCCESSFULLY EXECUTE A DATE.
INTERESTING WAY TO PHRASE IT. BUT I THINK I GET THE IDEA.
FIRST THING TO REMEMBER--NOW, YOU MAY WANT TO TAKE THIS DOWN.
CLICK!
A DATE IS NOT JUST ANOTHER CASUAL SOCIAL ENCOUNTER. IT'S A STAGE. YOUR STAGE, THAT YOU SET TO SHOW YOURSELF IN YOUR BEST LIGHT.

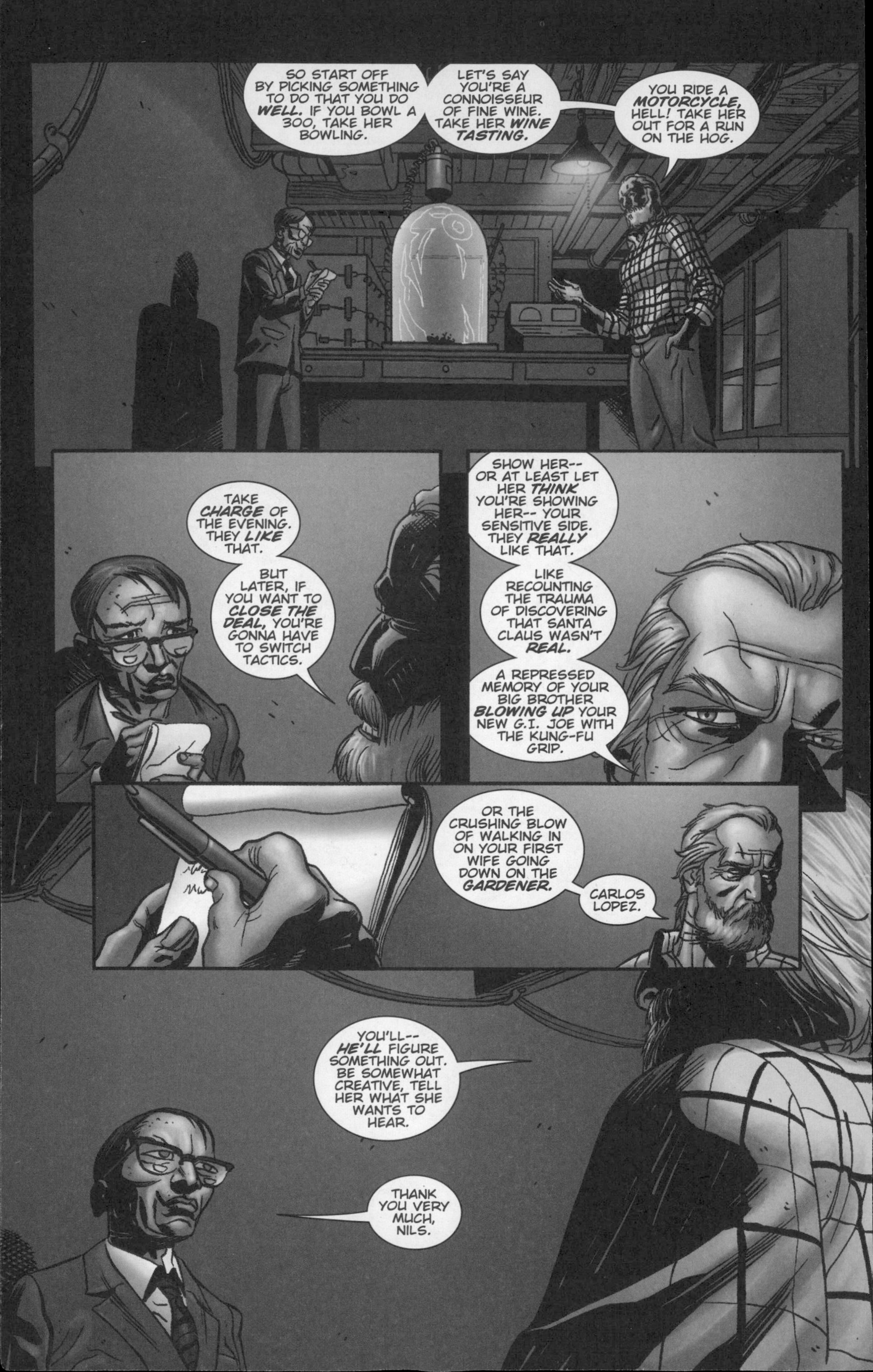
SO START OFF BY PICKING SOMETHING TO DO THAT YOU DO WELL. IF YOU BOWL A 300, TAKE HER BOWLING.
LET'S SAY YOU'RE A CONNOISSEUR OF FINE WINE. TAKE HER WINE TASTING.
YOU RIDE A MOTORCYCLE, HELL! TAKE HER OUT FOR A RUN ON THE HOG.
TAKE CHARGE OF THE EVENING. THEY LIKE THAT.
BUT LATER, IF YOU WANT TO CLOSE THE DEAL, YOU'RE GONNA HAVE TO SWITCH TACTICS.
SHOW HER-- OR AT LEAST LET HER THINK YOU'RE SHOWING HER-- YOUR SENSITIVE SIDE. THEY REALLY LIKE THAT.
LIKE RECOUNTING THE TRAUMA OF DISCOVERING THAT SANTA CLAUS WASN'T REAL.
A REPRESSED MEMORY OF YOUR BIG BROTHER BLOWING UP YOUR NEW G.I. JOE WITH THE KUNG-FU GRIP.
OR THE CRUSHING BLOW OF WALKING IN ON YOUR FIRST WIFE GOING DOWN ON THE GARDENER.
CARLOS LOPEZ.
YOU'LL-- HE'LL FIGURE SOMETHING OUT. BE SOMEWHAT CREATIVE, TELL HER WHAT SHE WANTS TO HEAR.
THANK YOU VERY MUCH, NILS.

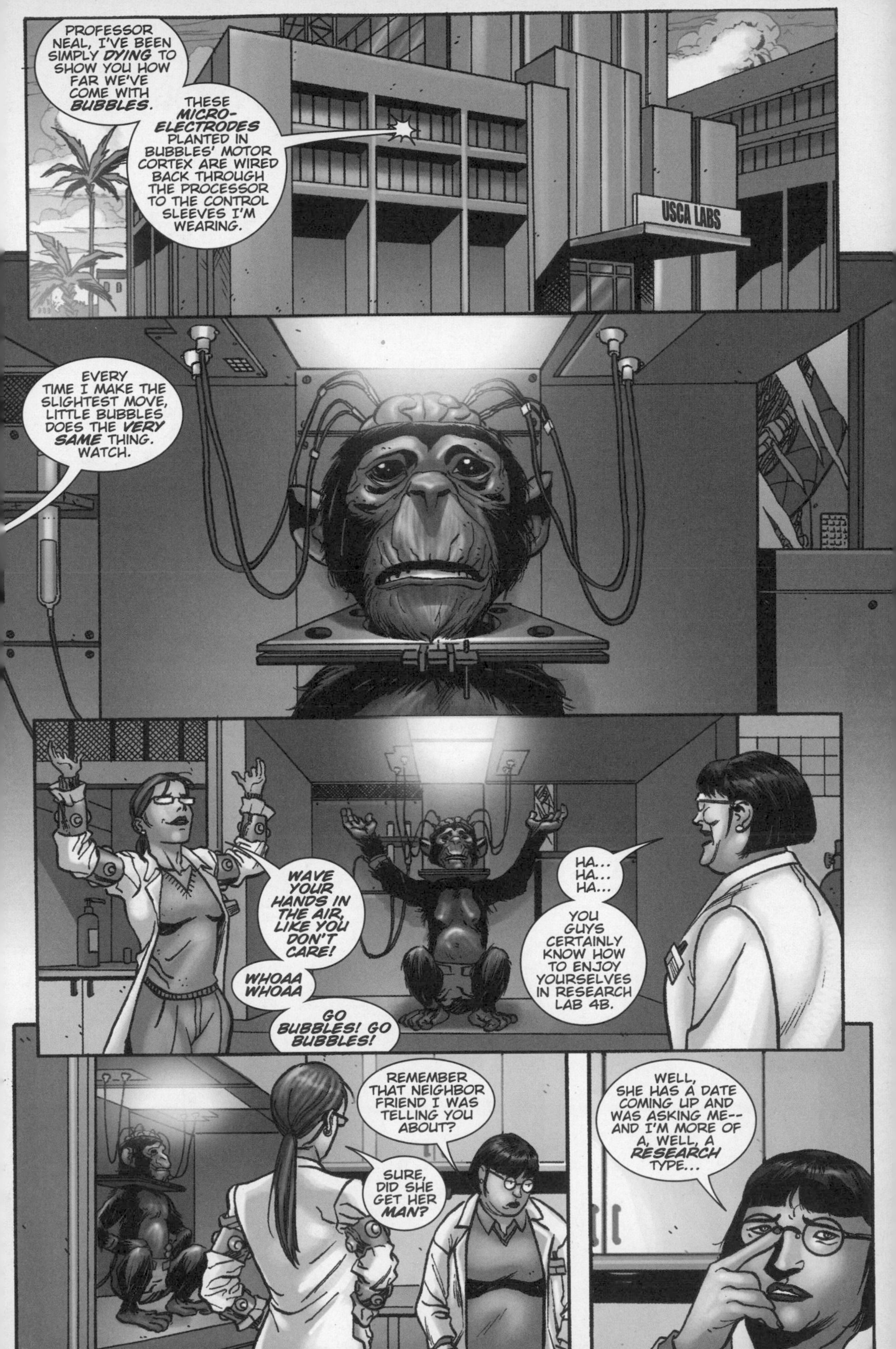

PROFESSOR NEAL, I'VE BEEN SIMPLY *DYING* TO SHOW YOU HOW FAR WE'VE COME WITH *BUBBLES*.
THESE *MICRO-ELECTRODES* PLANTED IN BUBBLES' MOTOR CORTEX ARE WIRED BACK THROUGH THE PROCESSOR TO THE CONTROL SLEEVES I'M WEARING.
USCA LABS
EVERY TIME I MAKE THE SLIGHTEST MOVE, LITTLE BUBBLES DOES THE *VERY SAME* THING. WATCH.
WAVE YOUR HANDS IN THE AIR, LIKE YOU DON'T CARE!
WHOAA WHOAA
GO BUBBLES! GO BUBBLES!
HA... HA... HA...
YOU GUYS CERTAINLY KNOW HOW TO ENJOY YOURSELVES IN RESEARCH LAB 4B.
REMEMBER THAT NEIGHBOR FRIEND I WAS TELLING YOU ABOUT?
SURE, DID SHE GET HER *MAN?*
WELL, SHE HAS A DATE COMING UP AND WAS ASKING ME-- AND I'M MORE OF A, WELL, A *RESEARCH* TYPE...

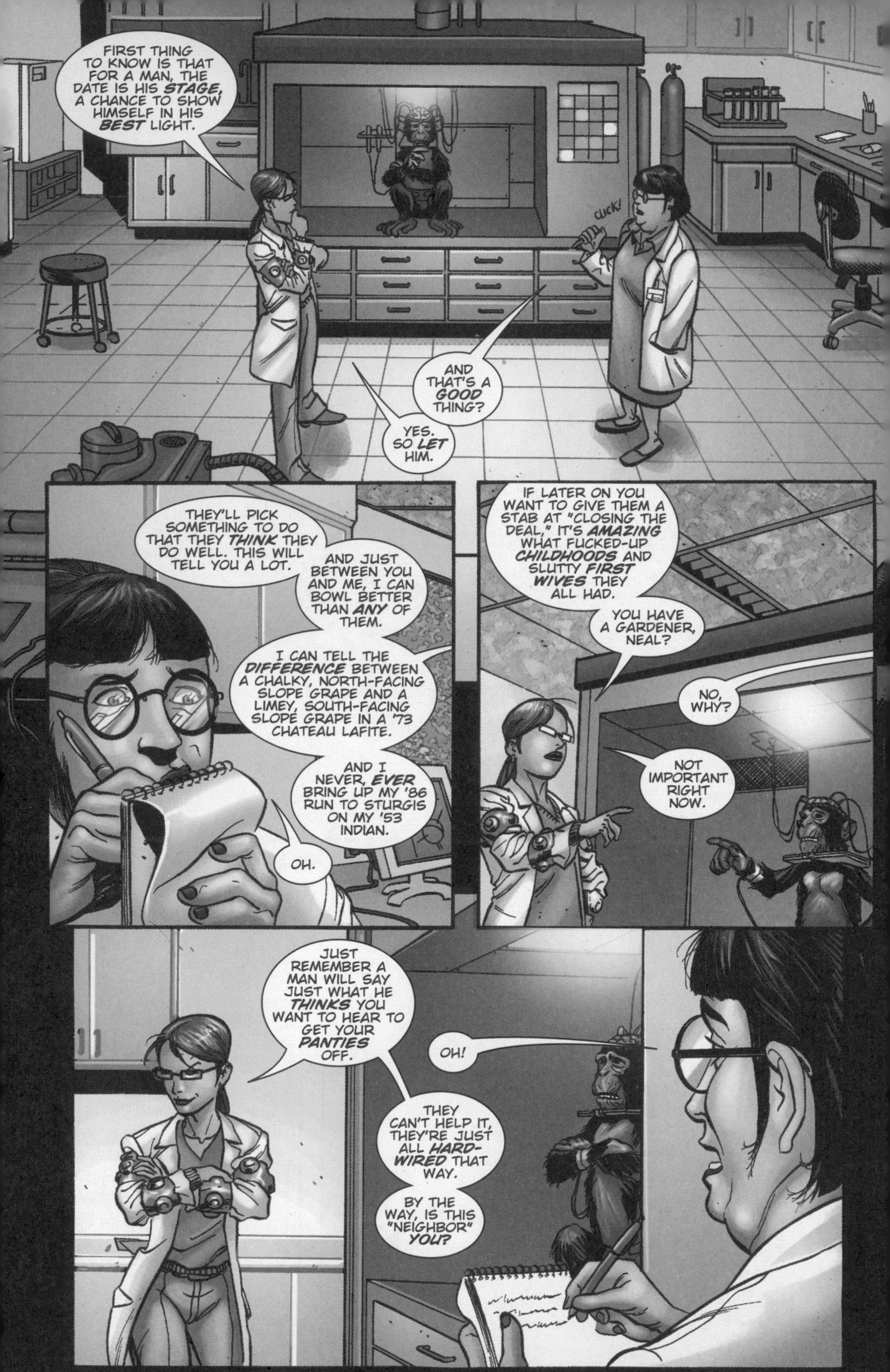
FIRST THING TO KNOW IS THAT FOR A MAN, THE DATE IS HIS STAGE, A CHANCE TO SHOW HIMSELF IN HIS BEST LIGHT.
CLICK!
AND THAT'S A GOOD THING?
YES. SO LET HIM.
THEY'LL PICK SOMETHING TO DO THAT THEY THINK THEY DO WELL. THIS WILL TELL YOU A LOT.
AND JUST BETWEEN YOU AND ME, I CAN BOWL BETTER THAN ANY OF THEM.
I CAN TELL THE DIFFERENCE BETWEEN A CHALKY, NORTH-FACING SLOPE GRAPE AND A LIMEY, SOUTH-FACING SLOPE GRAPE IN A '73 CHATEAU LAFITE.
AND I NEVER, EVER BRING UP MY '86 RUN TO STURGIS ON MY '53 INDIAN.
OH.
IF LATER ON YOU WANT TO GIVE THEM A STAB AT "CLOSING THE DEAL," IT'S AMAZING WHAT FUCKED-UP CHILDHOODS AND SLUTTY FIRST WIVES THEY ALL HAD.
YOU HAVE A GARDENER, NEAL?
NO, WHY?
NOT IMPORTANT RIGHT NOW.
JUST REMEMBER A MAN WILL SAY JUST WHAT HE THINKS YOU WANT TO HEAR TO GET YOUR PANTIES OFF.
OH!
THEY CAN'T HELP IT, THEY'RE JUST ALL HARD-WIRED THAT WAY.
BY THE WAY, IS THIS "NEIGHBOR" YOU?

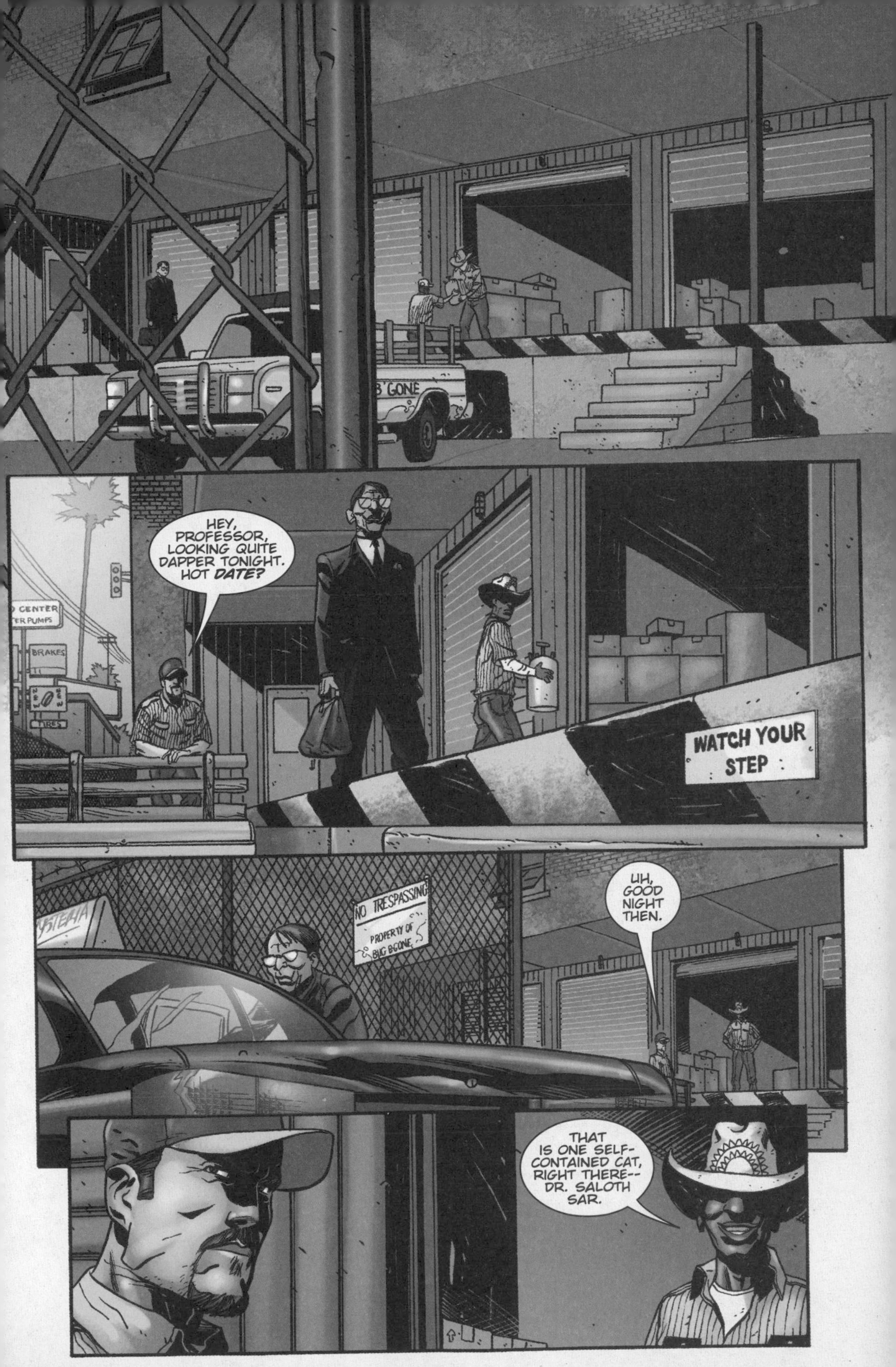
B GONE
HEY, PROFESSOR, LOOKING QUITE DAPPER TONIGHT. HOT *DATE?*
BRAKES
TIRES
WATCH YOUR STEP
NO TRESPASSING
PROPERTY OF BUG-B-GONE
UH, GOOD NIGHT THEN.
THAT IS ONE SELF-CONTAINED CAT, RIGHT THERE-- DR. SALOTH SAR.

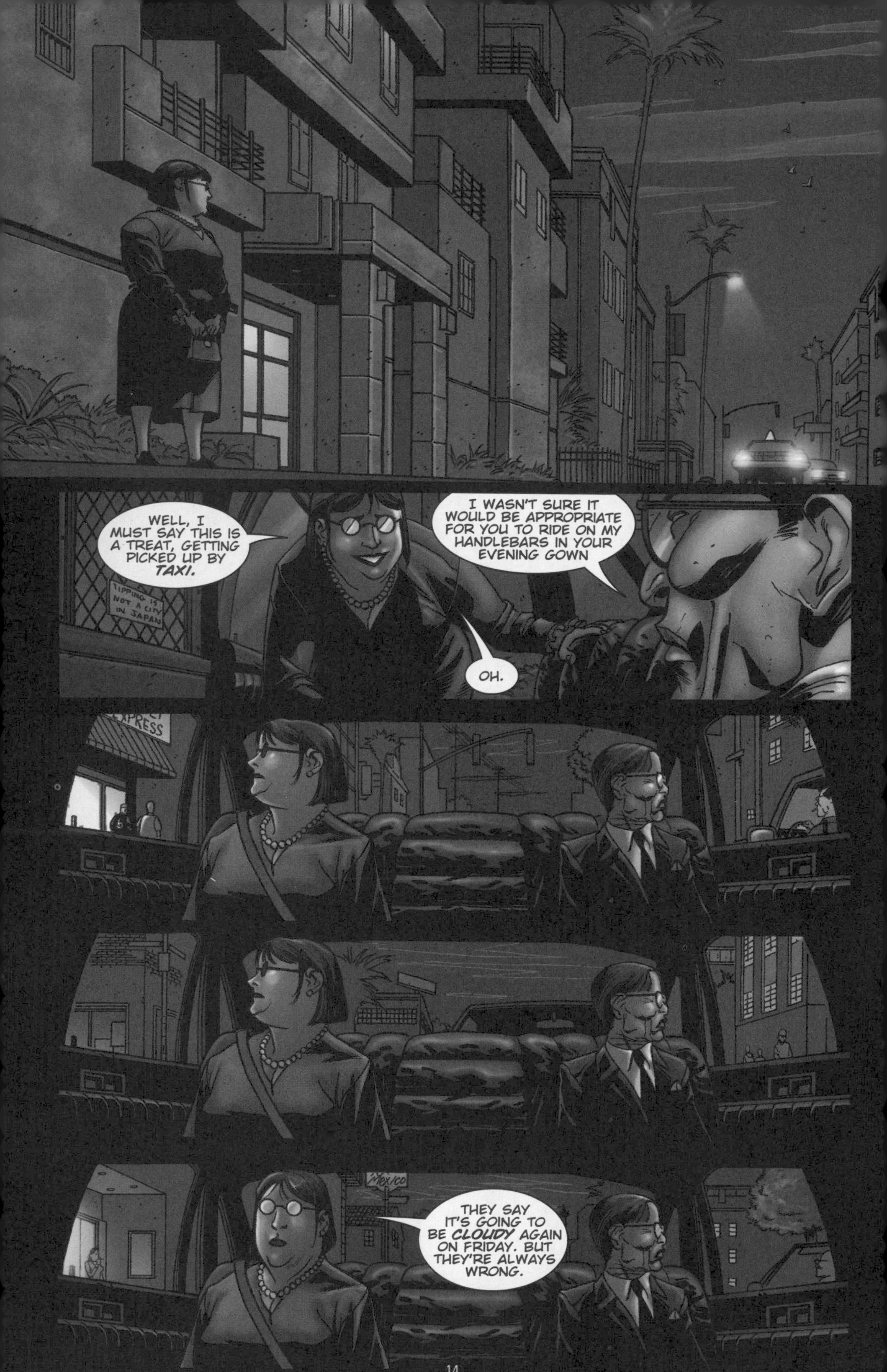
WELL, I MUST SAY THIS IS A TREAT, GETTING PICKED UP BY *TAXI.*
TIPPING IS NOT A CITY IN JAPAN
I WASN'T SURE IT WOULD BE APPROPRIATE FOR YOU TO RIDE ON MY HANDLEBARS IN YOUR EVENING GOWN
OH.
THEY SAY IT'S *GOING* TO BE ***CLOUDY*** AGAIN ON FRIDAY. BUT THEY'RE ALWAYS WRONG.

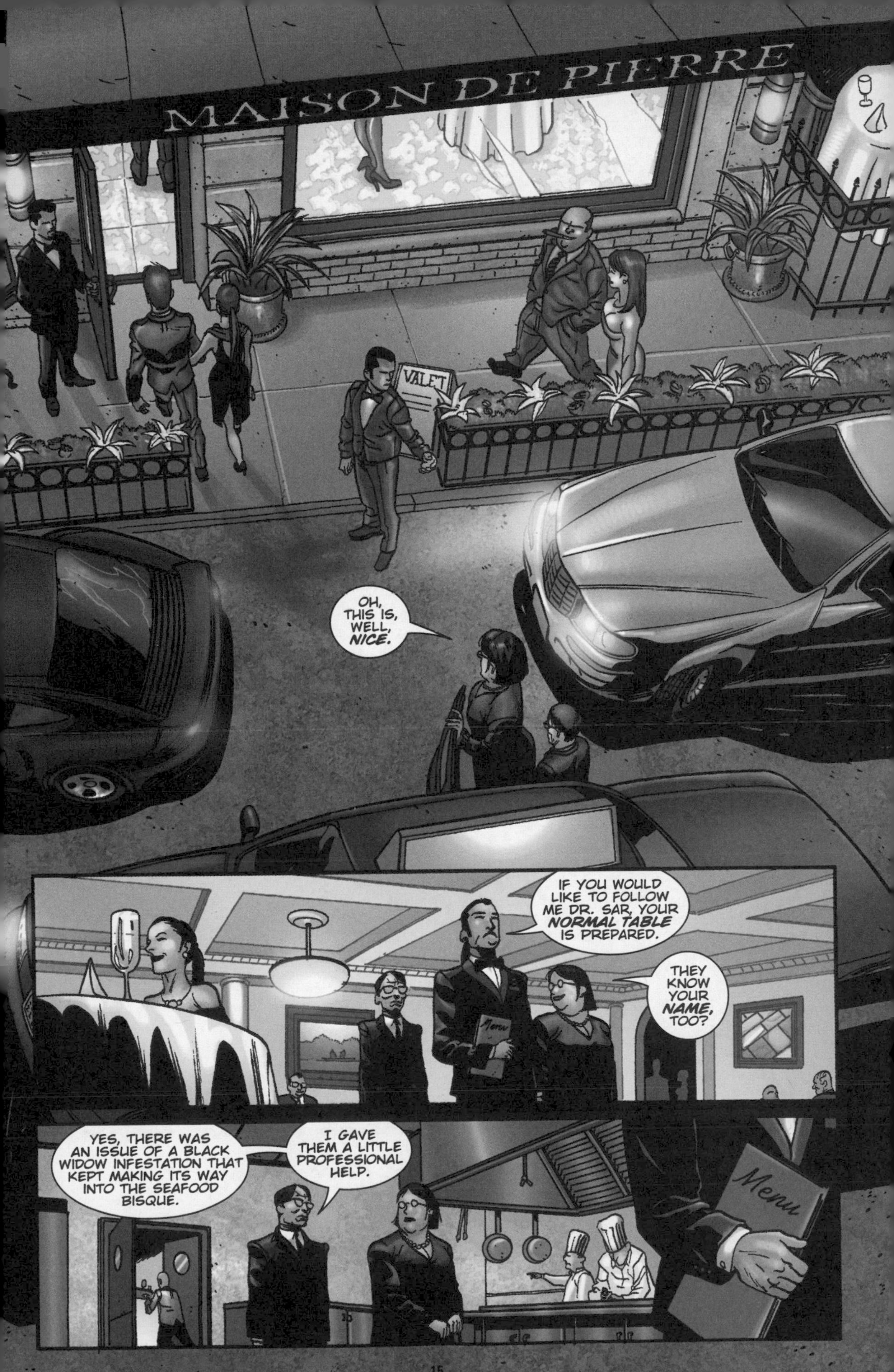
MAISON DE PIERRE
VALET
OH, THIS IS, WELL, NICE.
IF YOU WOULD LIKE TO FOLLOW ME DR. SAR, YOUR NORMAL TABLE IS PREPARED.
THEY KNOW YOUR NAME, TOO?
YES, THERE WAS AN ISSUE OF A BLACK WIDOW INFESTATION THAT KEPT MAKING ITS WAY INTO THE SEAFOOD BISQUE.
I GAVE THEM A LITTLE PROFESSIONAL HELP.
Menu

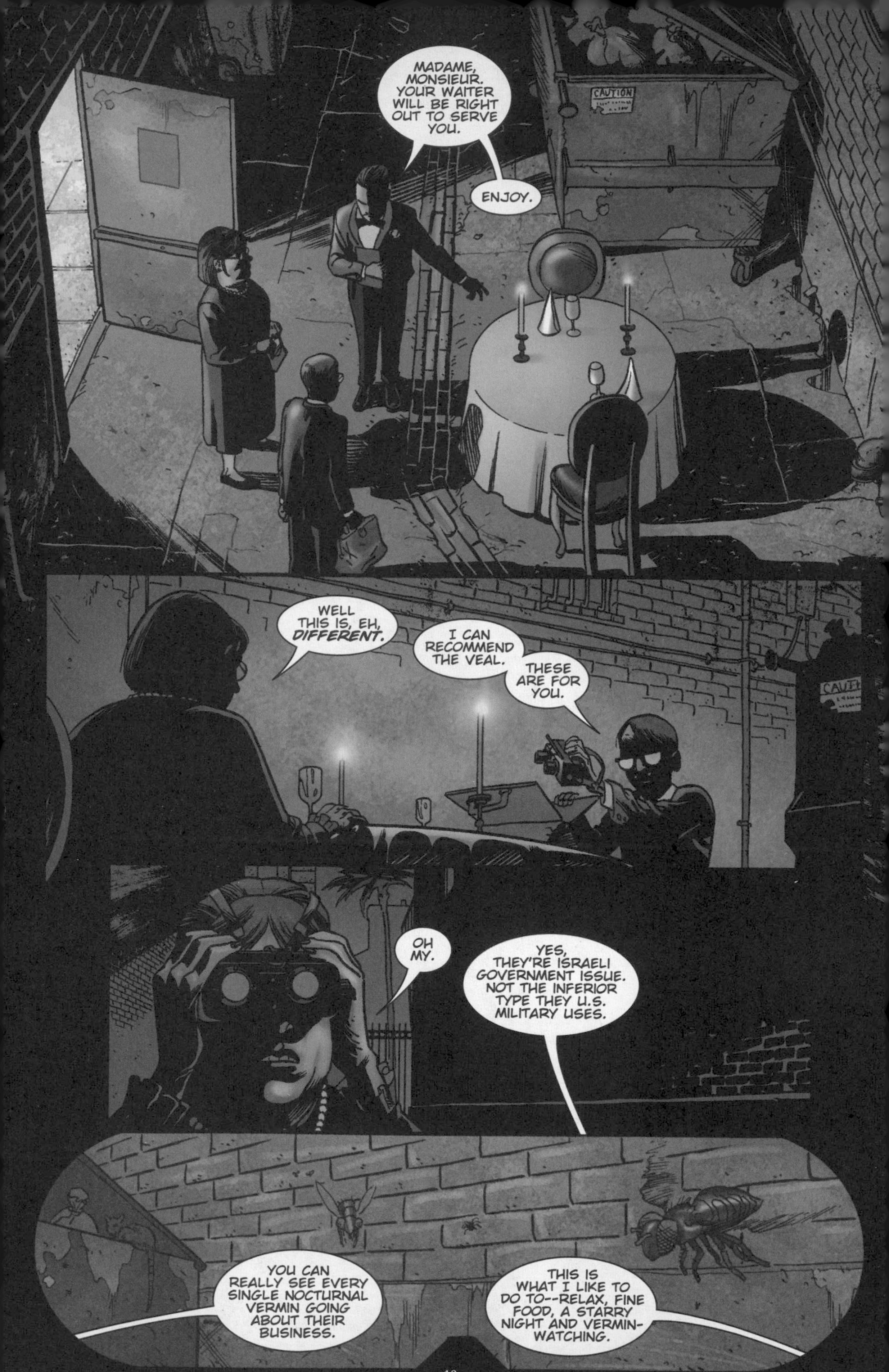
MADAME, MONSIEUR. YOUR WAITER WILL BE RIGHT OUT TO SERVE YOU.
ENJOY.
CAUTION
WELL THIS IS, EH, DIFFERENT.
I CAN RECOMMEND THE VEAL.
THESE ARE FOR YOU.
OH MY.
YES, THEY'RE ISRAELI GOVERNMENT ISSUE. NOT THE INFERIOR TYPE THEY U.S. MILITARY USES.
YOU CAN REALLY SEE EVERY SINGLE NOCTURNAL VERMIN GOING ABOUT THEIR BUSINESS.
THIS IS WHAT I LIKE TO DO TO--RELAX, FINE FOOD, A STARRY NIGHT AND VERMIN-WATCHING.

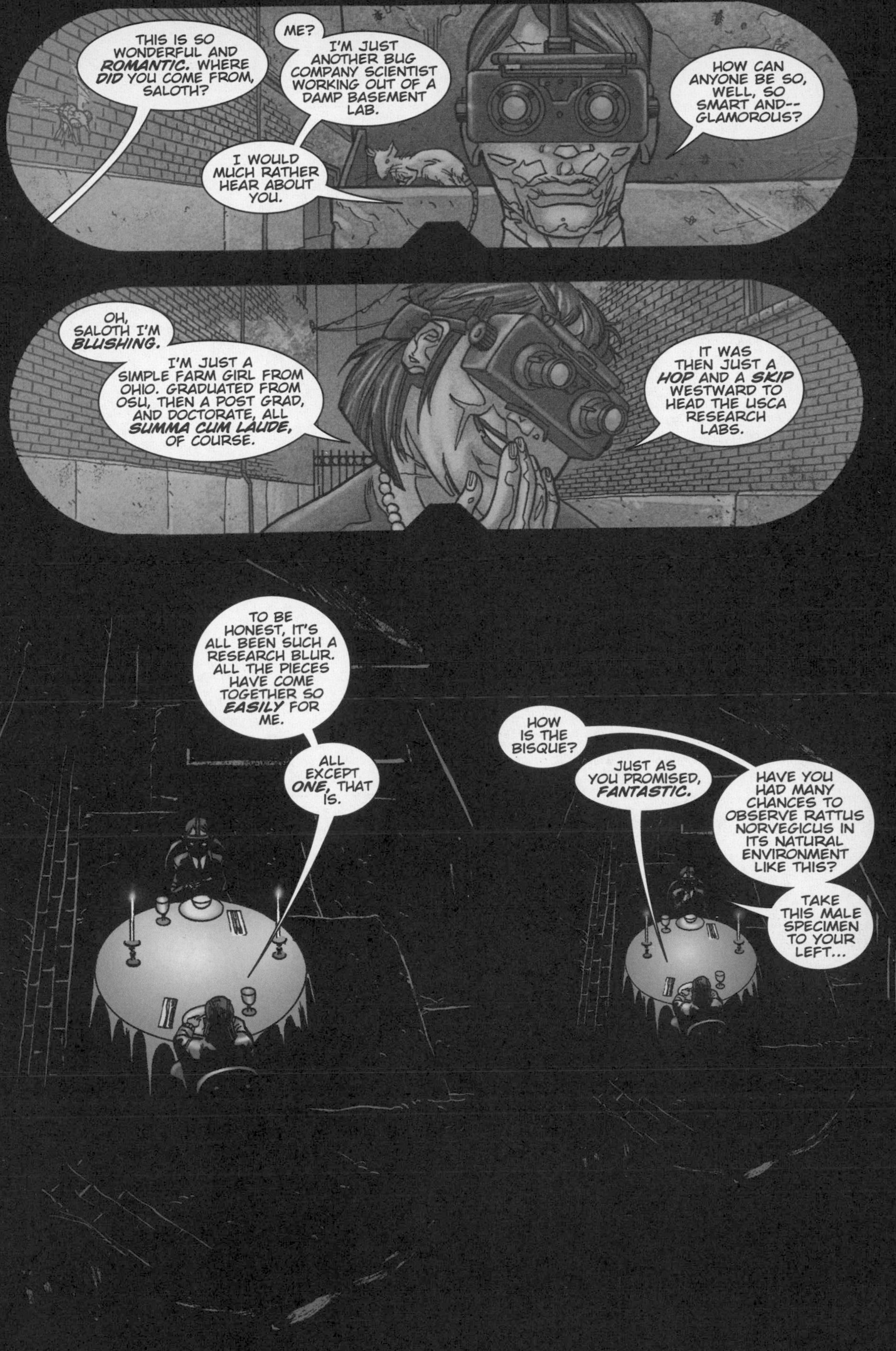
THIS IS SO WONDERFUL AND ROMANTIC. WHERE DID YOU COME FROM, SALOTH?
ME?
I'M JUST ANOTHER BUG COMPANY SCIENTIST WORKING OUT OF A DAMP BASEMENT LAB.
I WOULD MUCH RATHER HEAR ABOUT YOU.
HOW CAN ANYONE BE SO, WELL, SO SMART AND--GLAMOROUS?
OH, SALOTH I'M BLUSHING.
I'M JUST A SIMPLE FARM GIRL FROM OHIO. GRADUATED FROM OSU, THEN A POST GRAD, AND DOCTORATE, ALL SUMMA CUM LAUDE, OF COURSE.
IT WAS THEN JUST A HOP AND A SKIP WESTWARD TO HEAD THE USCA RESEARCH LABS.
TO BE HONEST, IT'S ALL BEEN SUCH A RESEARCH BLUR. ALL THE PIECES HAVE COME TOGETHER SO EASILY FOR ME.
ALL EXCEPT ONE, THAT IS.
HOW IS THE BISQUE?
JUST AS YOU PROMISED, FANTASTIC.
HAVE YOU HAD MANY CHANCES TO OBSERVE RATTUS NORVEGICUS IN ITS NATURAL ENVIRONMENT LIKE THIS?
TAKE THIS MALE SPECIMEN TO YOUR LEFT...

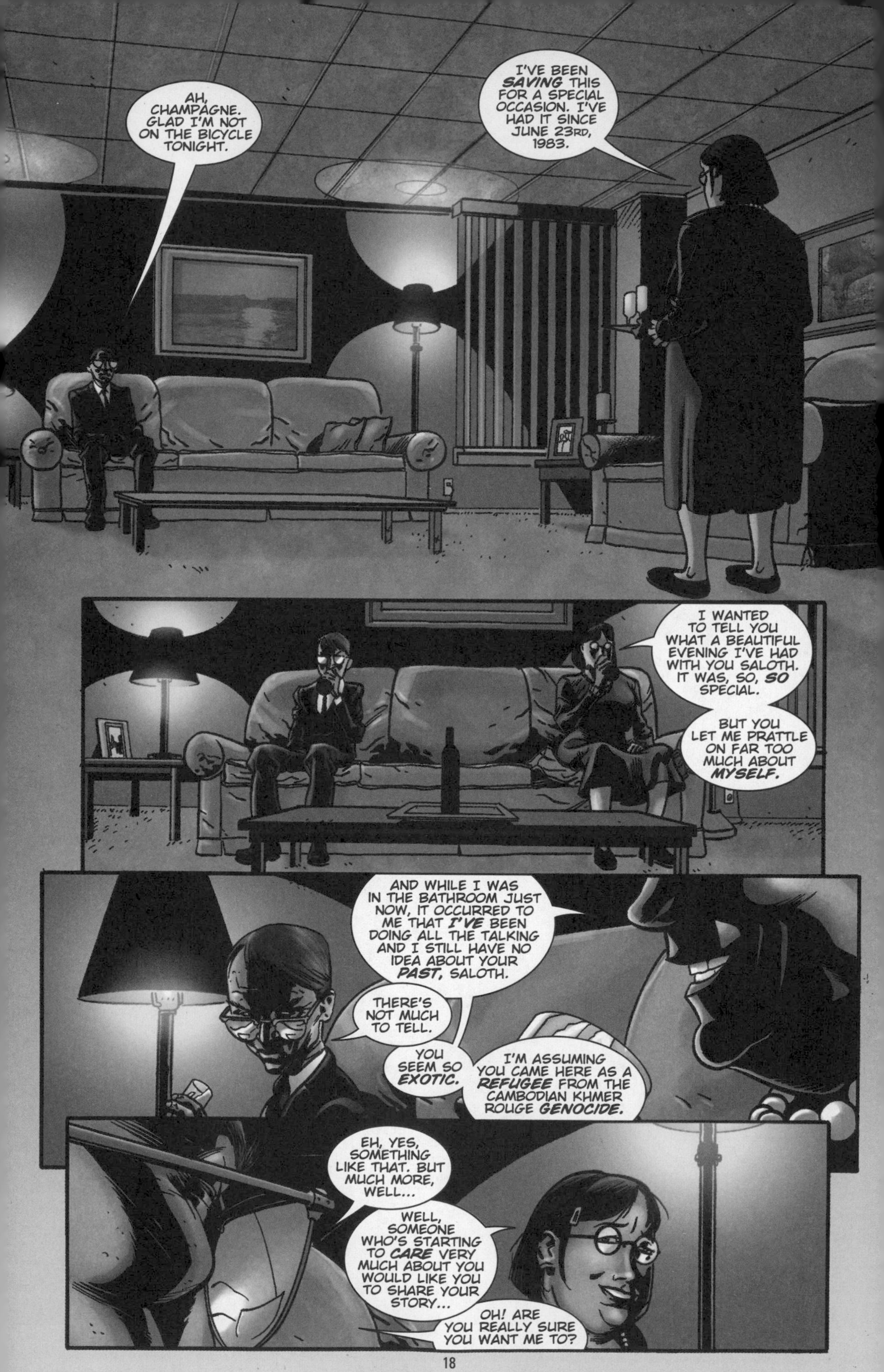
AH, CHAMPAGNE. GLAD I'M NOT ON THE BICYCLE TONIGHT.
I'VE BEEN SAVING THIS FOR A SPECIAL OCCASION. I'VE HAD IT SINCE JUNE 23RD, 1983.
I WANTED TO TELL YOU WHAT A BEAUTIFUL EVENING I'VE HAD WITH YOU SALOTH. IT WAS, SO, SO SPECIAL.
BUT YOU LET ME PRATTLE ON FAR TOO MUCH ABOUT MYSELF.
AND WHILE I WAS IN THE BATHROOM JUST NOW, IT OCCURRED TO ME THAT I'VE BEEN DOING ALL THE TALKING AND I STILL HAVE NO IDEA ABOUT YOUR PAST, SALOTH.
THERE'S NOT MUCH TO TELL.
YOU SEEM SO EXOTIC.
I'M ASSUMING YOU CAME HERE AS A REFUGEE FROM THE CAMBODIAN KHMER ROUGE GENOCIDE.
EH, YES, SOMETHING LIKE THAT. BUT MUCH MORE, WELL...
WELL, SOMEONE WHO'S STARTING TO CARE VERY MUCH ABOUT YOU WOULD LIKE YOU TO SHARE YOUR STORY...
OH! ARE YOU REALLY SURE YOU WANT ME TO?

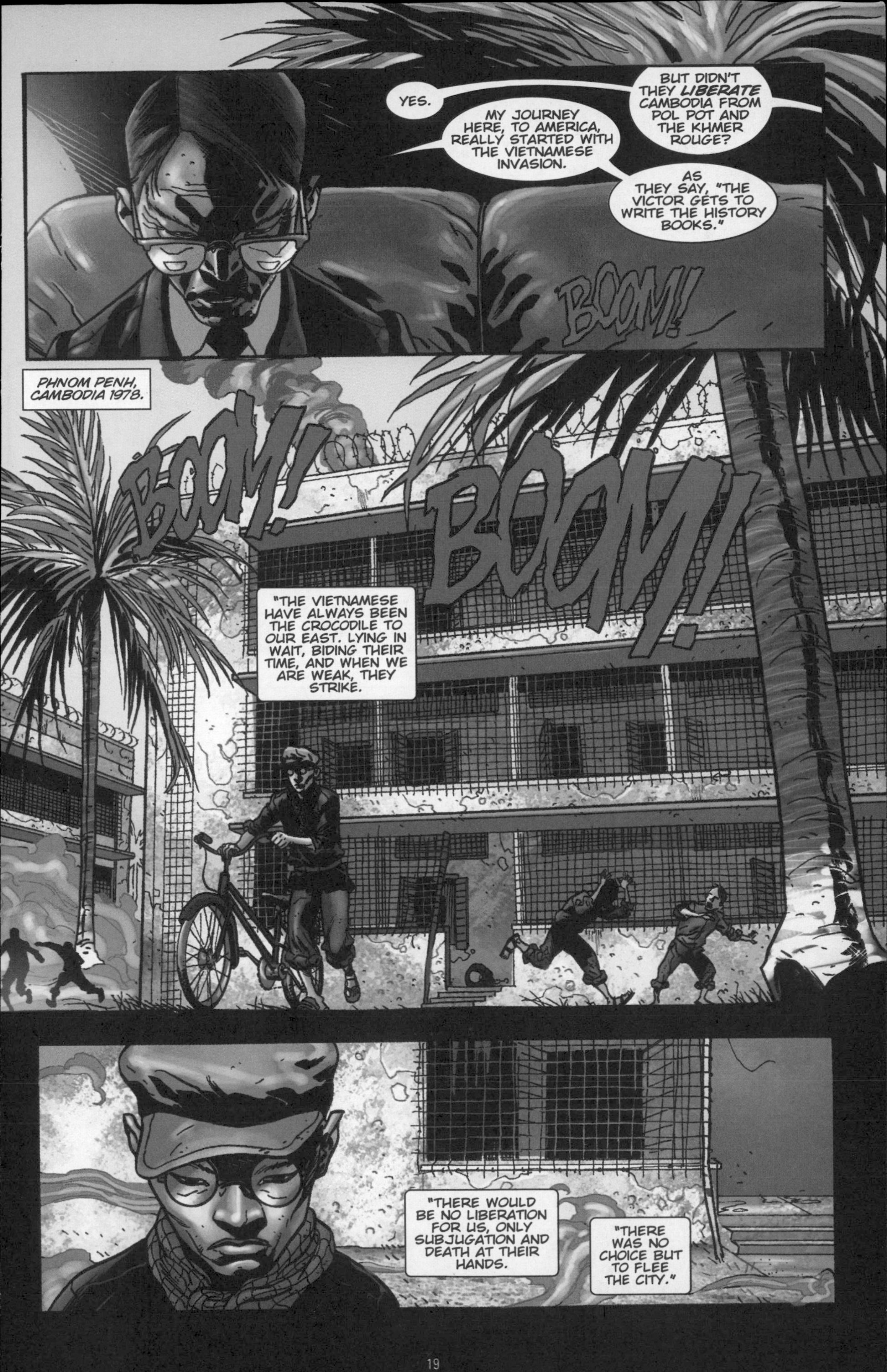
YES.
MY JOURNEY HERE, TO AMERICA, REALLY STARTED WITH THE VIETNAMESE INVASION.
BUT DIDN'T THEY LIBERATE CAMBODIA FROM POL POT AND THE KHMER ROUGE?
AS THEY SAY, "THE VICTOR GETS TO WRITE THE HISTORY BOOKS."
BOOM!
PHNOM PENH, CAMBODIA 1978.
BOOM!
BOOM!
"THE VIETNAMESE HAVE ALWAYS BEEN THE CROCODILE TO OUR EAST. LYING IN WAIT, BIDING THEIR TIME, AND WHEN WE ARE WEAK, THEY STRIKE.
"THERE WOULD BE NO LIBERATION FOR US, ONLY SUBJUGATION AND DEATH AT THEIR HANDS.
"THERE WAS NO CHOICE BUT TO FLEE THE CITY."

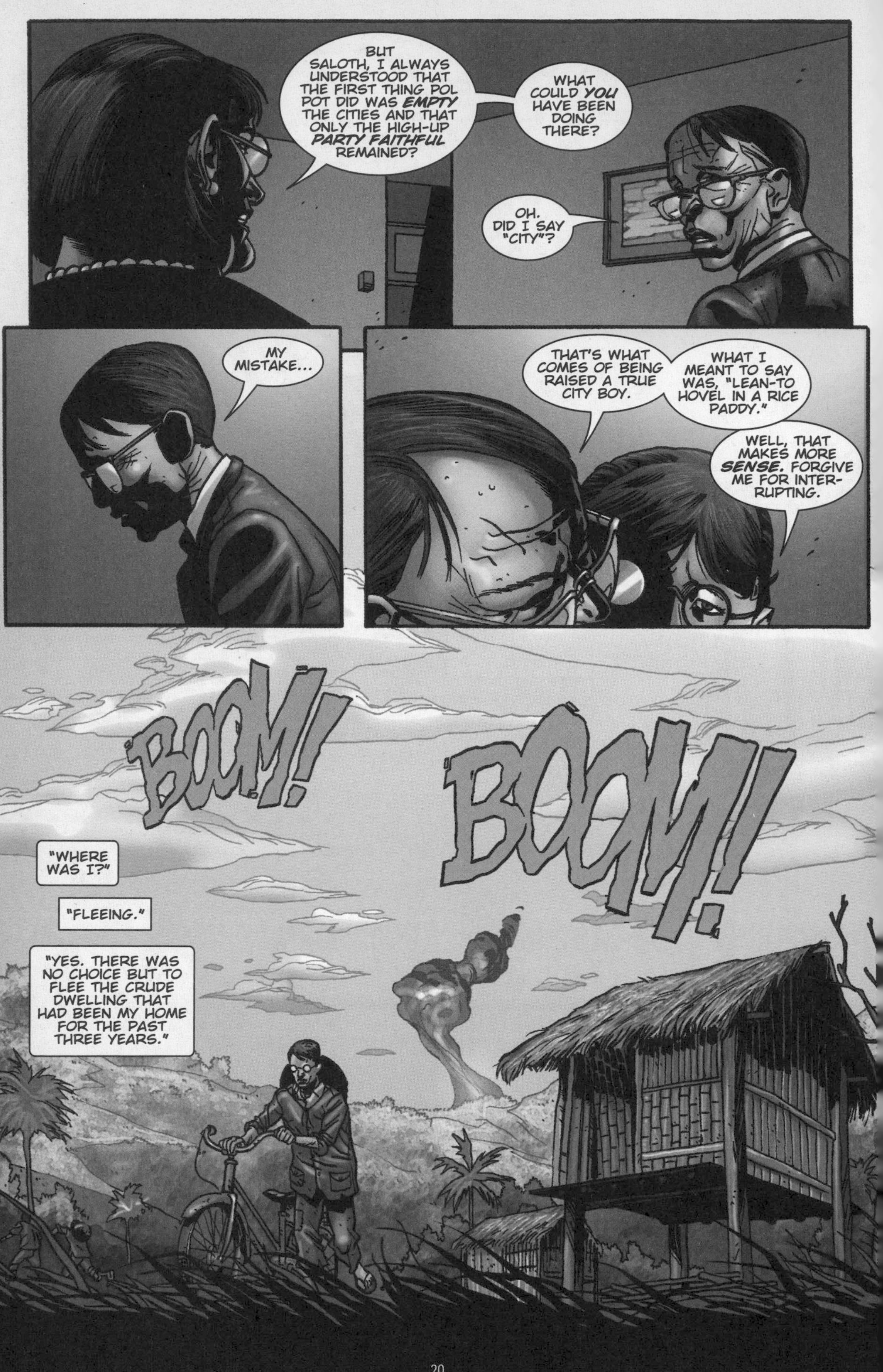

BUT SALOTH, I ALWAYS UNDERSTOOD THAT THE FIRST THING POL POT DID WAS EMPTY THE CITIES AND THAT ONLY THE HIGH-UP PARTY FAITHFUL REMAINED?
WHAT COULD YOU HAVE BEEN DOING THERE?
OH. DID I SAY "CITY"?
MY MISTAKE...
THAT'S WHAT COMES OF BEING RAISED A TRUE CITY BOY.
WHAT I MEANT TO SAY WAS, "LEAN-TO HOVEL IN A RICE PADDY."
WELL, THAT MAKES MORE SENSE. FORGIVE ME FOR INTER-RUPTING.
BOOM!
BOOM!
"WHERE WAS I?"
"FLEEING."
"YES. THERE WAS NO CHOICE BUT TO FLEE THE CRUDE DWELLING THAT HAD BEEN MY HOME FOR THE PAST THREE YEARS."

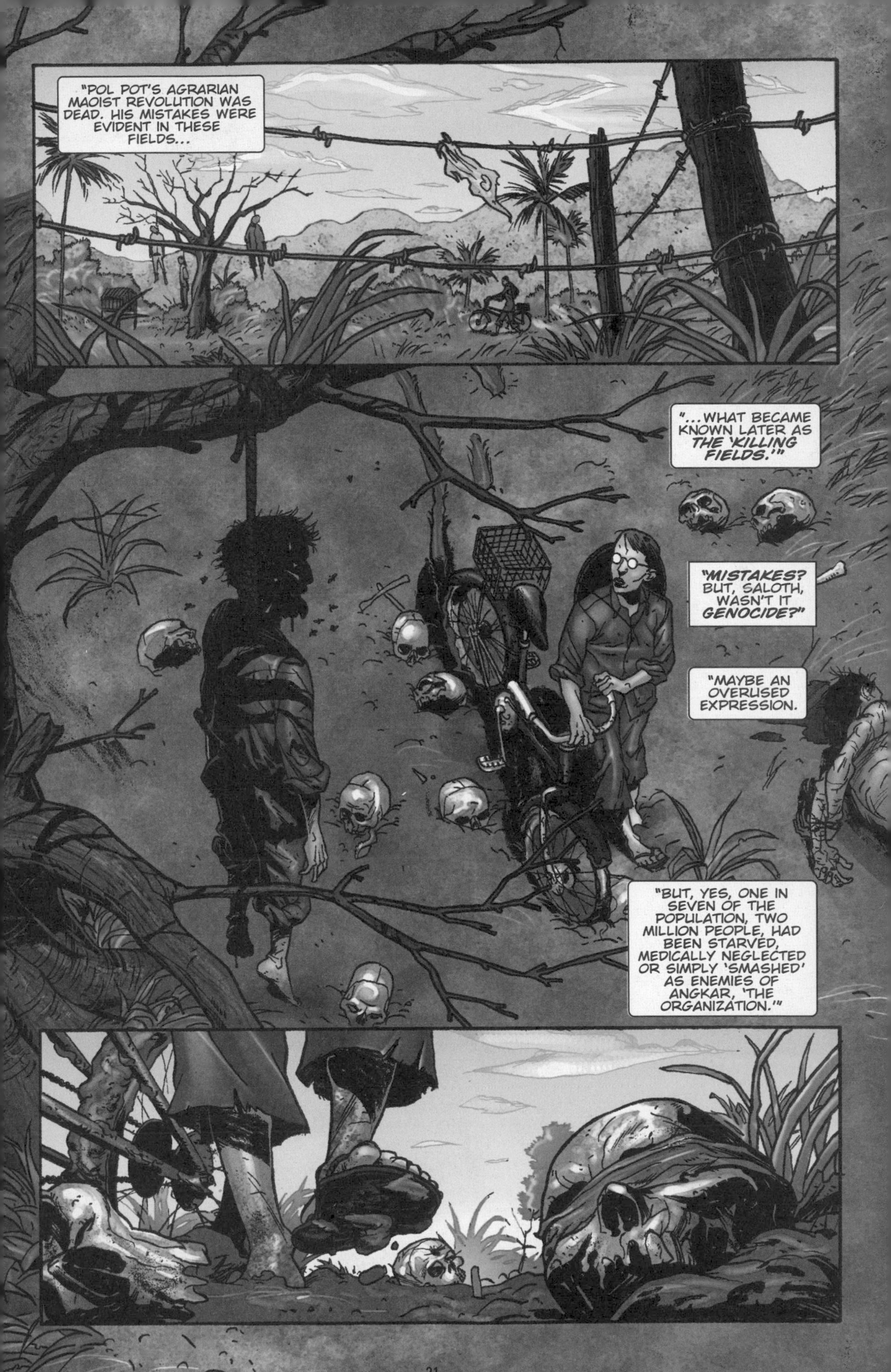
"POL POT'S AGRARIAN MAOIST REVOLUTION WAS DEAD. HIS MISTAKES WERE EVIDENT IN THESE FIELDS...
"...WHAT BECAME KNOWN LATER AS THE 'KILLING FIELDS.'"
"MISTAKES? BUT, SALOTH, WASN'T IT GENOCIDE?"
"MAYBE AN OVERUSED EXPRESSION.
"BUT, YES, ONE IN SEVEN OF THE POPULATION, TWO MILLION PEOPLE, HAD BEEN STARVED, MEDICALLY NEGLECTED OR SIMPLY 'SMASHED' AS ENEMIES OF ANGKAR, 'THE ORGANIZATION.'"

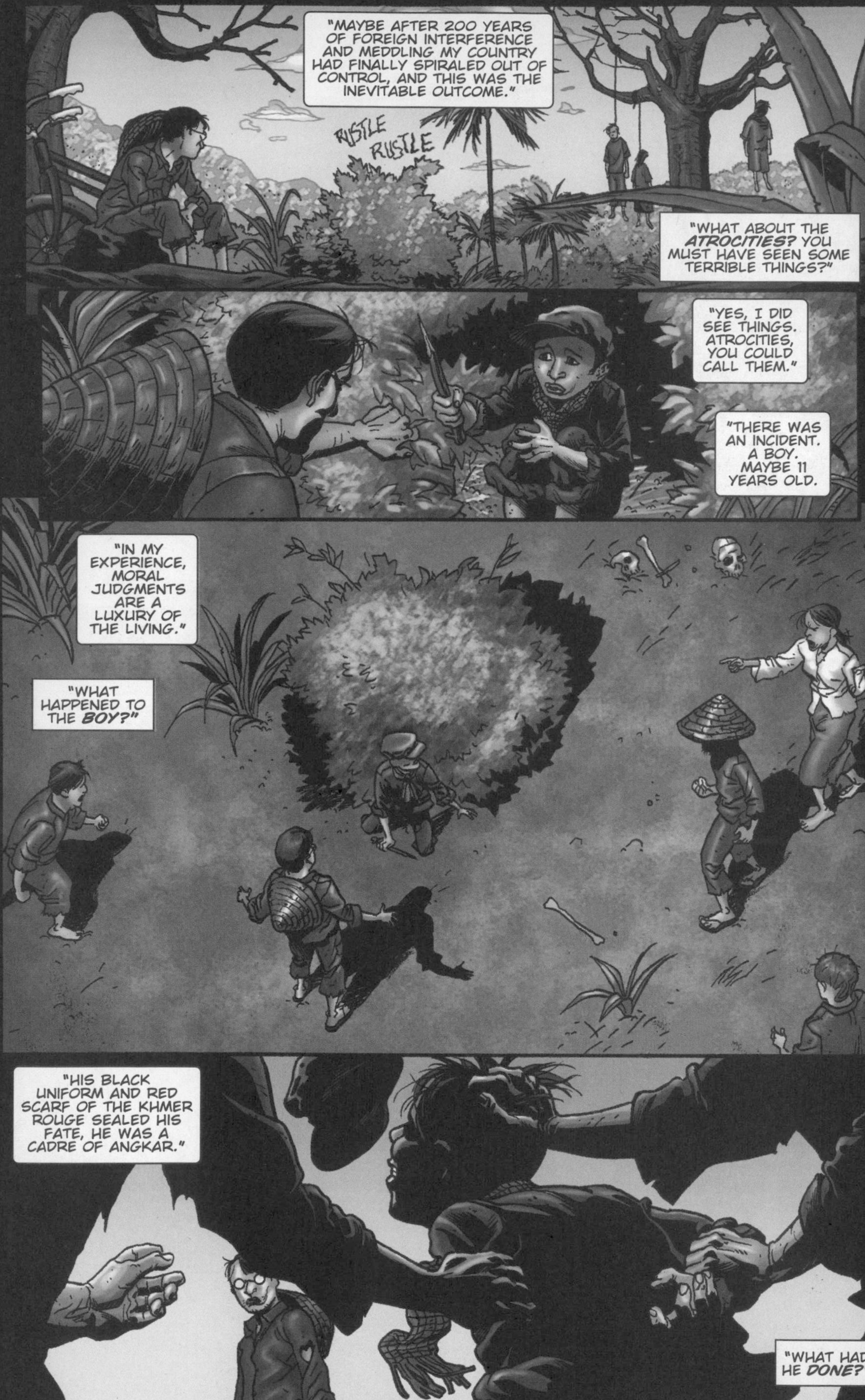
"MAYBE AFTER 200 YEARS OF FOREIGN INTERFERENCE AND MEDDLING MY COUNTRY HAD FINALLY SPIRALED OUT OF CONTROL, AND THIS WAS THE INEVITABLE OUTCOME."
RUSTLE RUSTLE
"WHAT ABOUT THE ATROCITIES? YOU MUST HAVE SEEN SOME TERRIBLE THINGS?"
"YES, I DID SEE THINGS. ATROCITIES, YOU COULD CALL THEM."
"THERE WAS AN INCIDENT. A BOY. MAYBE 11 YEARS OLD.
"IN MY EXPERIENCE, MORAL JUDGMENTS ARE A LUXURY OF THE LIVING."
"WHAT HAPPENED TO THE BOY?"
"HIS BLACK UNIFORM AND RED SCARF OF THE KHMER ROUGE SEALED HIS FATE, HE WAS A CADRE OF ANGKAR."
"WHAT HAD HE DONE?"

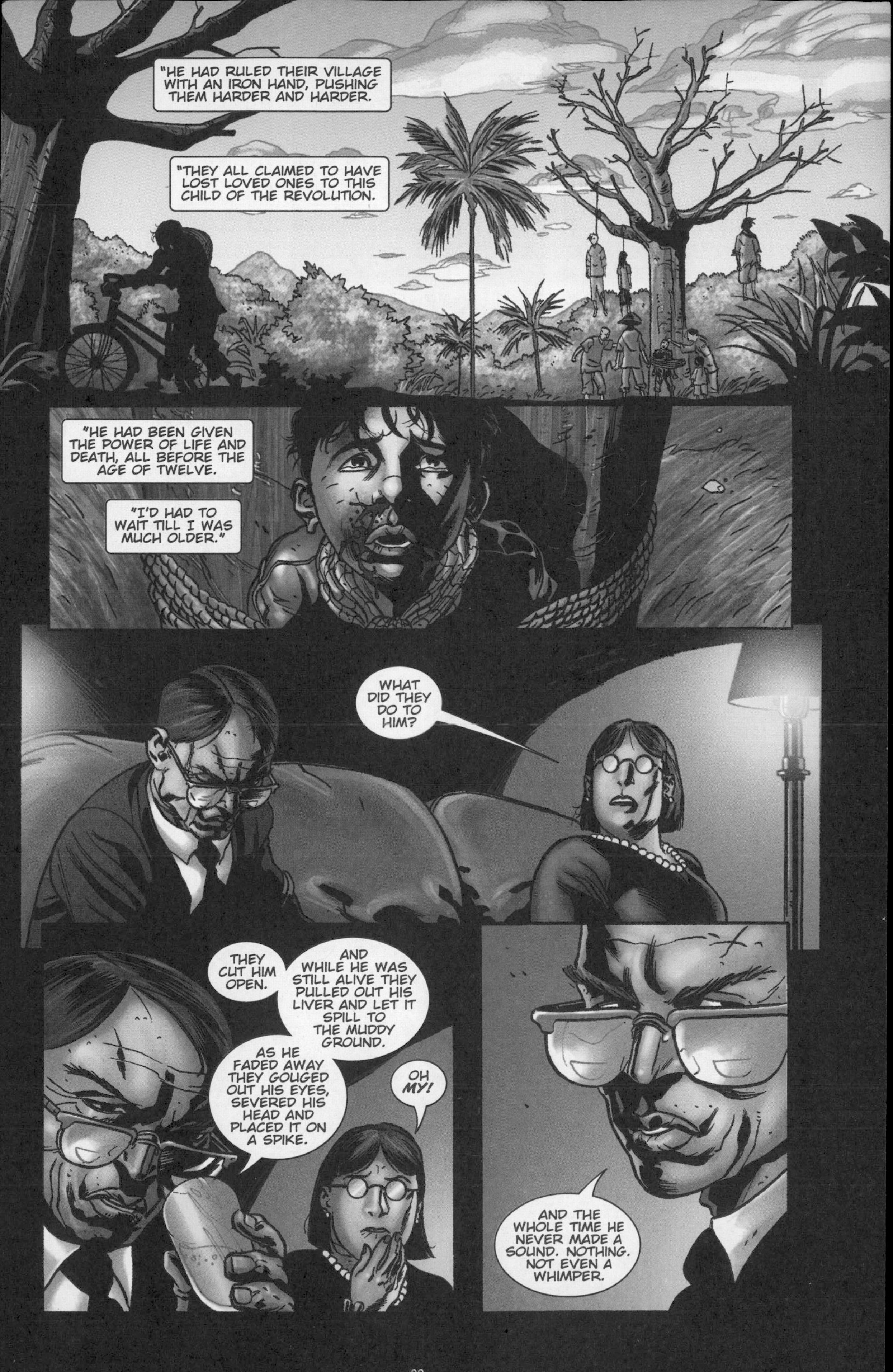
"HE HAD RULED THEIR VILLAGE WITH AN IRON HAND, PUSHING THEM HARDER AND HARDER.
"THEY ALL CLAIMED TO HAVE LOST LOVED ONES TO THIS CHILD OF THE REVOLUTION.
"HE HAD BEEN GIVEN THE POWER OF LIFE AND DEATH, ALL BEFORE THE AGE OF TWELVE.
"I'D HAD TO WAIT TILL I WAS MUCH OLDER."
WHAT DID THEY DO TO HIM?
THEY CUT HIM OPEN.
AND WHILE HE WAS STILL ALIVE THEY PULLED OUT HIS LIVER AND LET IT SPILL TO THE MUDDY GROUND.
AS HE FADED AWAY THEY GOUGED OUT HIS EYES, SEVERED HIS HEAD AND PLACED IT ON A SPIKE.
OH MY!
AND THE WHOLE TIME HE NEVER MADE A SOUND. NOTHING. NOT EVEN A WHIMPER.

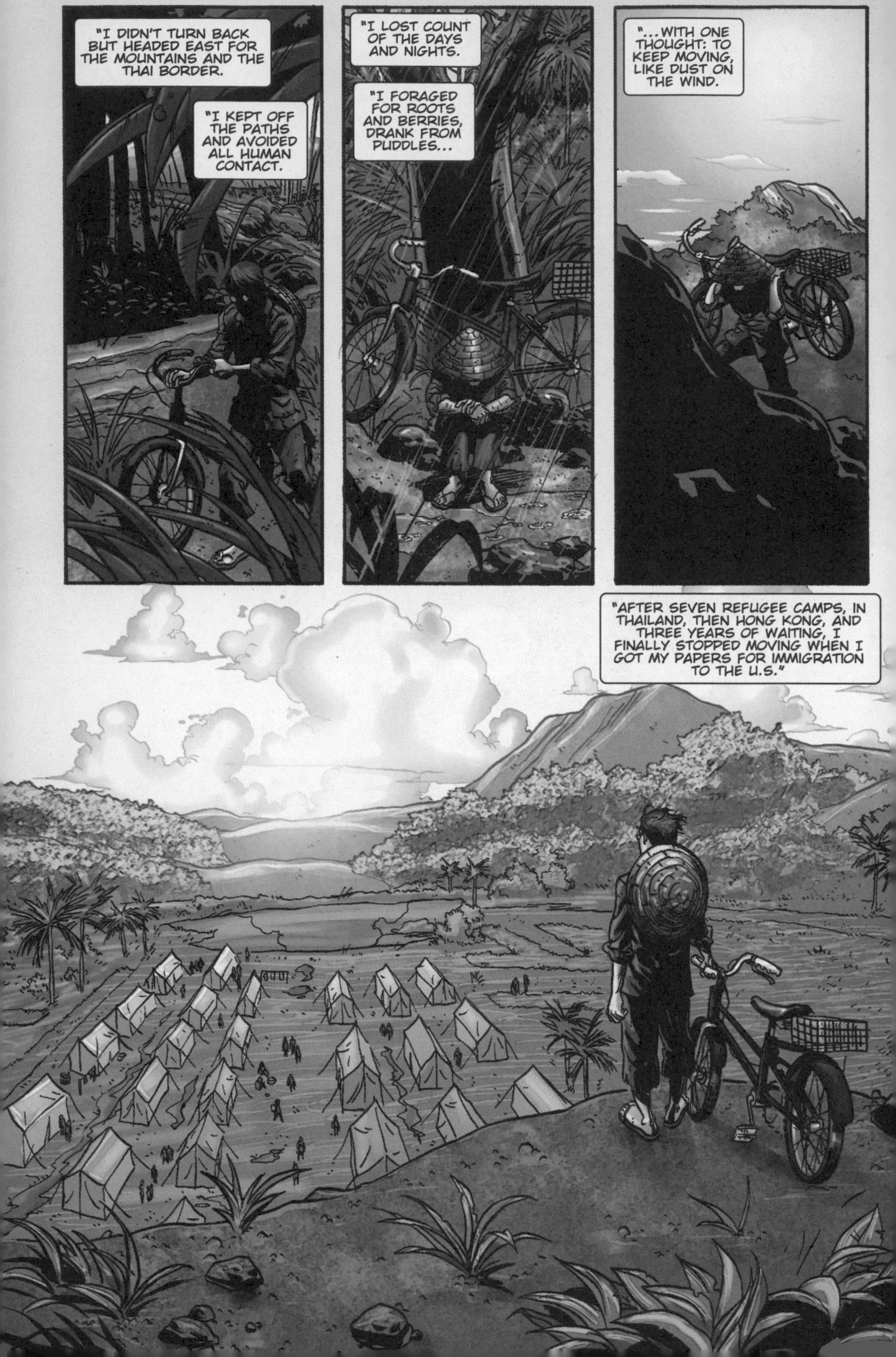
"I DIDN'T TURN BACK BUT HEADED EAST FOR THE MOUNTAINS AND THE THAI BORDER.
"I KEPT OFF THE PATHS AND AVOIDED ALL HUMAN CONTACT.
"I LOST COUNT OF THE DAYS AND NIGHTS.
"I FORAGED FOR ROOTS AND BERRIES, DRANK FROM PUDDLES...
"...WITH ONE THOUGHT: TO KEEP MOVING, LIKE DUST ON THE WIND.
"AFTER SEVEN REFUGEE CAMPS, IN THAILAND, THEN HONG KONG, AND THREE YEARS OF WAITING, I FINALLY STOPPED MOVING WHEN I GOT MY PAPERS FOR IMMIGRATION TO THE U.S."

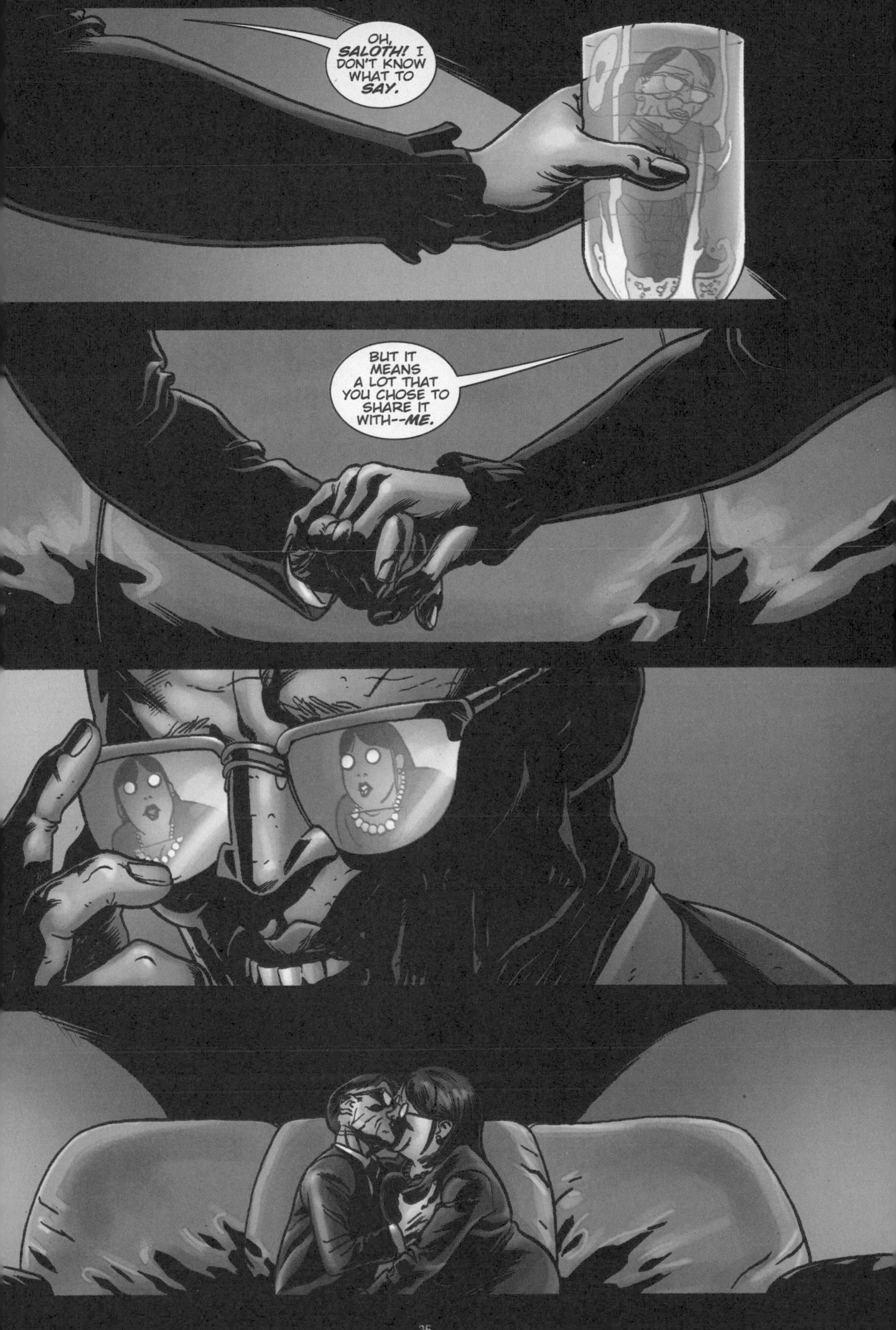
OH, SALOTH! I DON'T KNOW WHAT TO SAY.
BUT IT MEANS A LOT THAT YOU CHOSE TO SHARE IT WITH--ME.

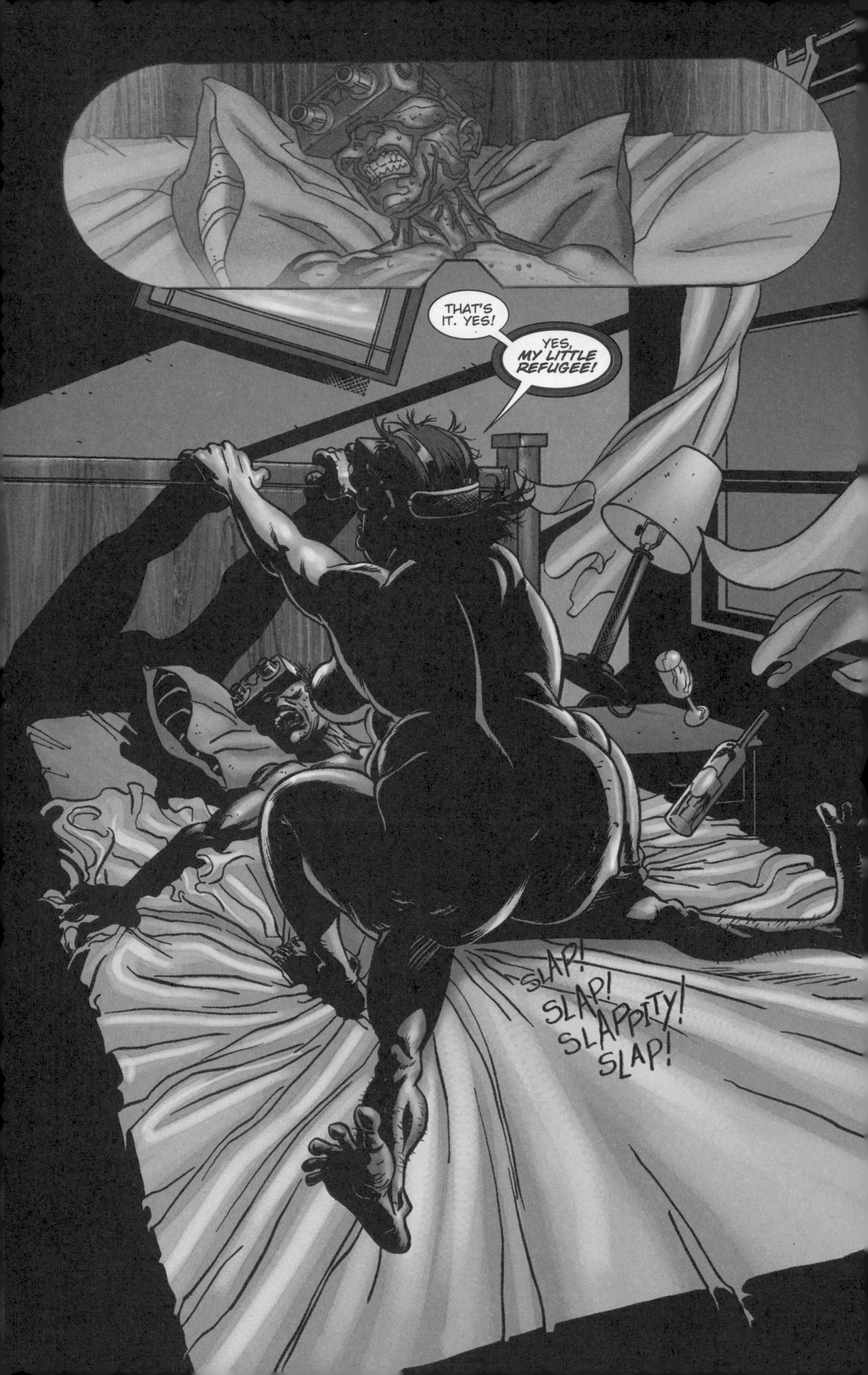
THAT'S IT. YES!
YES, MY LITTLE REFUGEE!
SLAP! SLAP! SLAPPITY! SLAP!

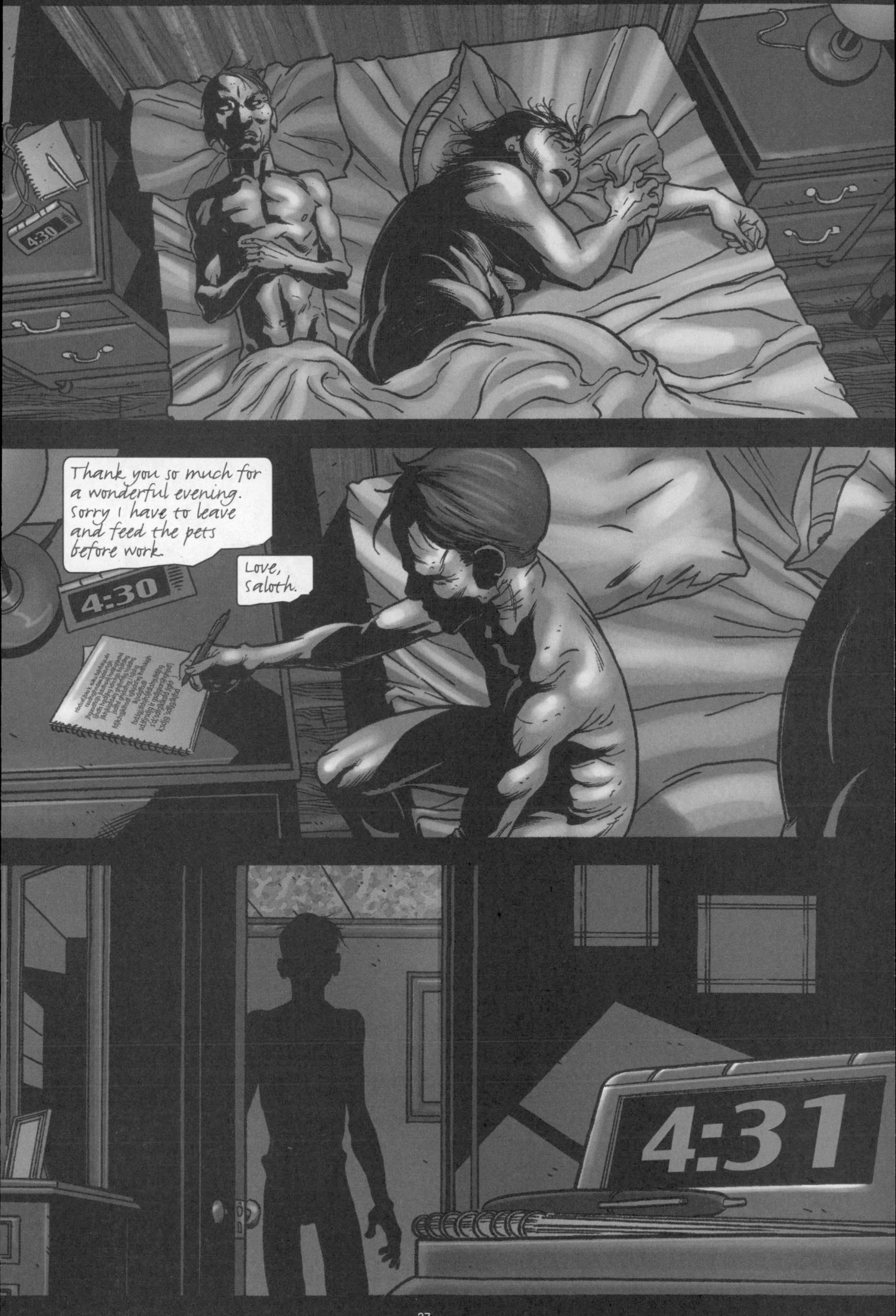
4:30
Thank you so much for a wonderful evening. Sorry I have to leave and feed the pets before work.
Love, Saloth.
4:30
4:31

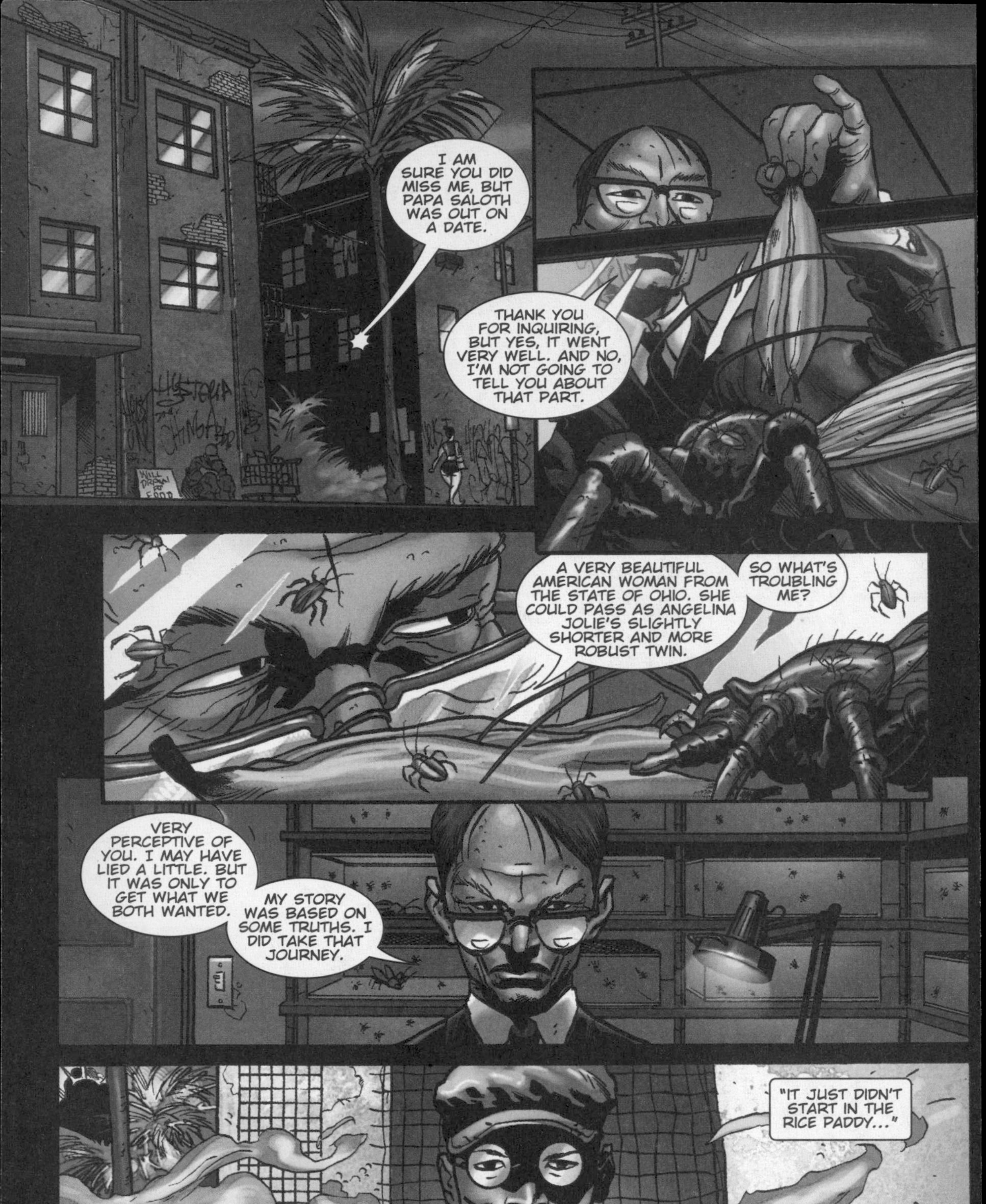
I AM SURE YOU DID MISS ME, BUT PAPA SALOTH WAS OUT ON A DATE.
THANK YOU FOR INQUIRING, BUT YES, IT WENT VERY WELL. AND NO, I'M NOT GOING TO TELL YOU ABOUT THAT PART.
A VERY BEAUTIFUL AMERICAN WOMAN FROM THE STATE OF OHIO. SHE COULD PASS AS ANGELINA JOLIE'S SLIGHTLY SHORTER AND MORE ROBUST TWIN.
SO WHAT'S TROUBLING ME?
VERY PERCEPTIVE OF YOU. I MAY HAVE LIED A LITTLE. BUT IT WAS ONLY TO GET WHAT WE BOTH WANTED.
MY STORY WAS BASED ON SOME TRUTHS. I DID TAKE THAT JOURNEY.
"IT JUST DIDN'T START IN THE RICE PADDY..."

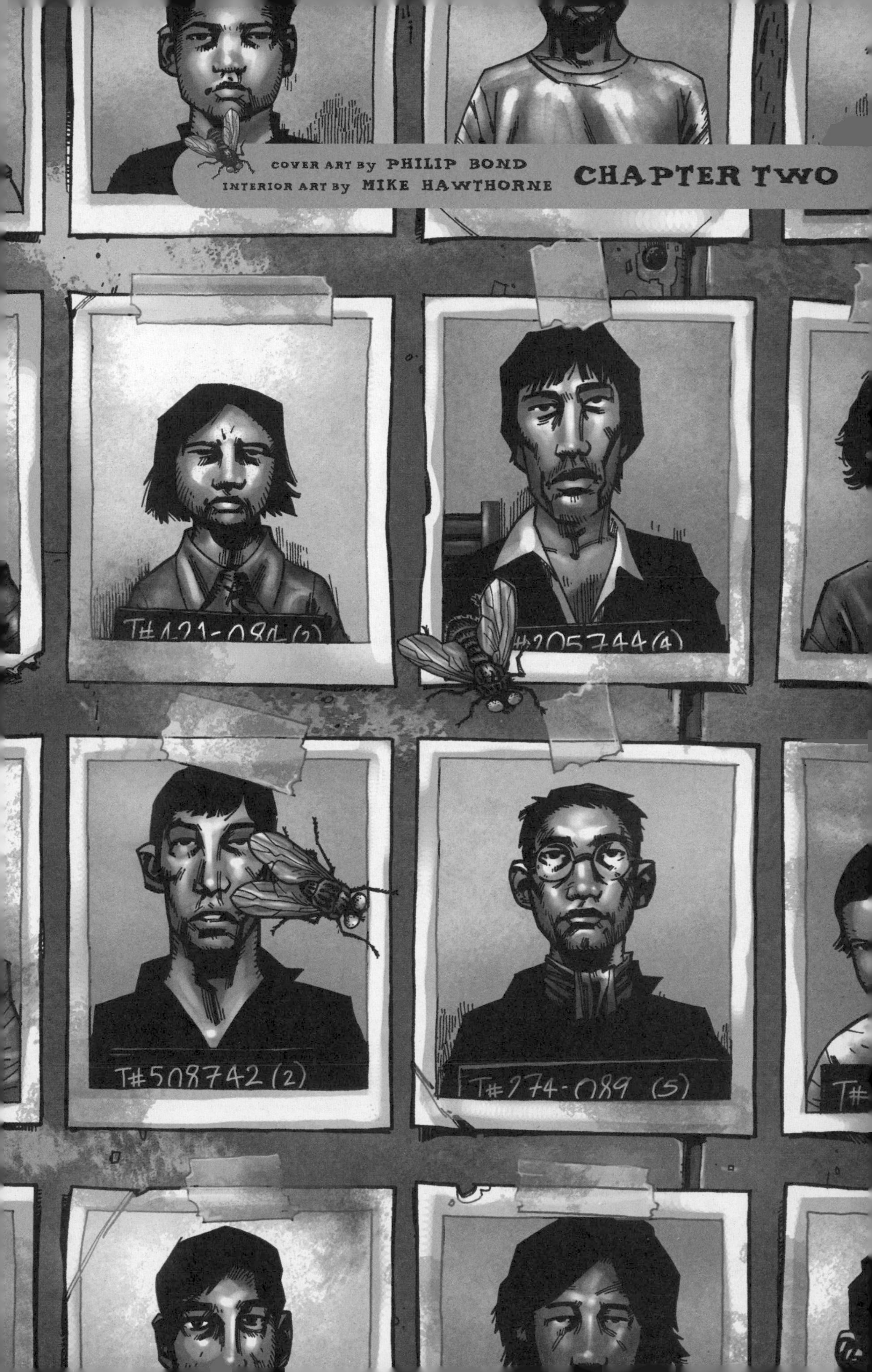
COVER ART BY PHILIP BOND
INTERIOR ART BY MIKE HAWTHORNE
CHAPTER TWO
T#508742 (2)

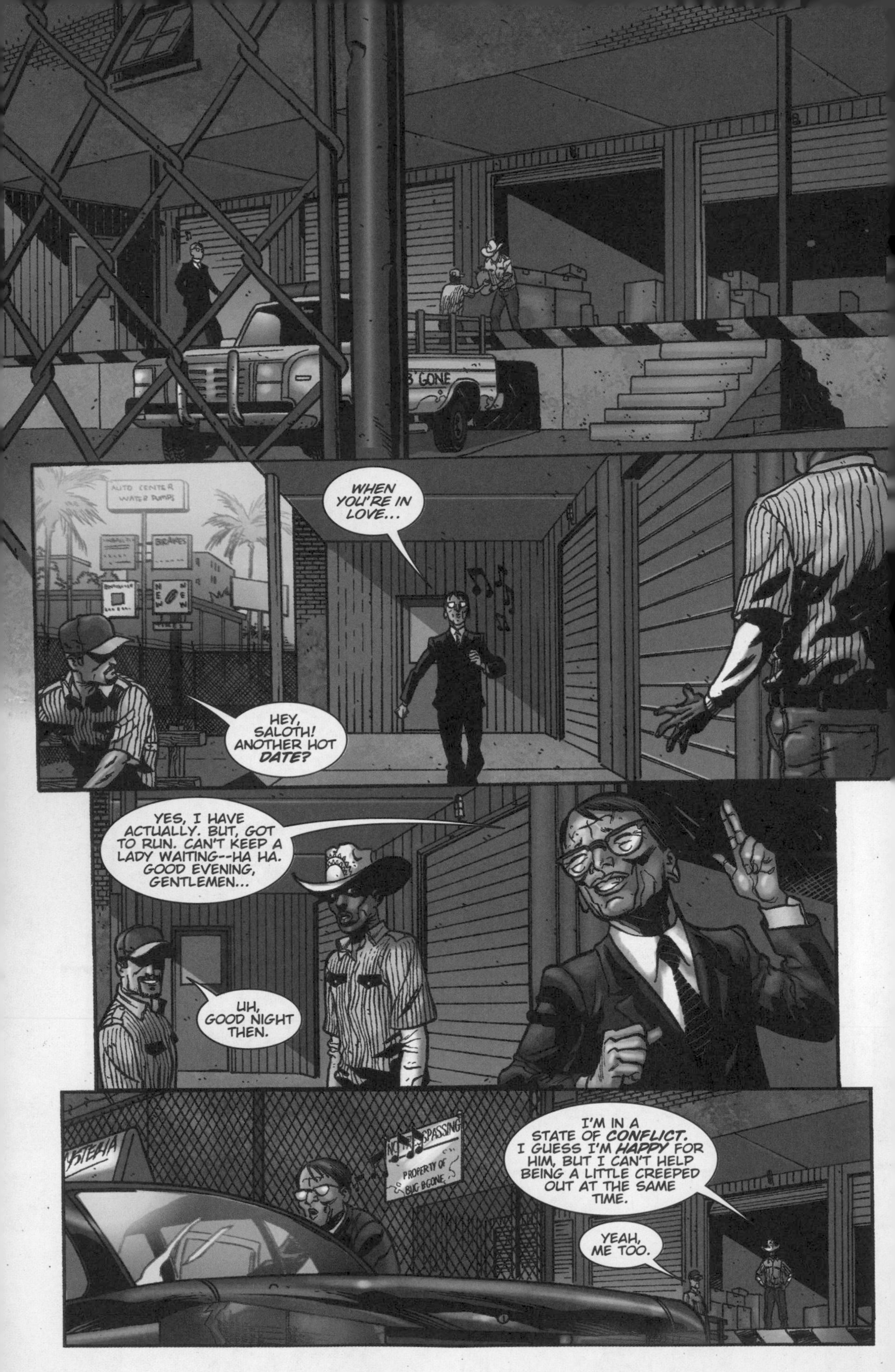
WHEN YOU'RE IN LOVE...
HEY, SALOTH! ANOTHER HOT DATE?
YES, I HAVE ACTUALLY. BUT, GOT TO RUN. CAN'T KEEP A LADY WAITING--HA HA. GOOD EVENING, GENTLEMEN...
UH, GOOD NIGHT THEN.
I'M IN A STATE OF CONFLICT. I GUESS I'M HAPPY FOR HIM, BUT I CAN'T HELP BEING A LITTLE CREEPED OUT AT THE SAME TIME.
YEAH, ME TOO.

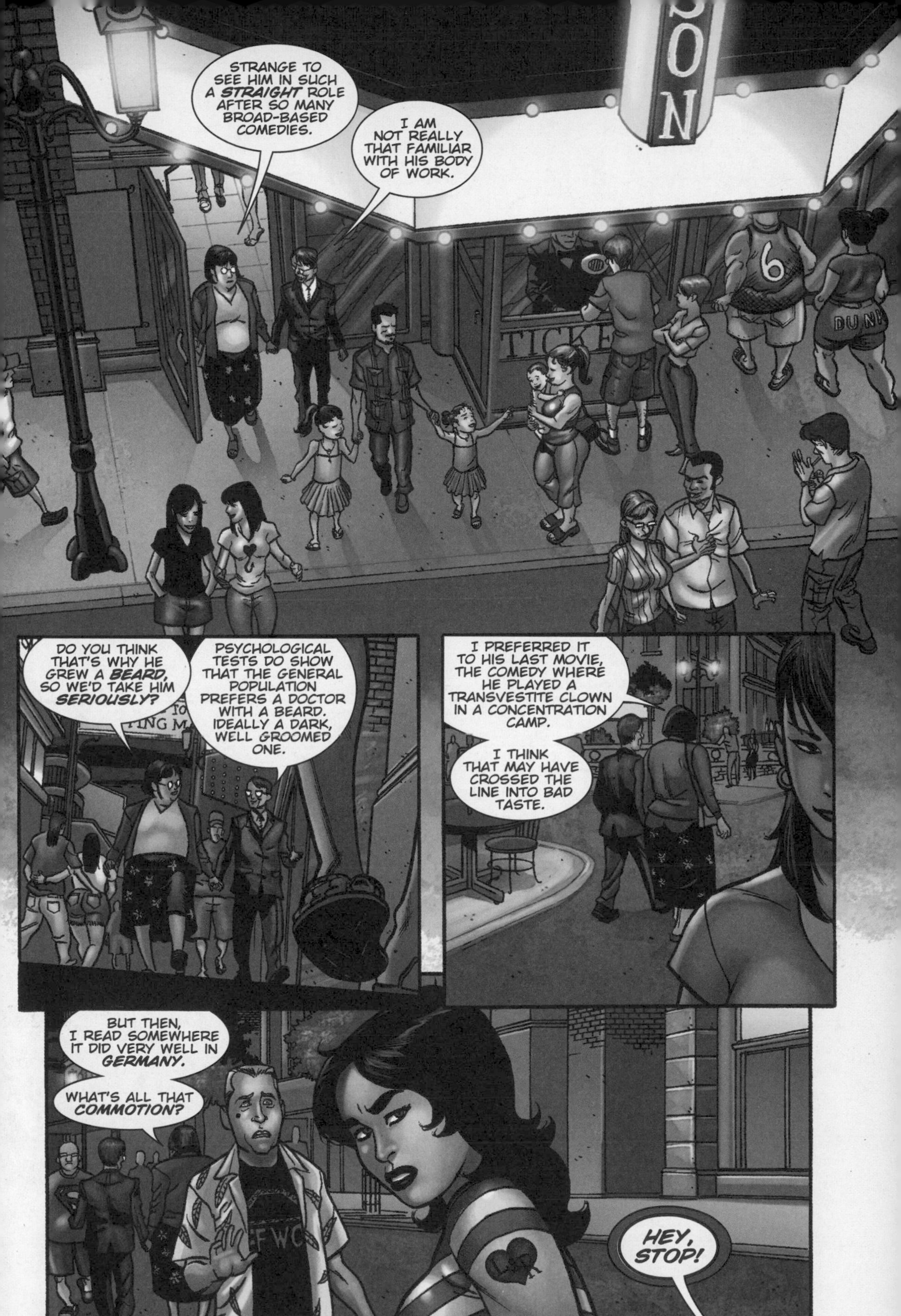
STRANGE TO SEE HIM IN SUCH A STRAIGHT ROLE AFTER SO MANY BROAD-BASED COMEDIES.
I AM NOT REALLY THAT FAMILIAR WITH HIS BODY OF WORK.
DO YOU THINK THAT'S WHY HE GREW A BEARD, SO WE'D TAKE HIM SERIOUSLY?
PSYCHOLOGICAL TESTS DO SHOW THAT THE GENERAL POPULATION PREFERS A DOCTOR WITH A BEARD. IDEALLY A DARK, WELL GROOMED ONE.
I PREFERRED IT TO HIS LAST MOVIE, THE COMEDY WHERE HE PLAYED A TRANSVESTITE CLOWN IN A CONCENTRATION CAMP.
I THINK THAT MAY HAVE CROSSED THE LINE INTO BAD TASTE.
BUT THEN, I READ SOMEWHERE IT DID VERY WELL IN GERMANY.
WHAT'S ALL THAT COMMOTION?
HEY, STOP!

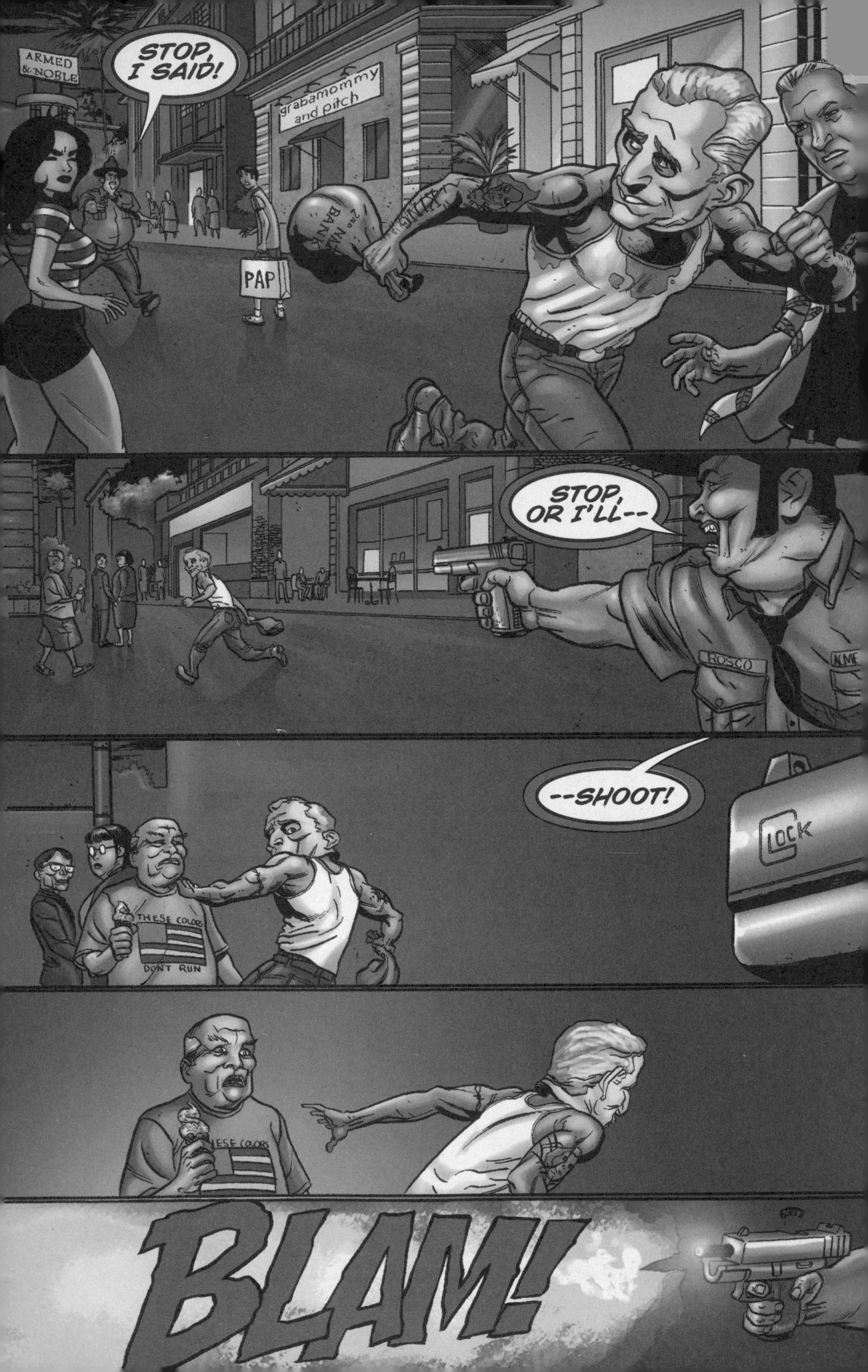
ARMED & NOBLE
STOP, I SAID!
grabamommy and pitch
PAP
2ND NAT BANK
STOP, OR I'LL--
ROSCO
--SHOOT!
GLOCK
THESE COLORS DONT RUN
BLAM!

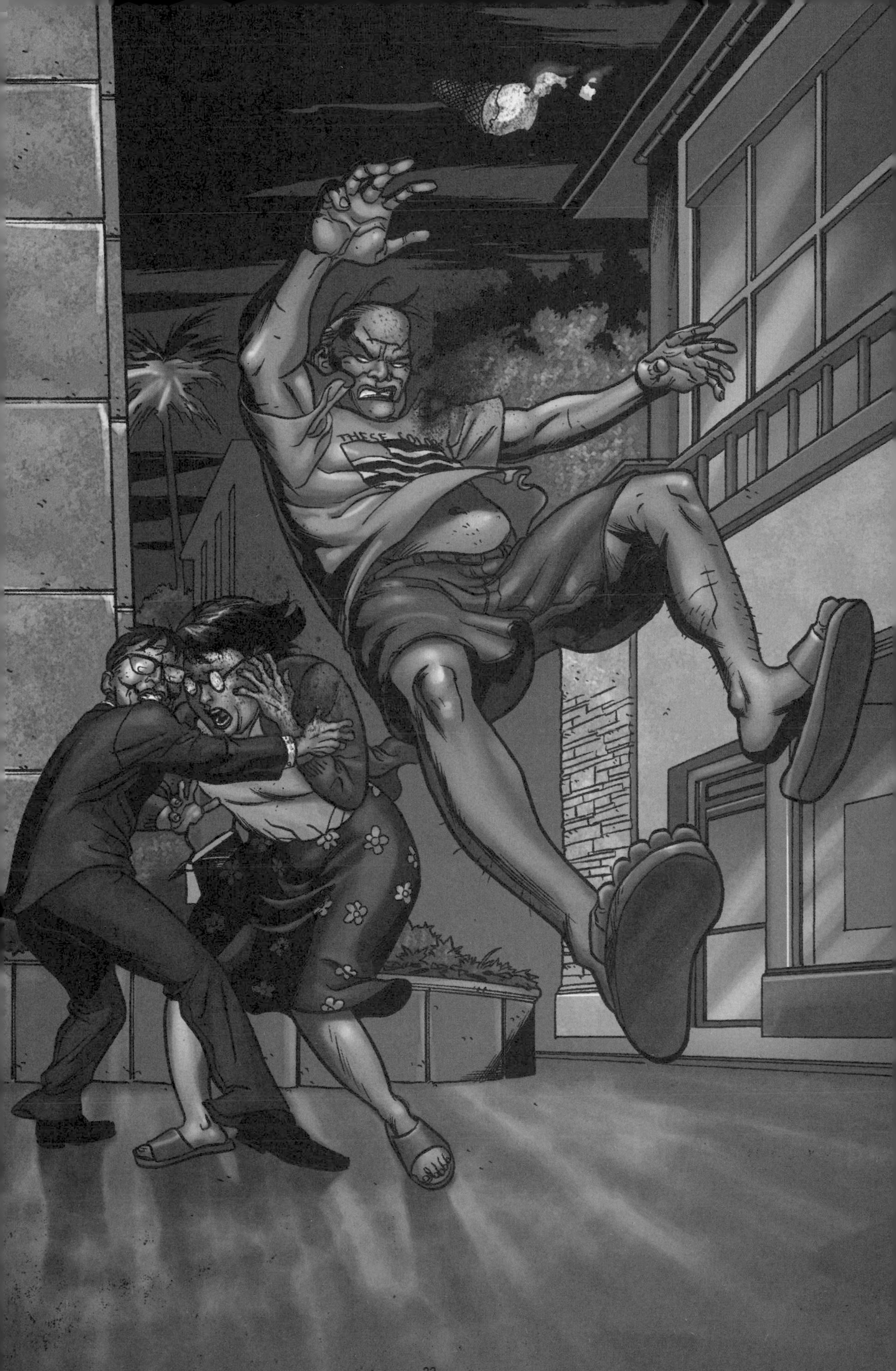
THESE

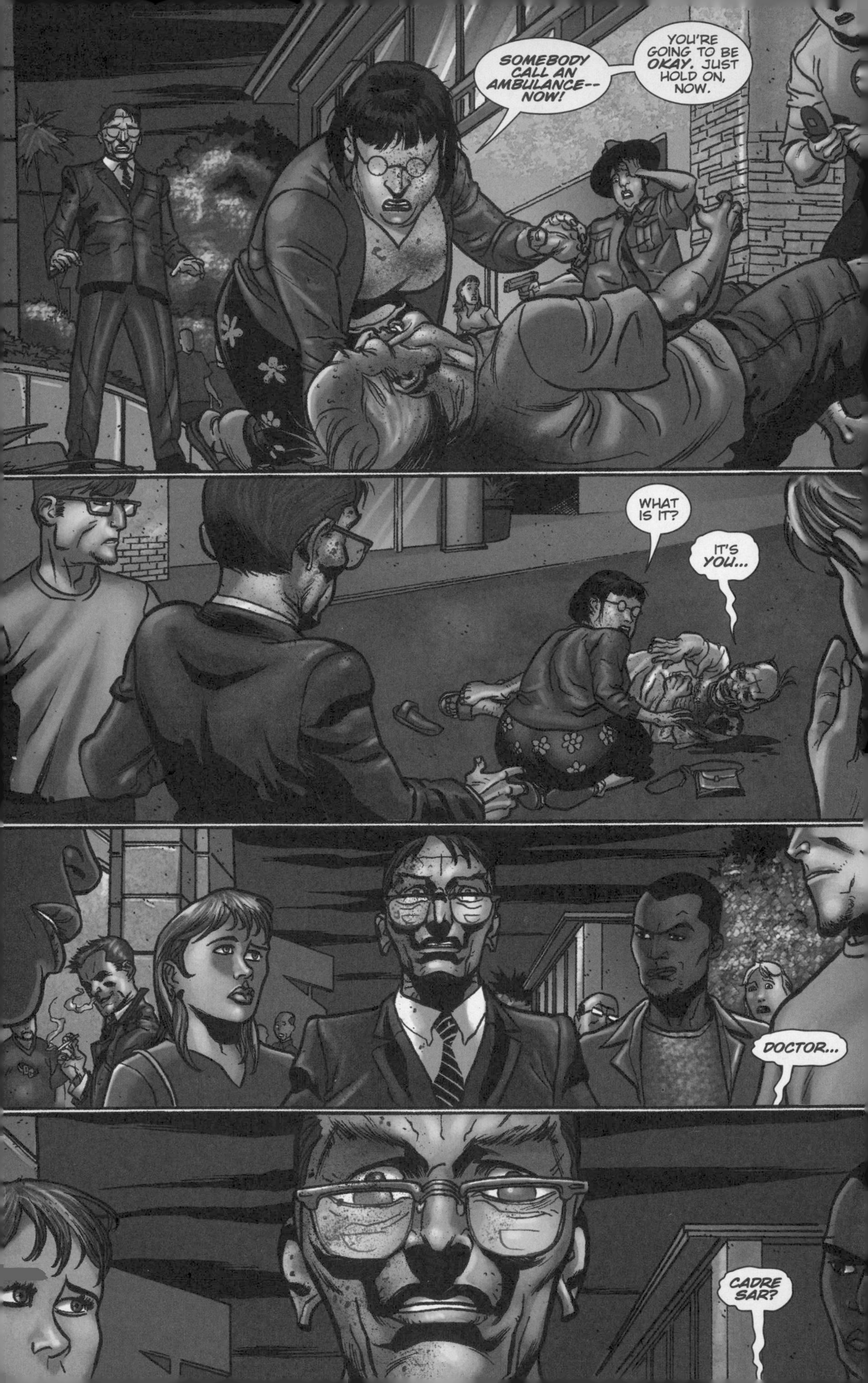
SOMEBODY CALL AN AMBULANCE-- NOW!
YOU'RE GOING TO BE OKAY. JUST HOLD ON, NOW.
WHAT IS IT?
IT'S YOU...
DOCTOR...
CADRE SAR?

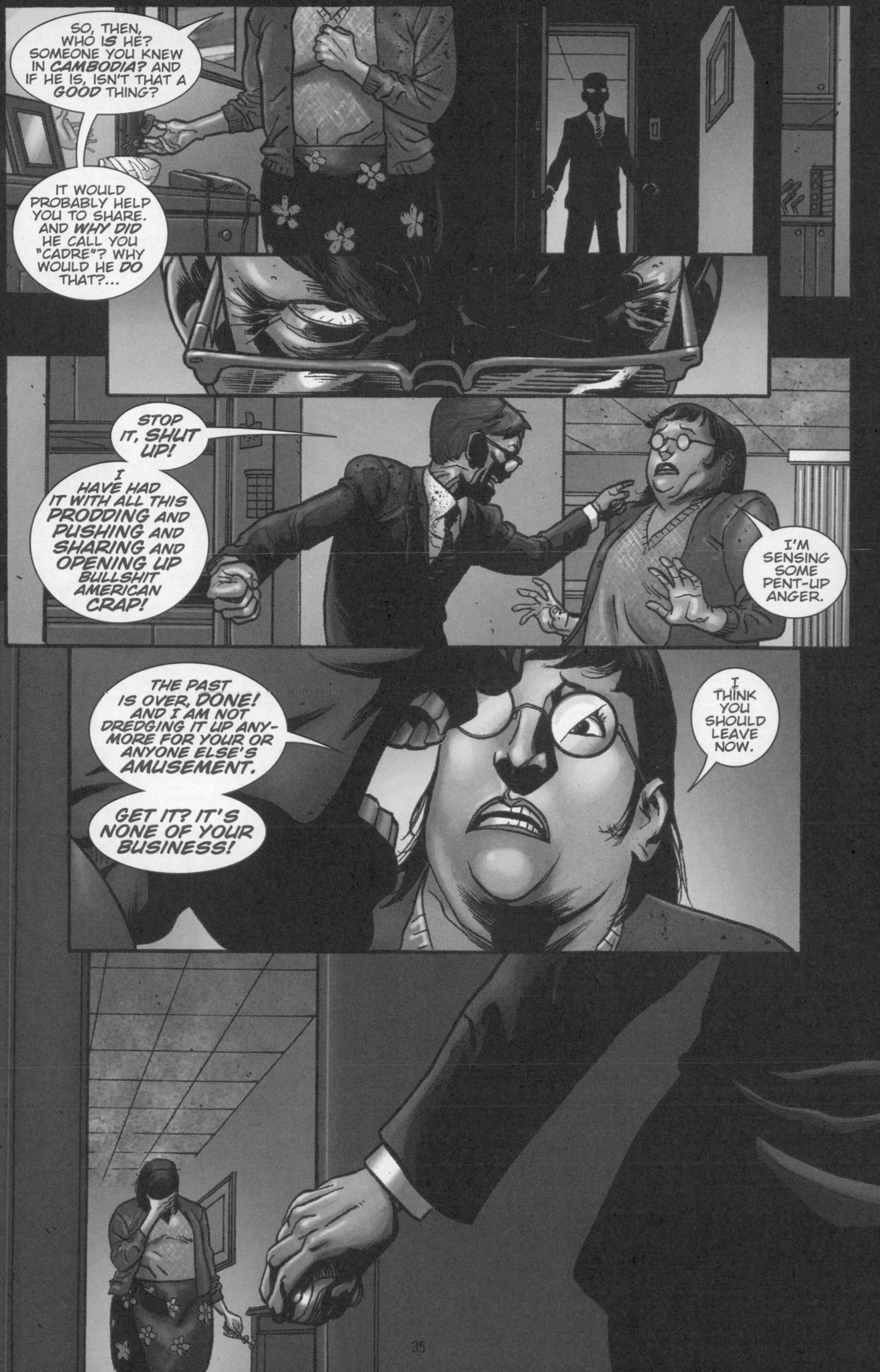
SO, THEN, WHO IS HE? SOMEONE YOU KNEW IN CAMBODIA? AND IF HE IS, ISN'T THAT A GOOD THING?
IT WOULD PROBABLY HELP YOU TO SHARE. AND WHY DID HE CALL YOU "CADRE"? WHY WOULD HE DO THAT?...
STOP IT, SHUT UP!
I HAVE HAD IT WITH ALL THIS PRODDING AND PUSHING AND SHARING AND OPENING UP BULLSHIT AMERICAN CRAP!
I'M SENSING SOME PENT-UP ANGER.
THE PAST IS OVER, DONE! AND I AM NOT DREDGING IT UP ANY-MORE FOR YOUR OR ANYONE ELSE'S AMUSEMENT.
GET IT? IT'S NONE OF YOUR BUSINESS!
I THINK YOU SHOULD LEAVE NOW.

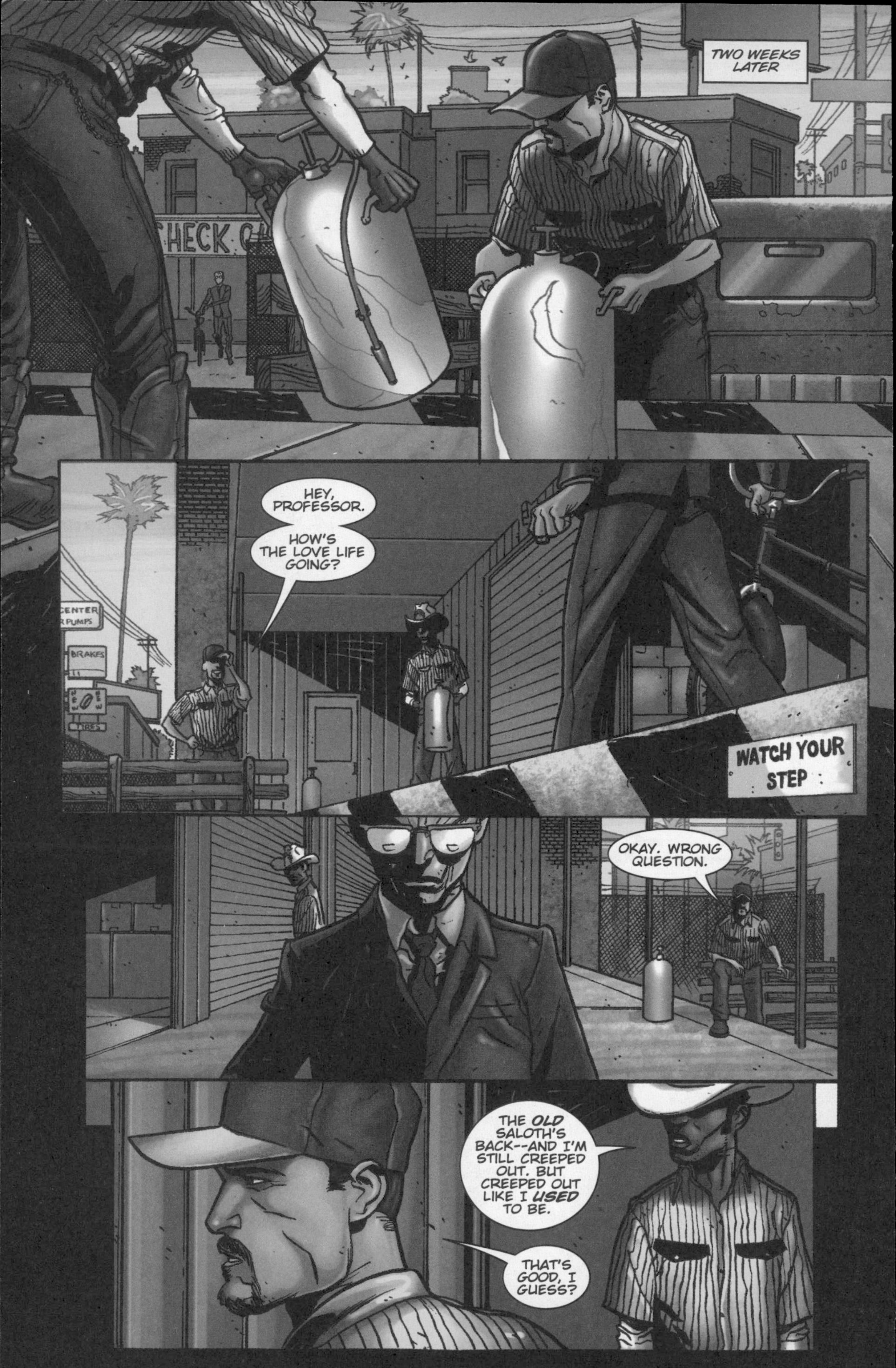
TWO WEEKS LATER
CHECK C
HEY, PROFESSOR.
HOW'S THE LOVE LIFE GOING?
CENTER
BRAKES
TIRES
WATCH YOUR STEP
OKAY. WRONG QUESTION.
THE *OLD* SALOTH'S BACK--AND I'M STILL CREEPED OUT. BUT CREEPED OUT LIKE I *USED* TO BE.
THAT'S GOOD, I GUESS?

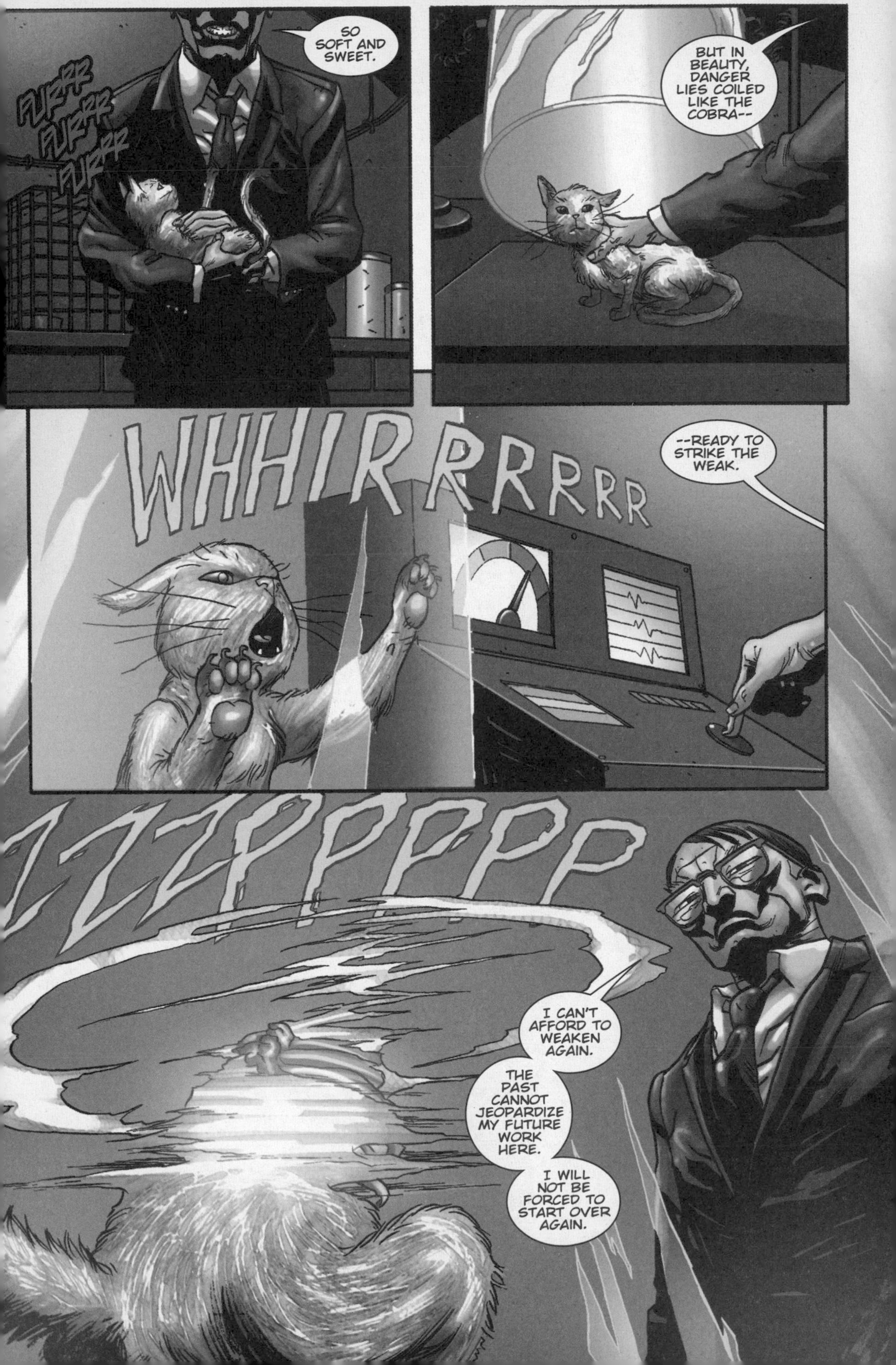

SO SOFT AND SWEET.
FURRR FURRR FURRR
BUT IN BEAUTY, DANGER LIES COILED LIKE THE COBRA--
WHHIRRRRRR
--READY TO STRIKE THE WEAK.
ZZZPPPPPP
I CAN'T AFFORD TO WEAKEN AGAIN.
THE PAST CANNOT JEOPARDIZE MY FUTURE WORK HERE.
I WILL NOT BE FORCED TO START OVER AGAIN.

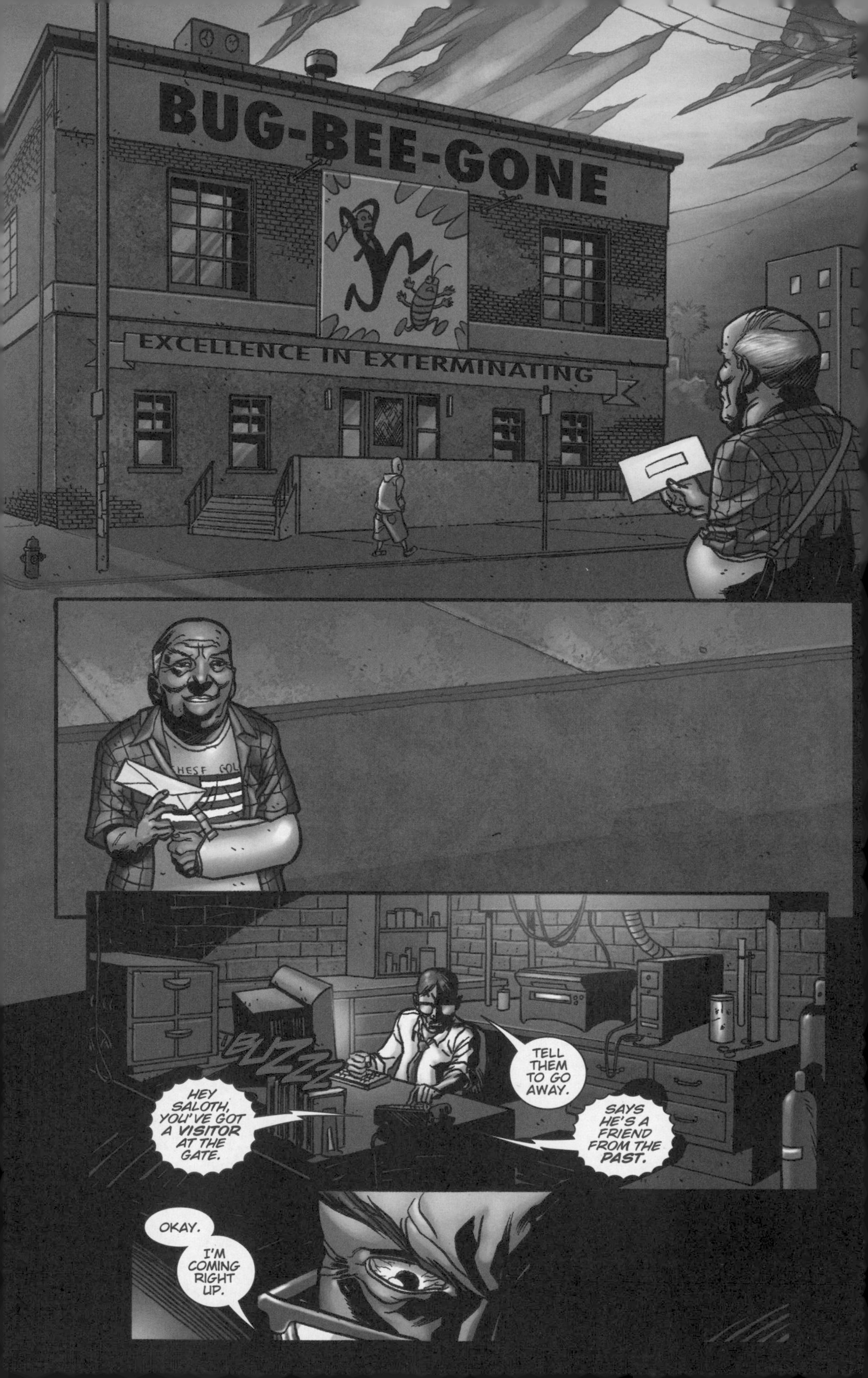
BUG-BEE-GONE
EXCELLENCE IN EXTERMINATING
BUZZZ
HEY SALOTH, YOU'VE GOT A VISITOR AT THE GATE.
TELL THEM TO GO AWAY.
SAYS HE'S A FRIEND FROM THE PAST.
OKAY.
I'M COMING RIGHT UP.

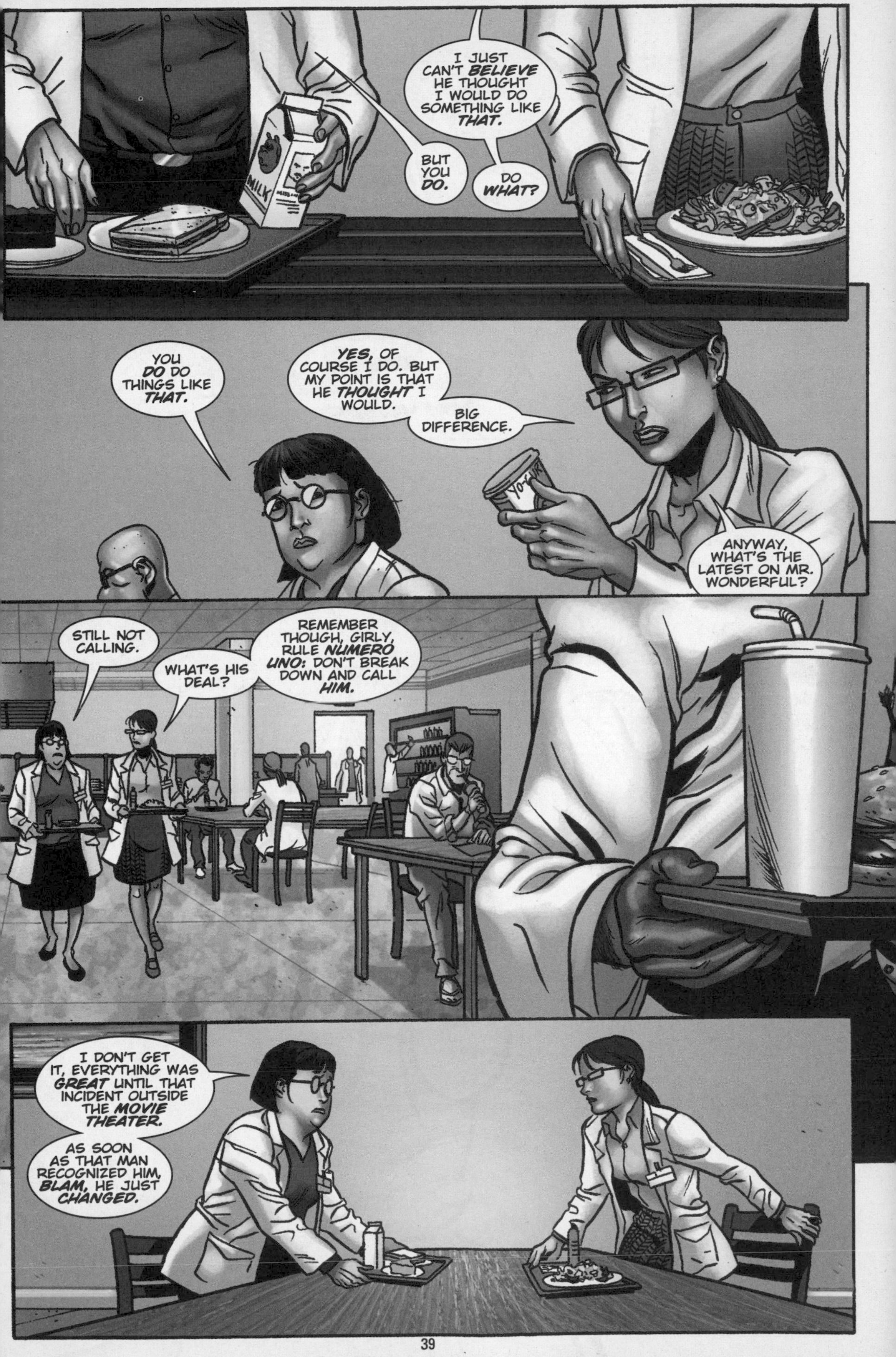
I JUST CAN'T BELIEVE HE THOUGHT I WOULD DO SOMETHING LIKE THAT.
BUT YOU DO.
DO WHAT?
MILK
YOU DO DO THINGS LIKE THAT.
YES, OF COURSE I DO. BUT MY POINT IS THAT HE THOUGHT I WOULD.
BIG DIFFERENCE.
ANYWAY, WHAT'S THE LATEST ON MR. WONDERFUL?
STILL NOT CALLING.
WHAT'S HIS DEAL?
REMEMBER THOUGH, GIRLY, RULE NUMERO UNO: DON'T BREAK DOWN AND CALL HIM.
I DON'T GET IT, EVERYTHING WAS GREAT UNTIL THAT INCIDENT OUTSIDE THE MOVIE THEATER.
AS SOON AS THAT MAN RECOGNIZED HIM, BLAM, HE JUST CHANGED.

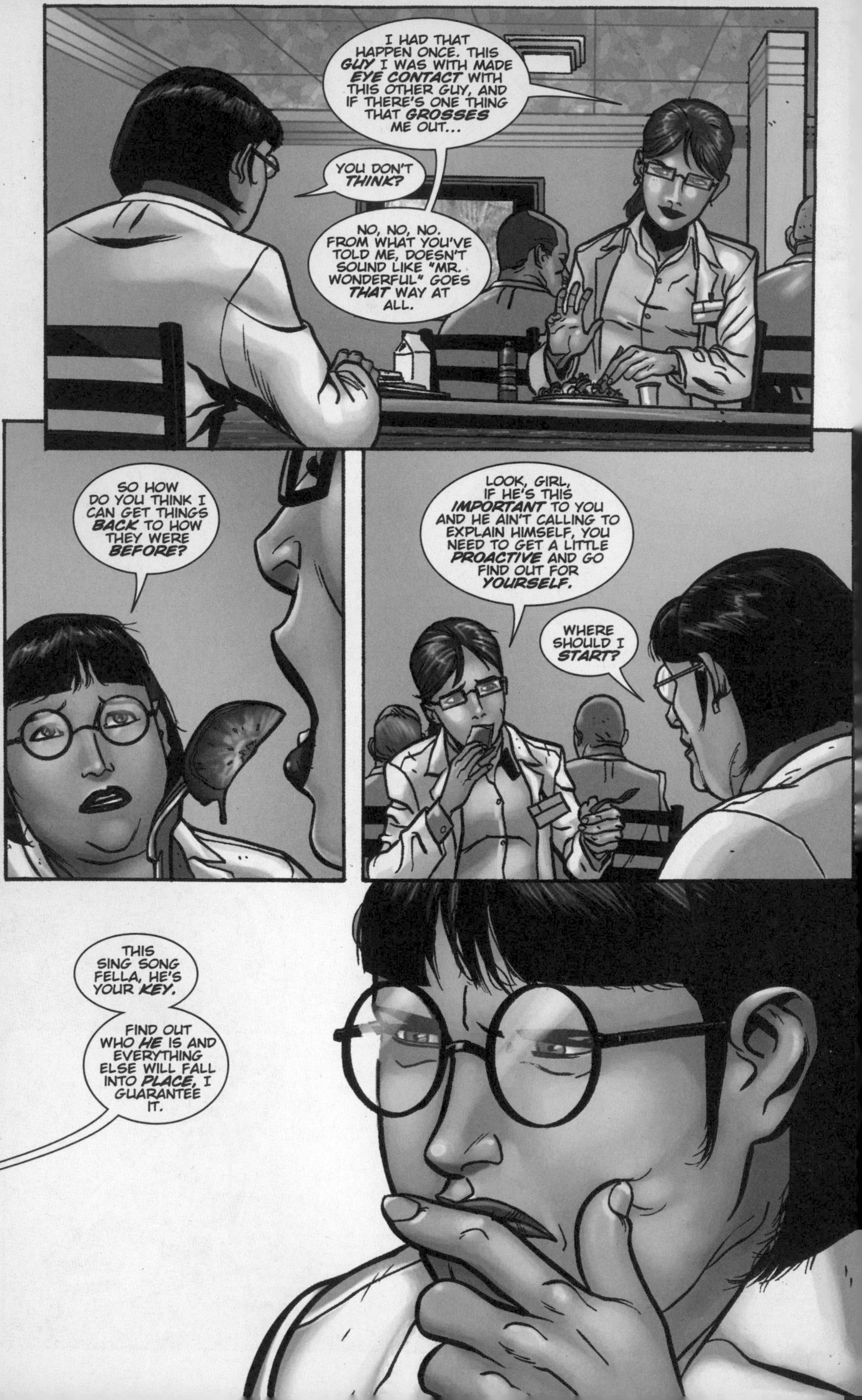
I HAD THAT HAPPEN ONCE. THIS GUY I WAS WITH MADE EYE CONTACT WITH THIS OTHER GUY, AND IF THERE'S ONE THING THAT GROSSES ME OUT...
YOU DON'T THINK?
NO, NO, NO. FROM WHAT YOU'VE TOLD ME, DOESN'T SOUND LIKE "MR. WONDERFUL" GOES THAT WAY AT ALL.
SO HOW DO YOU THINK I CAN GET THINGS BACK TO HOW THEY WERE BEFORE?
LOOK, GIRL, IF HE'S THIS IMPORTANT TO YOU AND HE AIN'T CALLING TO EXPLAIN HIMSELF, YOU NEED TO GET A LITTLE PROACTIVE AND GO FIND OUT FOR YOURSELF.
WHERE SHOULD I START?
THIS SING SONG FELLA, HE'S YOUR KEY.
FIND OUT WHO HE IS AND EVERYTHING ELSE WILL FALL INTO PLACE, I GUARANTEE IT.

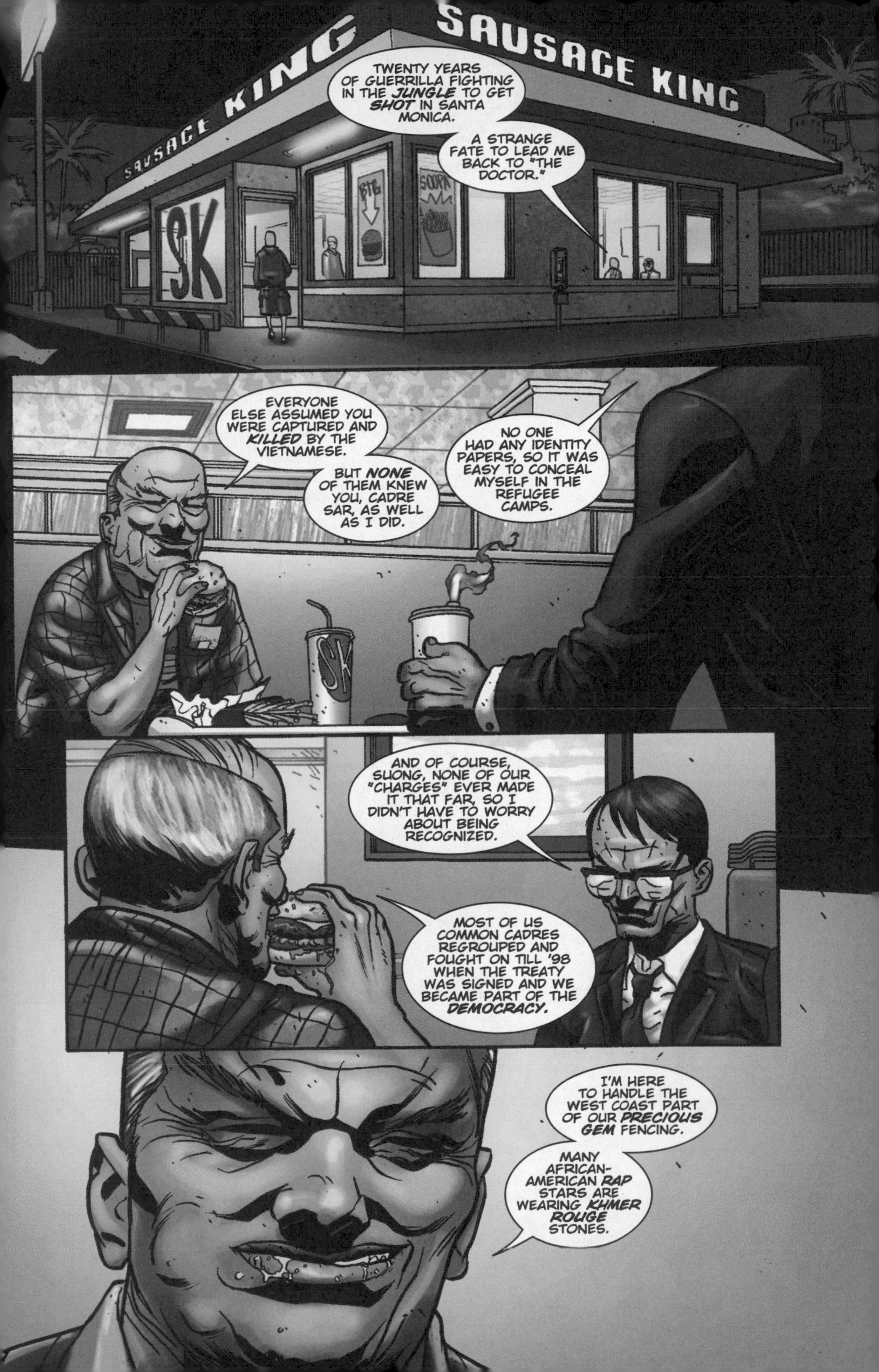
SAUSAGE KING
SAUSAGE KING
TWENTY YEARS OF GUERRILLA FIGHTING IN THE JUNGLE TO GET SHOT IN SANTA MONICA.
A STRANGE FATE TO LEAD ME BACK TO "THE DOCTOR."
SK
EVERYONE ELSE ASSUMED YOU WERE CAPTURED AND KILLED BY THE VIETNAMESE.
BUT NONE OF THEM KNEW YOU, CADRE SAR, AS WELL AS I DID.
NO ONE HAD ANY IDENTITY PAPERS, SO IT WAS EASY TO CONCEAL MYSELF IN THE REFUGEE CAMPS.
AND OF COURSE, SUONG, NONE OF OUR "CHARGES" EVER MADE IT THAT FAR, SO I DIDN'T HAVE TO WORRY ABOUT BEING RECOGNIZED.
MOST OF US COMMON CADRES REGROUPED AND FOUGHT ON TILL '98 WHEN THE TREATY WAS SIGNED AND WE BECAME PART OF THE DEMOCRACY.
I'M HERE TO HANDLE THE WEST COAST PART OF OUR PRECIOUS GEM FENCING.
MANY AFRICAN-AMERICAN RAP STARS ARE WEARING KHMER ROUGE STONES.

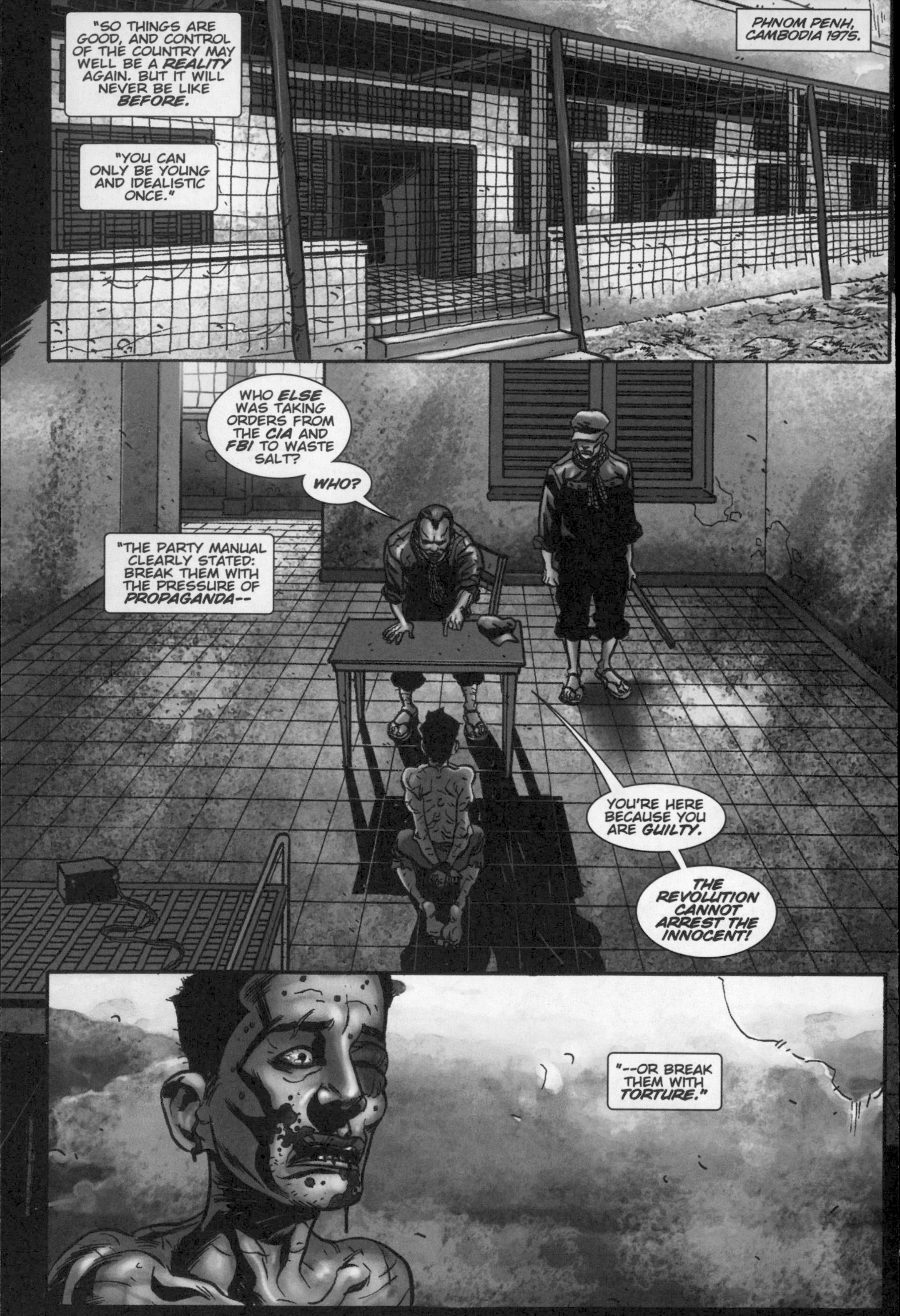
"SO THINGS ARE GOOD, AND CONTROL OF THE COUNTRY MAY WELL BE A REALITY AGAIN. BUT IT WILL NEVER BE LIKE BEFORE.
PHNOM PENH, CAMBODIA 1975.
"YOU CAN ONLY BE YOUNG AND IDEALISTIC ONCE."
WHO ELSE WAS TAKING ORDERS FROM THE CIA AND FBI TO WASTE SALT?
WHO?
"THE PARTY MANUAL CLEARLY STATED: BREAK THEM WITH THE PRESSURE OF PROPAGANDA--
YOU'RE HERE BECAUSE YOU ARE GUILTY.
THE REVOLUTION CANNOT ARREST THE INNOCENT!
"--OR BREAK THEM WITH TORTURE."

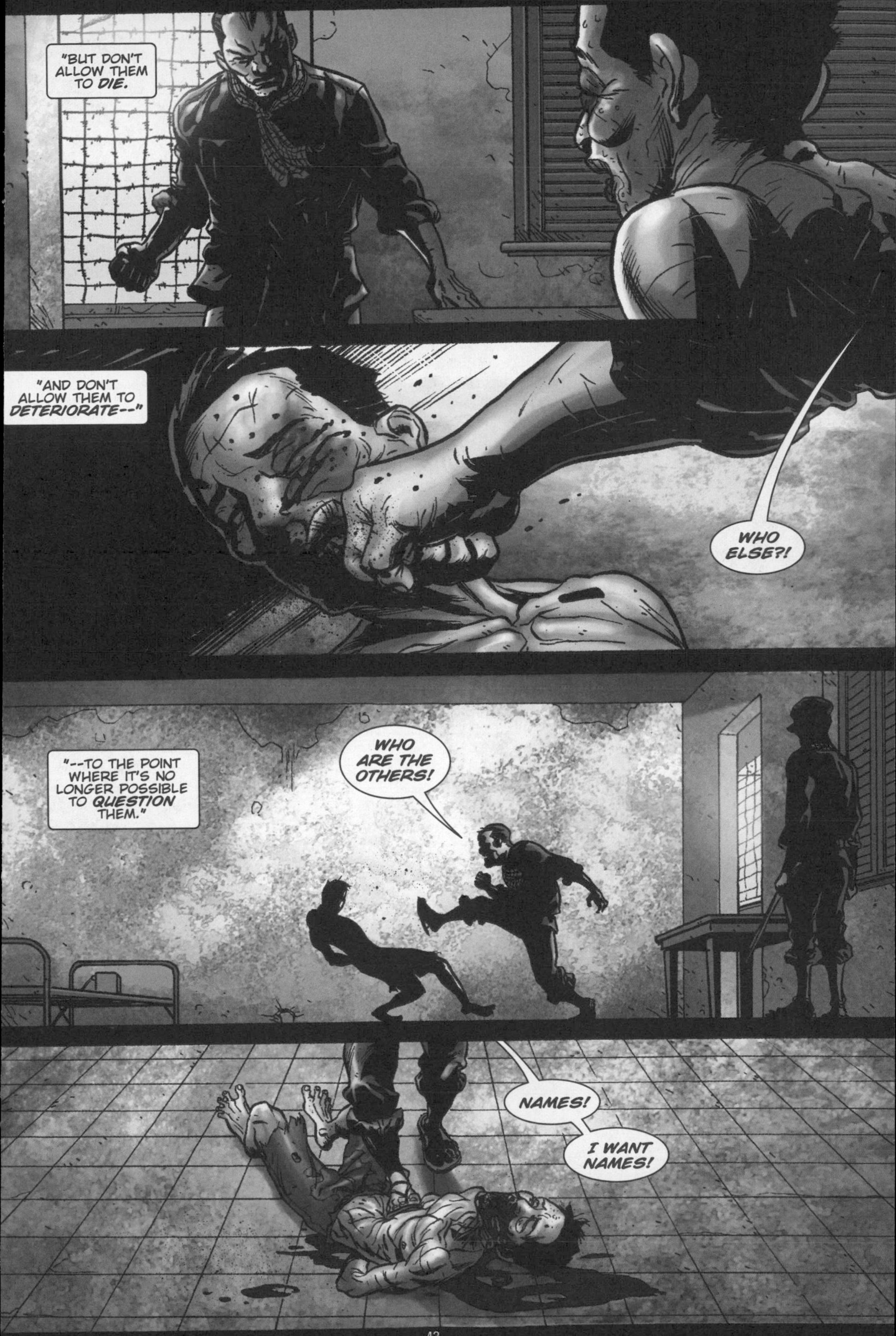
"BUT DON'T ALLOW THEM TO *DIE*.
"AND DON'T ALLOW THEM TO *DETERIORATE*--"
WHO ELSE?!
"--TO THE POINT WHERE IT'S NO LONGER POSSIBLE TO *QUESTION* THEM."
WHO ARE THE OTHERS!
NAMES!
I WANT NAMES!

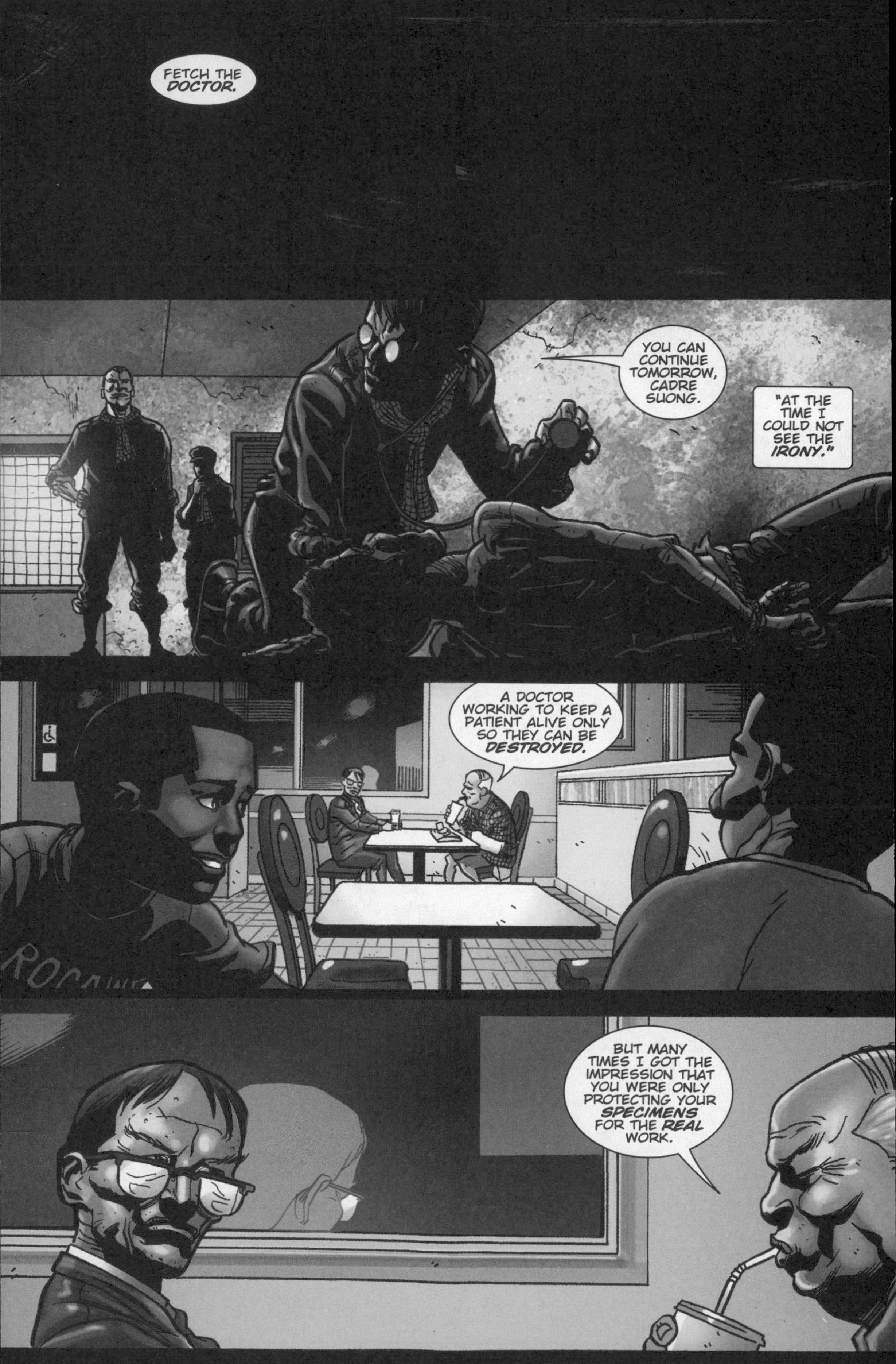
FETCH THE DOCTOR.
YOU CAN CONTINUE TOMORROW, CADRE SUONG.
"AT THE TIME I COULD NOT SEE THE IRONY."
A DOCTOR WORKING TO KEEP A PATIENT ALIVE ONLY SO THEY CAN BE DESTROYED.
BUT MANY TIMES I GOT THE IMPRESSION THAT YOU WERE ONLY PROTECTING YOUR SPECIMENS FOR THE REAL WORK.

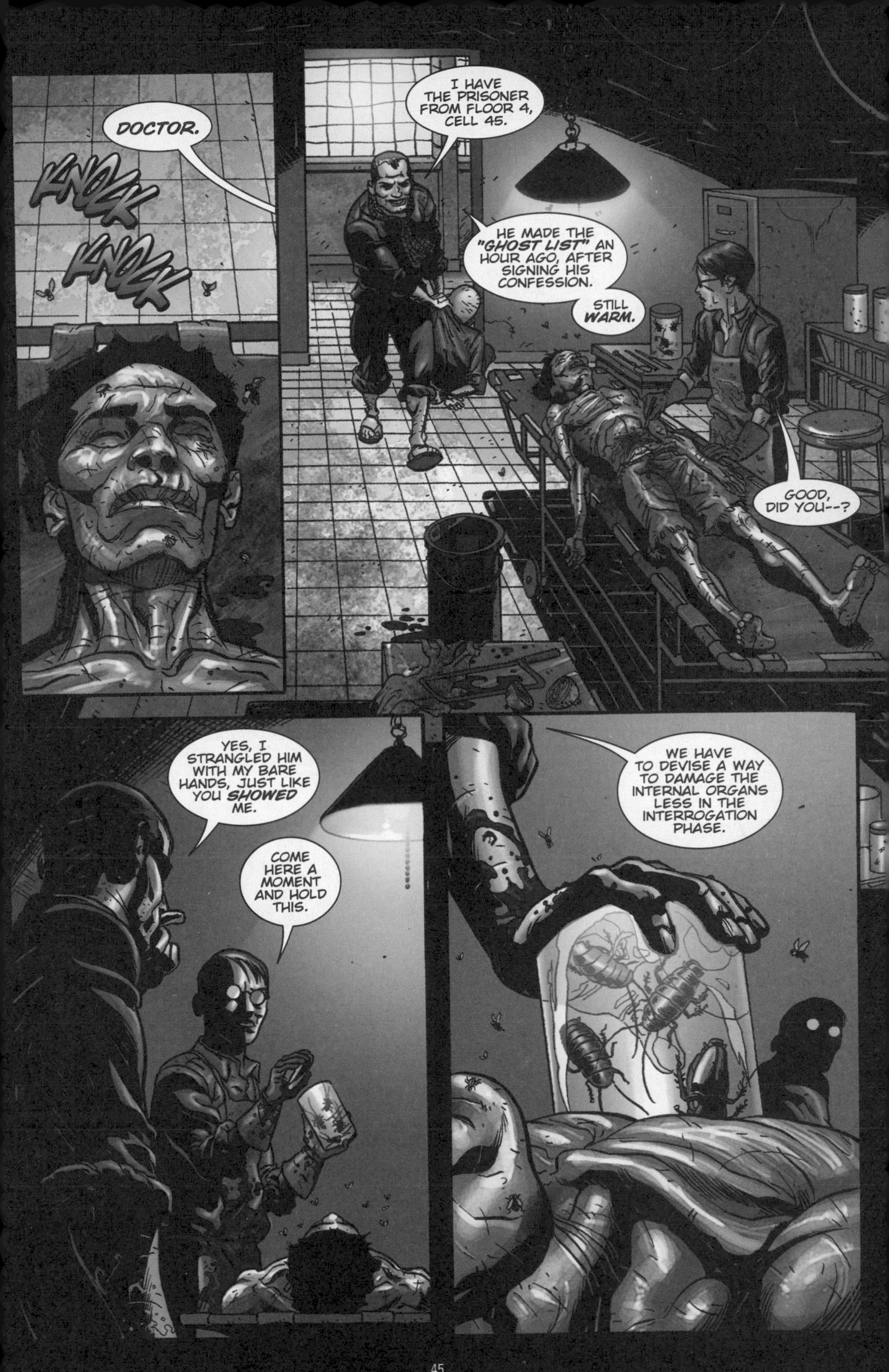
DOCTOR.
KNOCK KNOCK
I HAVE THE PRISONER FROM FLOOR 4, CELL 45.
HE MADE THE "GHOST LIST" AN HOUR AGO, AFTER SIGNING HIS CONFESSION.
STILL WARM.
GOOD, DID YOU--?
YES, I STRANGLED HIM WITH MY BARE HANDS, JUST LIKE YOU SHOWED ME.
COME HERE A MOMENT AND HOLD THIS.
WE HAVE TO DEVISE A WAY TO DAMAGE THE INTERNAL ORGANS LESS IN THE INTERROGATION PHASE.

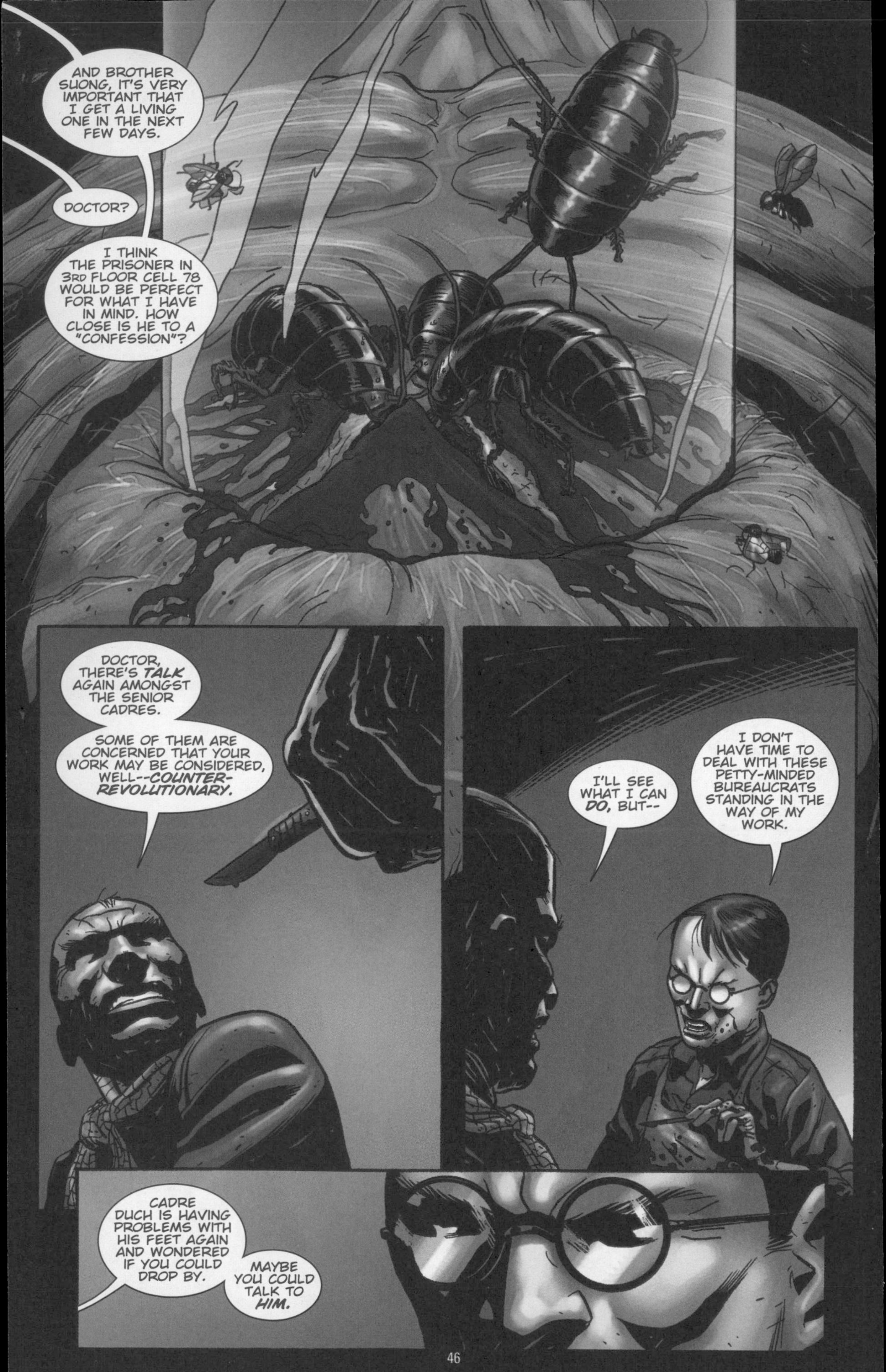
AND BROTHER SUONG, IT'S VERY IMPORTANT THAT I GET A LIVING ONE IN THE NEXT FEW DAYS.
DOCTOR?
I THINK THE PRISONER IN 3RD FLOOR CELL 78 WOULD BE PERFECT FOR WHAT I HAVE IN MIND. HOW CLOSE IS HE TO A "CONFESSION"?
DOCTOR, THERE'S TALK AGAIN AMONGST THE SENIOR CADRES.
SOME OF THEM ARE CONCERNED THAT YOUR WORK MAY BE CONSIDERED, WELL--COUNTER-REVOLUTIONARY.
I'LL SEE WHAT I CAN DO, BUT--
I DON'T HAVE TIME TO DEAL WITH THESE PETTY-MINDED BUREAUCRATS STANDING IN THE WAY OF MY WORK.
CADRE DUCH IS HAVING PROBLEMS WITH HIS FEET AGAIN AND WONDERED IF YOU COULD DROP BY.
MAYBE YOU COULD TALK TO HIM.

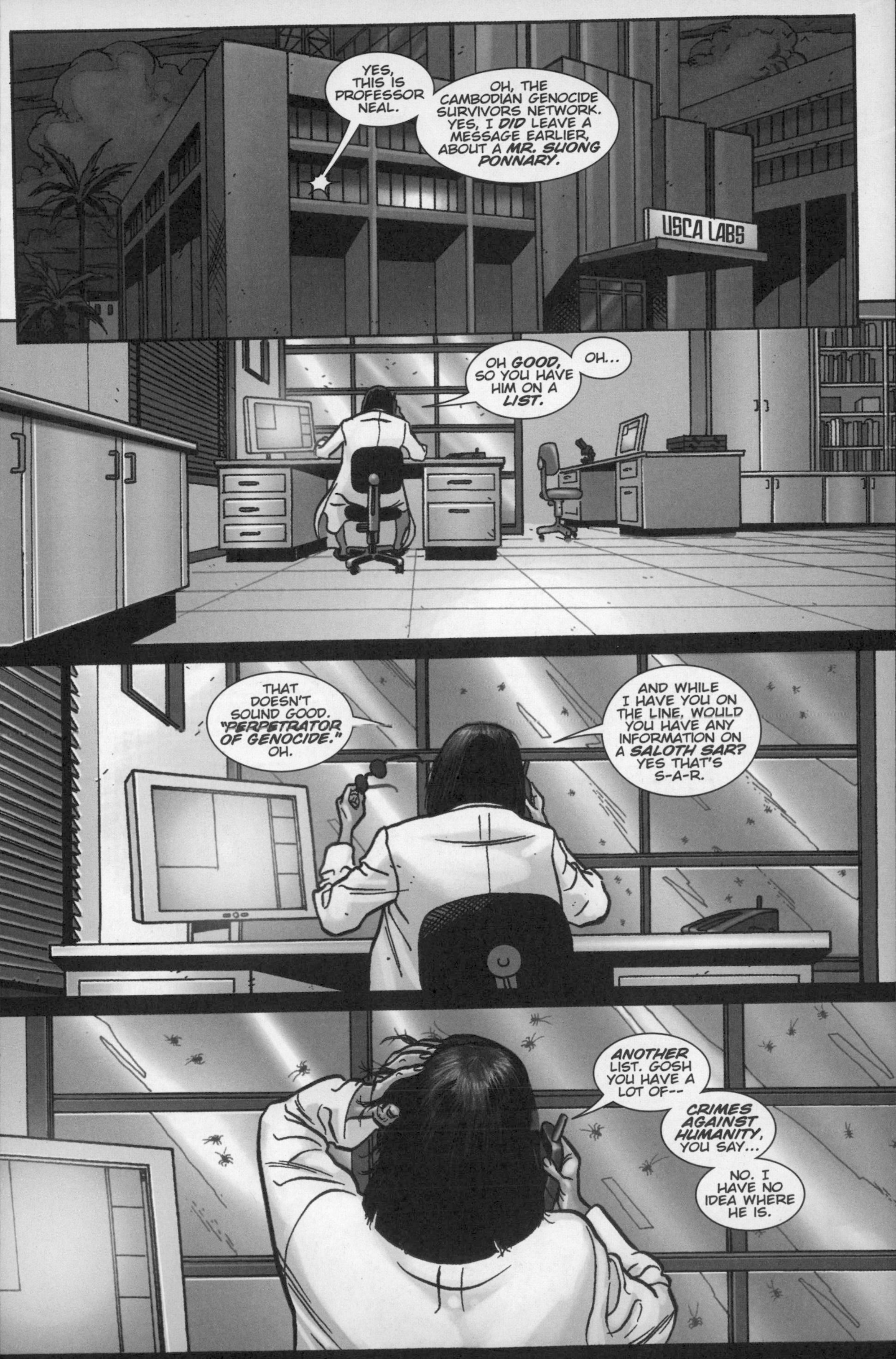
YES, THIS IS PROFESSOR NEAL.
OH, THE CAMBODIAN GENOCIDE SURVIVORS NETWORK. YES, I DID LEAVE A MESSAGE EARLIER, ABOUT A MR. SUONG PONNARY.
USCA LABS
OH GOOD, SO YOU HAVE HIM ON A LIST.
OH...
THAT DOESN'T SOUND GOOD. "PERPETRATOR OF GENOCIDE." OH.
AND WHILE I HAVE YOU ON THE LINE, WOULD YOU HAVE ANY INFORMATION ON A SALOTH SAR? YES THAT'S S-A-R.
ANOTHER LIST. GOSH YOU HAVE A LOT OF--
CRIMES AGAINST HUMANITY, YOU SAY...
NO. I HAVE NO IDEA WHERE HE IS.

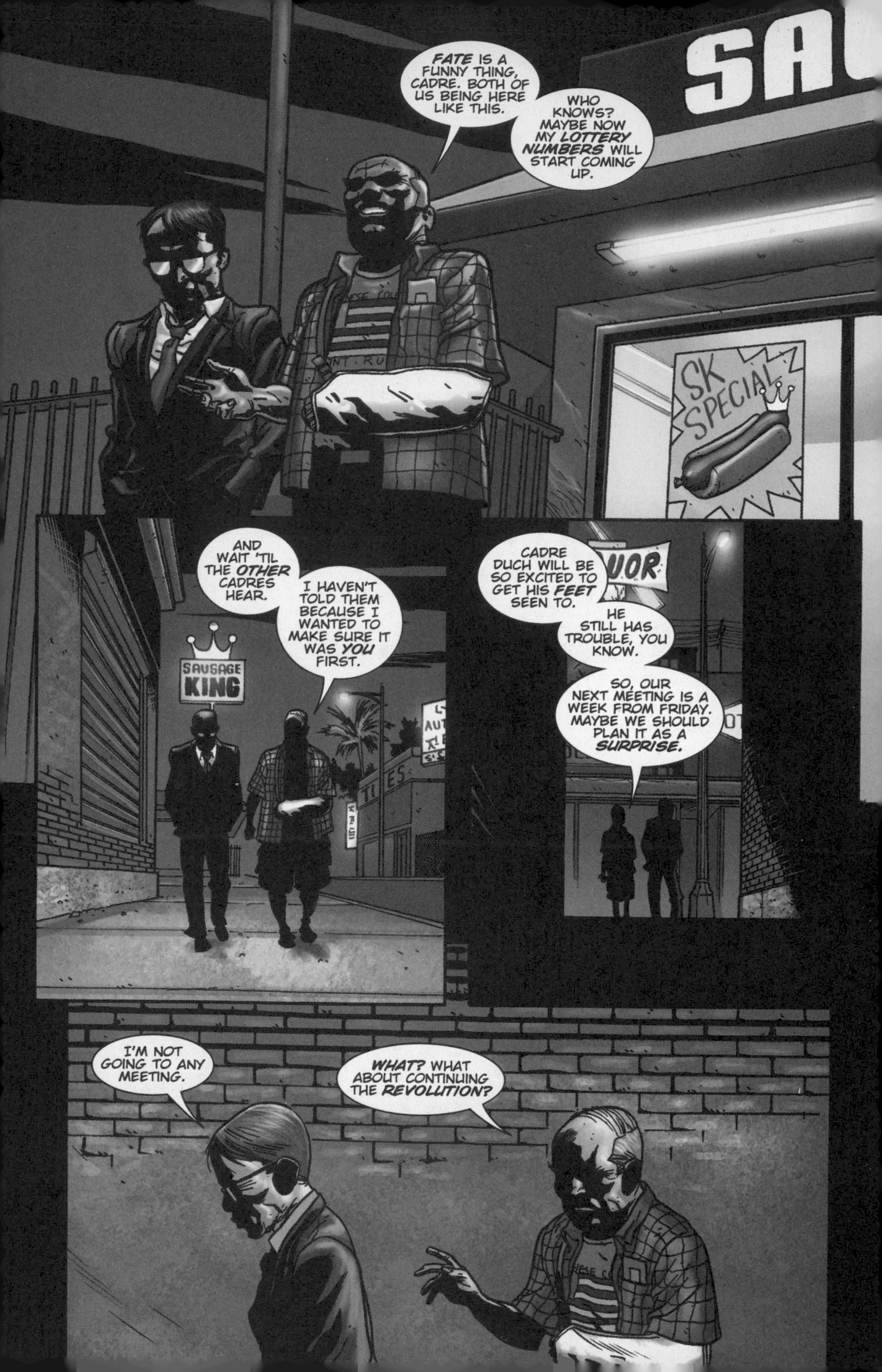
SAU
FATE IS A FUNNY THING, CADRE. BOTH OF US BEING HERE LIKE THIS.
WHO KNOWS? MAYBE NOW MY LOTTERY NUMBERS WILL START COMING UP.
SK SPECIAL
AND WAIT 'TIL THE OTHER CADRES HEAR.
I HAVEN'T TOLD THEM BECAUSE I WANTED TO MAKE SURE IT WAS YOU FIRST.
SAUSAGE KING
CADRE DUCH WILL BE SO EXCITED TO GET HIS FEET SEEN TO.
HE STILL HAS TROUBLE, YOU KNOW.
SO, OUR NEXT MEETING IS A WEEK FROM FRIDAY. MAYBE WE SHOULD PLAN IT AS A SURPRISE.
I'M NOT GOING TO ANY MEETING.
WHAT? WHAT ABOUT CONTINUING THE REVOLUTION?

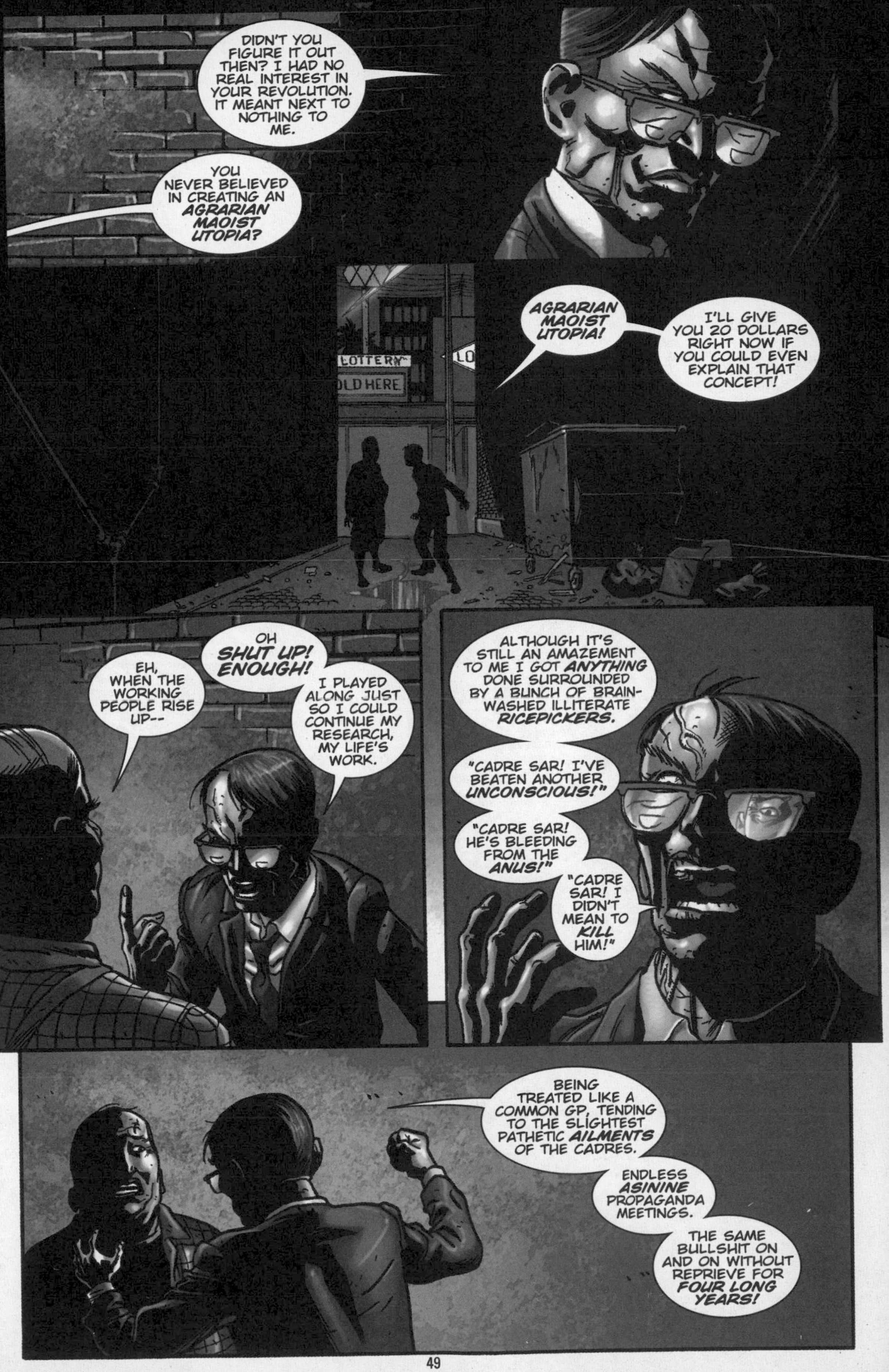
DIDN'T YOU FIGURE IT OUT THEN? I HAD NO REAL INTEREST IN YOUR REVOLUTION. IT MEANT NEXT TO NOTHING TO ME.
YOU NEVER BELIEVED IN CREATING AN AGRARIAN MAOIST UTOPIA?
LOTTERY
OLD HERE
LO
AGRARIAN MAOIST UTOPIA!
I'LL GIVE YOU 20 DOLLARS RIGHT NOW IF YOU COULD EVEN EXPLAIN THAT CONCEPT!
EH, WHEN THE WORKING PEOPLE RISE UP--
OH SHUT UP! ENOUGH!
I PLAYED ALONG JUST SO I COULD CONTINUE MY RESEARCH, MY LIFE'S WORK.
ALTHOUGH IT'S STILL AN AMAZEMENT TO ME I GOT ANYTHING DONE SURROUNDED BY A BUNCH OF BRAIN-WASHED ILLITERATE RICEPICKERS.
"CADRE SAR! I'VE BEATEN ANOTHER UNCONSCIOUS!"
"CADRE SAR! HE'S BLEEDING FROM THE ANUS!"
"CADRE SAR! I DIDN'T MEAN TO KILL HIM!"
BEING TREATED LIKE A COMMON GP, TENDING TO THE SLIGHTEST PATHETIC AILMENTS OF THE CADRES.
ENDLESS ASININE PROPAGANDA MEETINGS.
THE SAME BULLSHIT ON AND ON WITHOUT REPRIEVE FOR FOUR LONG YEARS!

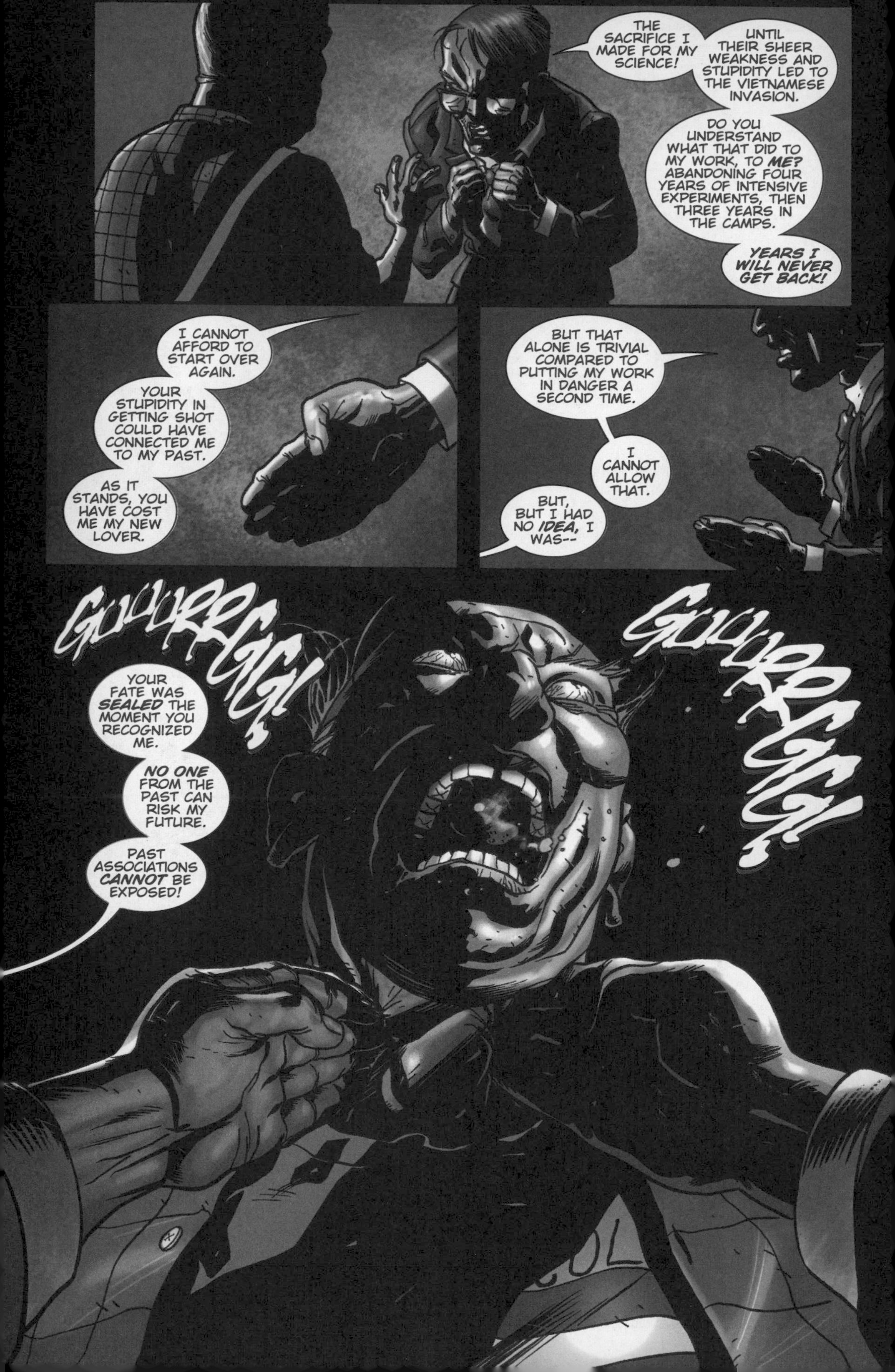
THE SACRIFICE I MADE FOR MY SCIENCE!
UNTIL THEIR SHEER WEAKNESS AND STUPIDITY LED TO THE VIETNAMESE INVASION.
DO YOU UNDERSTAND WHAT THAT DID TO MY WORK, TO *ME?* ABANDONING FOUR YEARS OF INTENSIVE EXPERIMENTS, THEN THREE YEARS IN THE CAMPS.
YEARS I WILL NEVER GET BACK!
I CANNOT AFFORD TO START OVER AGAIN.
YOUR STUPIDITY IN GETTING SHOT COULD HAVE CONNECTED ME TO MY PAST.
AS IT STANDS, YOU HAVE COST ME MY NEW LOVER.
BUT THAT ALONE IS TRIVIAL COMPARED TO PUTTING MY WORK IN DANGER A SECOND TIME.
I CANNOT ALLOW THAT.
BUT, BUT I HAD NO *IDEA,* I WAS--
GUURRGG!
GUURRGG!
YOUR FATE WAS *SEALED* THE MOMENT YOU RECOGNIZED ME.
NO ONE FROM THE PAST CAN RISK MY FUTURE.
PAST ASSOCIATIONS *CANNOT* BE EXPOSED!

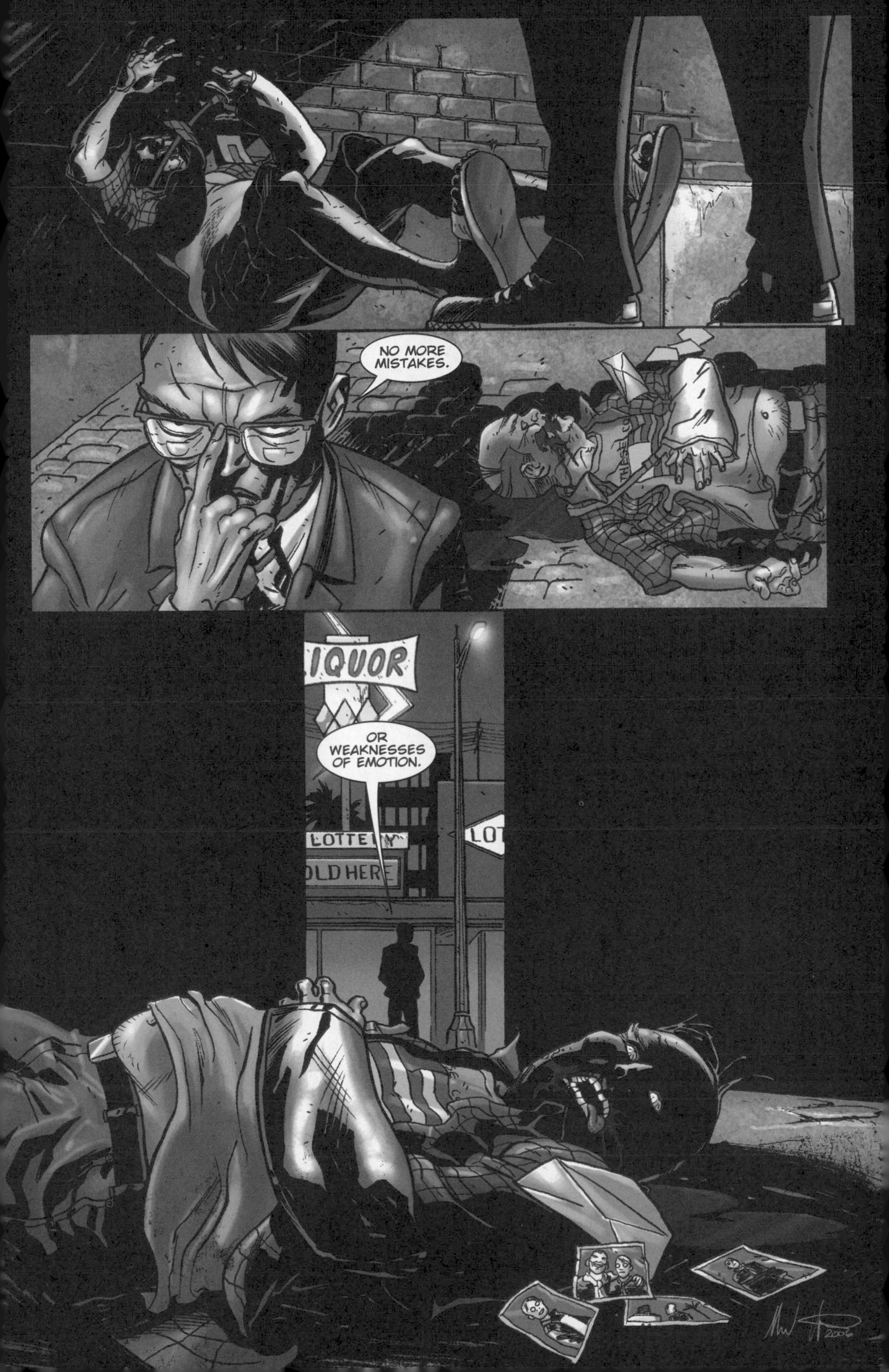
NO MORE MISTAKES.
LIQUOR
OR WEAKNESSES OF EMOTION.
LOTTERY
OLD HERE
LOT

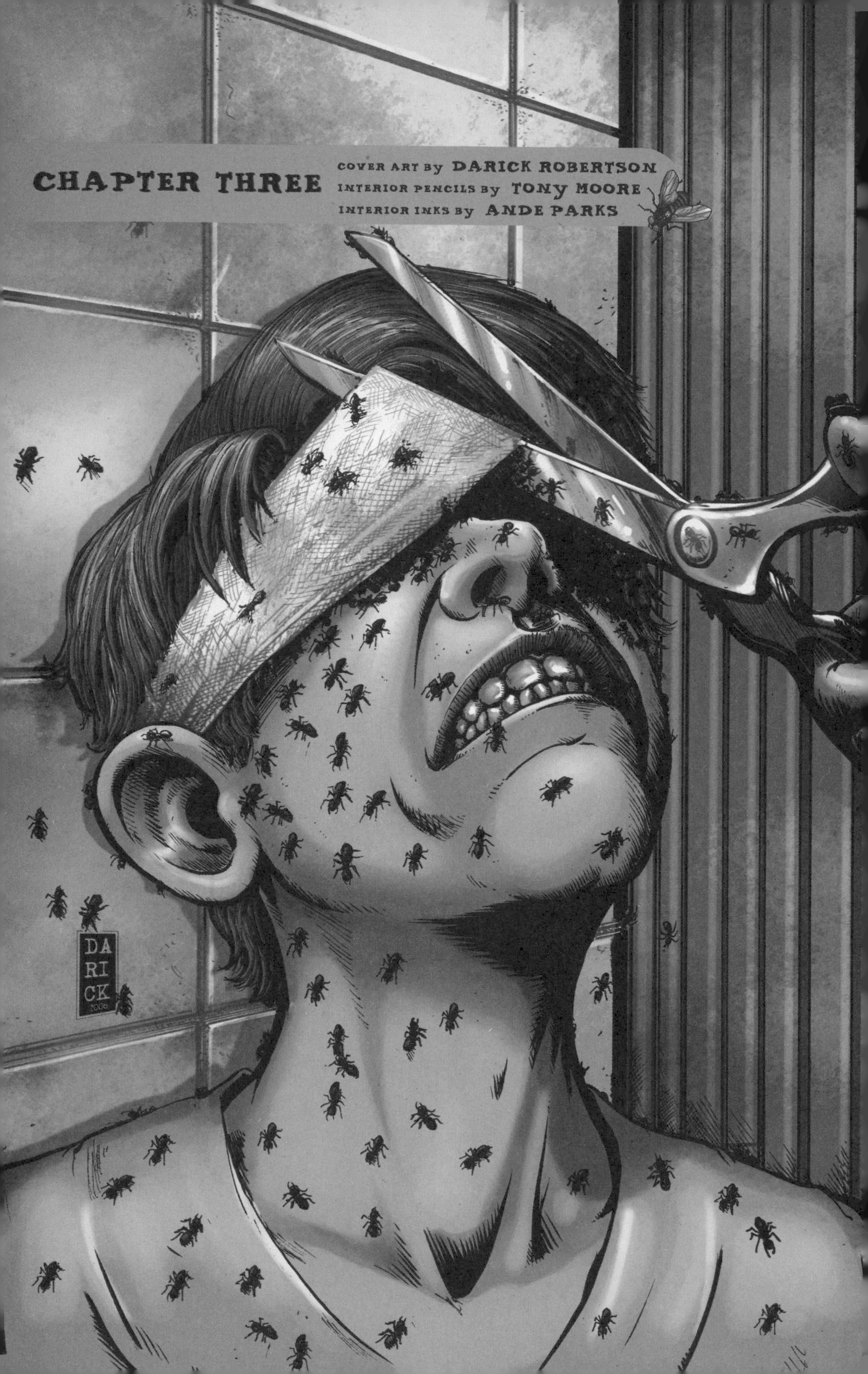
CHAPTER THREE
COVER ART BY DARICK ROBERTSON
INTERIOR PENCILS BY TONY MOORE
INTERIOR INKS BY ANDE PARKS
DARICK

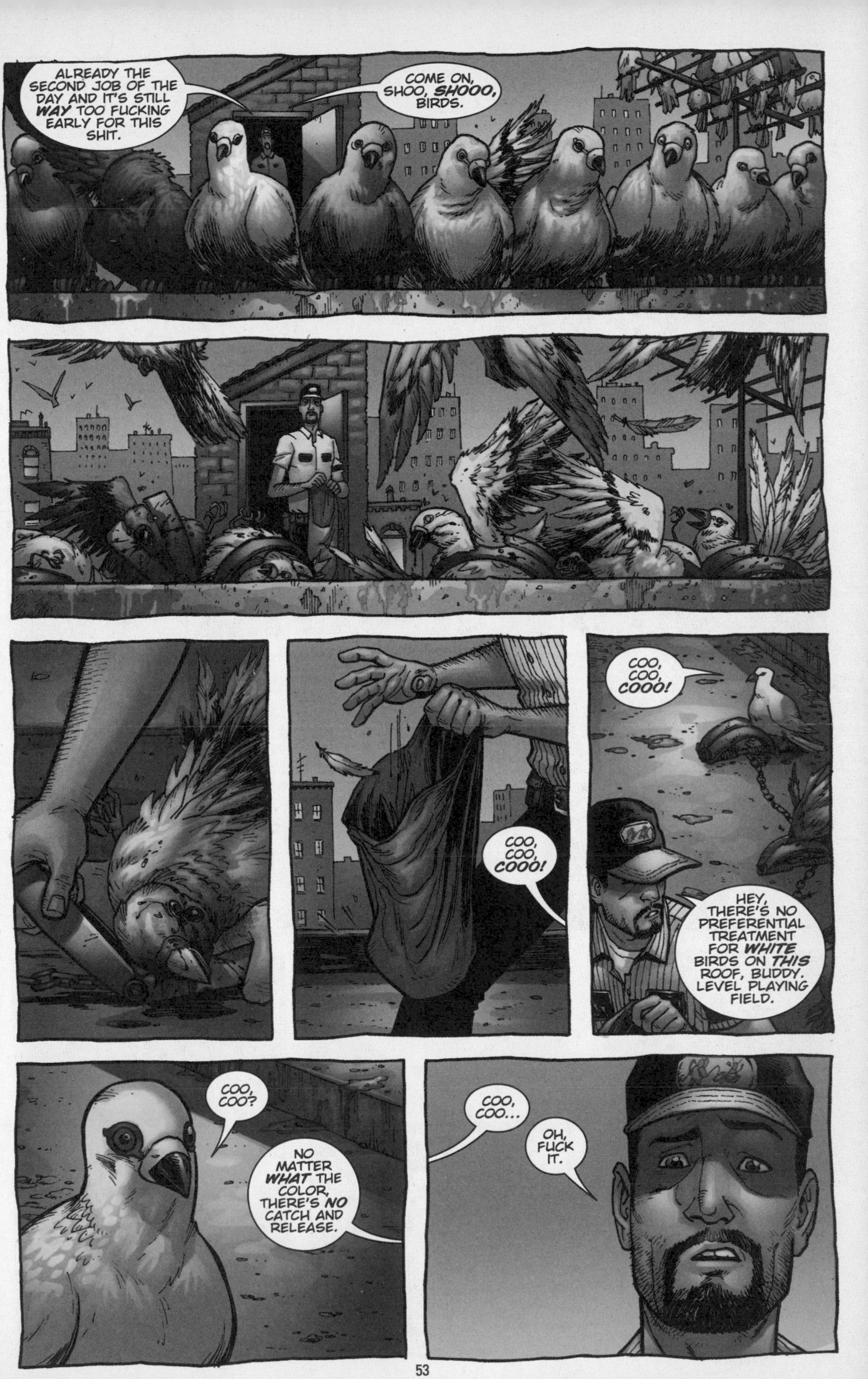

ALREADY THE SECOND JOB OF THE DAY AND IT'S STILL WAY TOO FUCKING EARLY FOR THIS SHIT.
COME ON, SHOO, SHOOO, BIRDS.
COO, COO, COOO!
COO, COO, COOO!
HEY, THERE'S NO PREFERENTIAL TREATMENT FOR WHITE BIRDS ON THIS ROOF, BUDDY. LEVEL PLAYING FIELD.
COO, COO?
NO MATTER WHAT THE COLOR, THERE'S NO CATCH AND RELEASE.
COO, COO...
OH, FUCK IT.

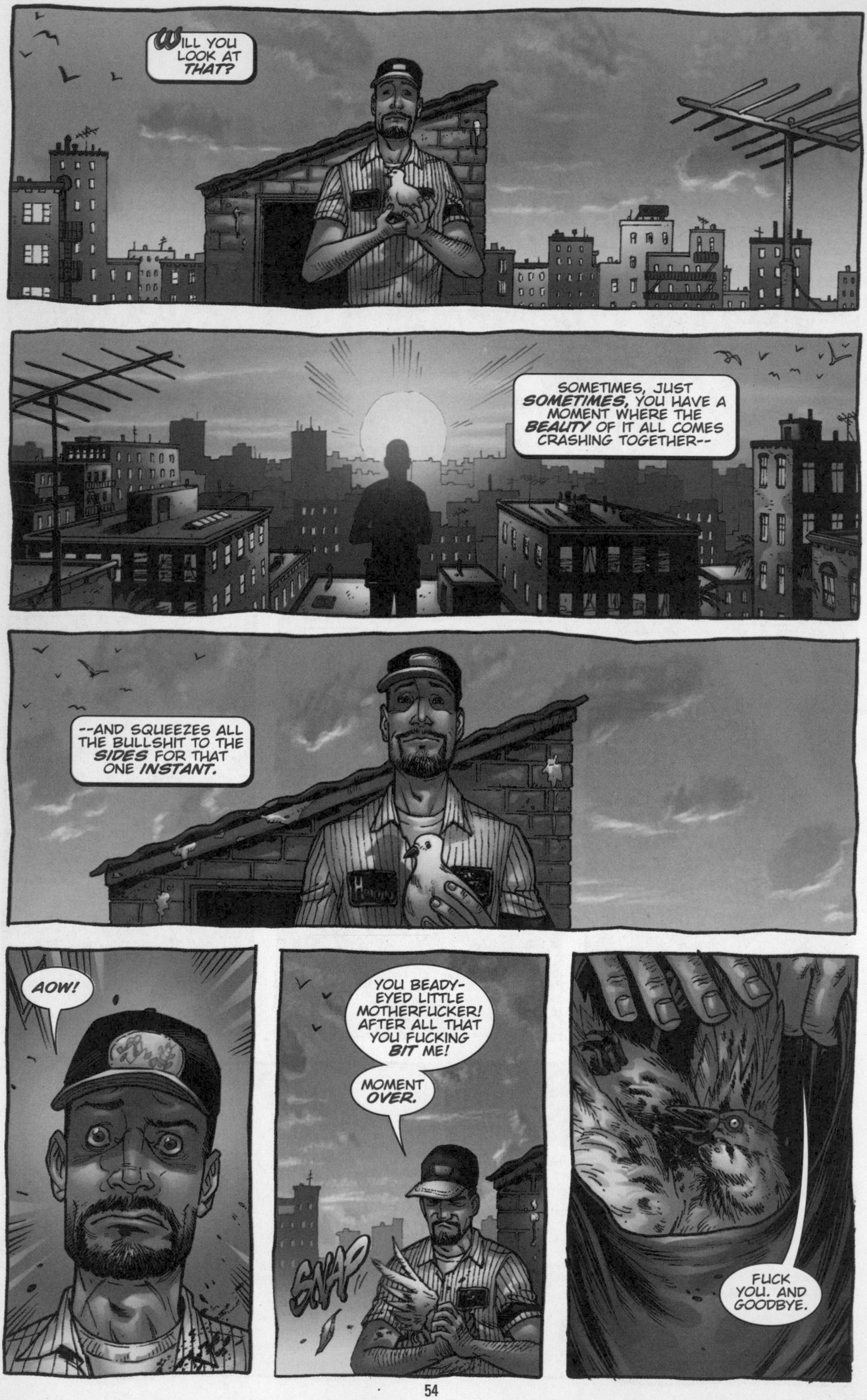
WILL YOU LOOK AT THAT?
SOMETIMES, JUST SOMETIMES, YOU HAVE A MOMENT WHERE THE BEAUTY OF IT ALL COMES CRASHING TOGETHER--
--AND SQUEEZES ALL THE BULLSHIT TO THE SIDES FOR THAT ONE INSTANT.
AOW!
YOU BEADY-EYED LITTLE MOTHERFUCKER! AFTER ALL THAT YOU FUCKING BIT ME!
MOMENT OVER.
SNAP
FUCK YOU. AND GOODBYE.

STEVIE, I WANT YOU TO COUNT VERY SLOWLY FROM 10, BACKWARDS.

AND WHEN I WAKE UP YOU PROMISE *MR. SNUGGLES* CAN HAVE VANILLA ICE CREAM?

AND IS VANILLA *MR. SNUGGLES'* FAVORITE FLAVOR?

YEAH WITH *SPRINKLES* AND--

--ZZZZZZzz

THE LITTLE FELLA'S *UNDER.*

*L*IFE'S JUST THE SHIT THAT HAPPENS BEFORE DEATH.

PATIENT'S ALL *READY* FOR HIS DOUBLE STRABISMUS, DOCTOR.

OKAY, SORRY I'M LATE. PILE-UP ON THE 405.

THEY SAID SOMETHING ABOUT A MASSIVE SWARM OF *BEES* ON THE RADIO.

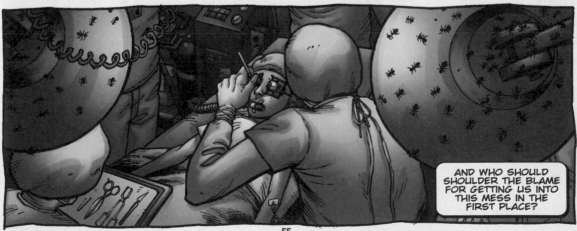

AND WHO SHOULD SHOULDER THE BLAME FOR GETTING US INTO THIS MESS IN THE FIRST PLACE?

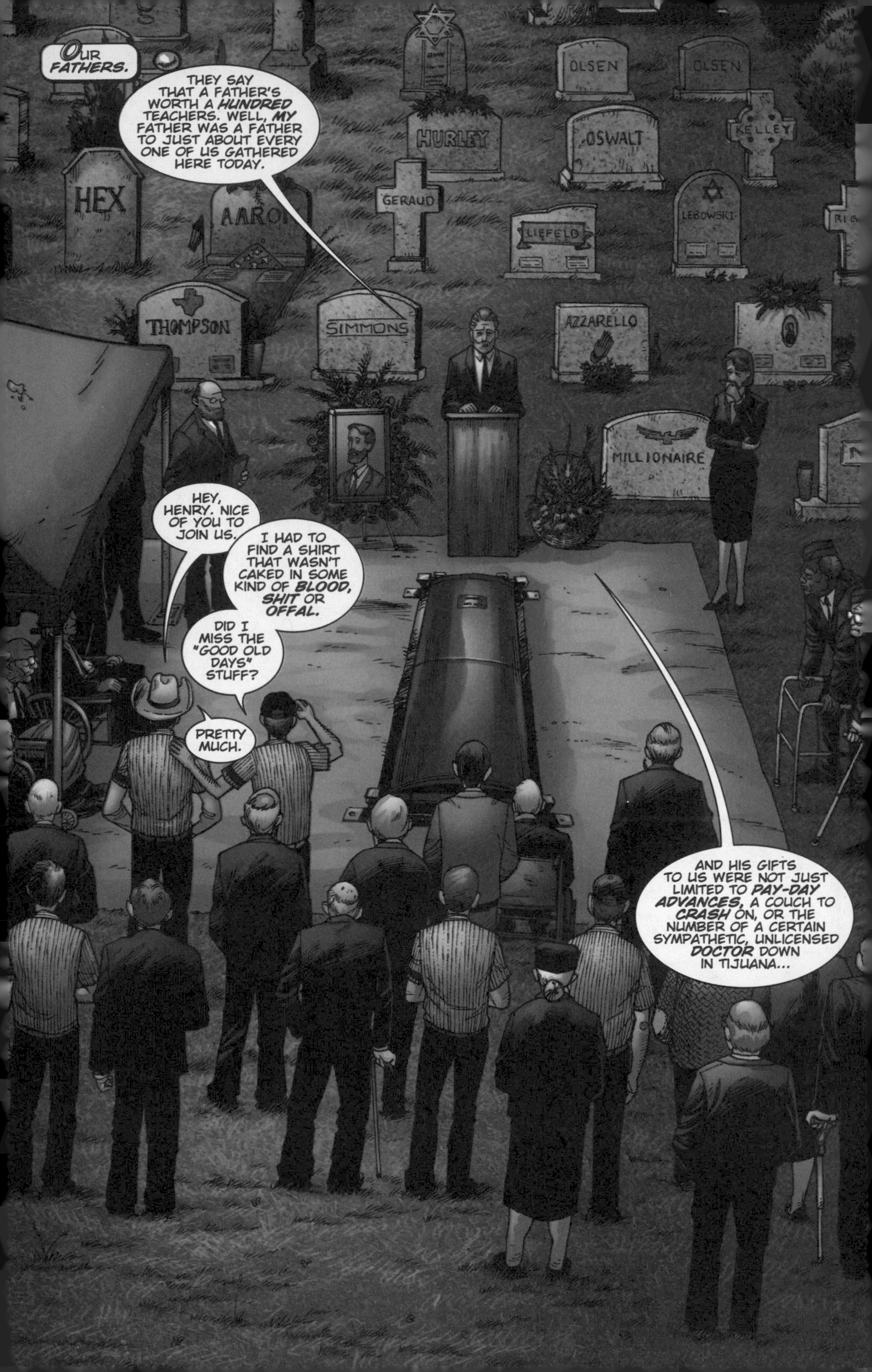
OUR FATHERS.
THEY SAY THAT A FATHER'S WORTH A HUNDRED TEACHERS. WELL, MY FATHER WAS A FATHER TO JUST ABOUT EVERY ONE OF US GATHERED HERE TODAY.
OLSEN
OLSEN
HURLEY
OSWALT
KELLEY
HEX
GERAUD
LEBOWSKI
LIEFELD
THOMPSON
SIMMONS
AZZARELLO
MILLIONAIRE
HEY, HENRY. NICE OF YOU TO JOIN US.
I HAD TO FIND A SHIRT THAT WASN'T CAKED IN SOME KIND OF BLOOD, SHIT OR OFFAL.
DID I MISS THE "GOOD OLD DAYS" STUFF?
PRETTY MUCH.
AND HIS GIFTS TO US WERE NOT JUST LIMITED TO PAY-DAY ADVANCES, A COUCH TO CRASH ON, OR THE NUMBER OF A CERTAIN SYMPATHETIC, UNLICENSED DOCTOR DOWN IN TIJUANA...

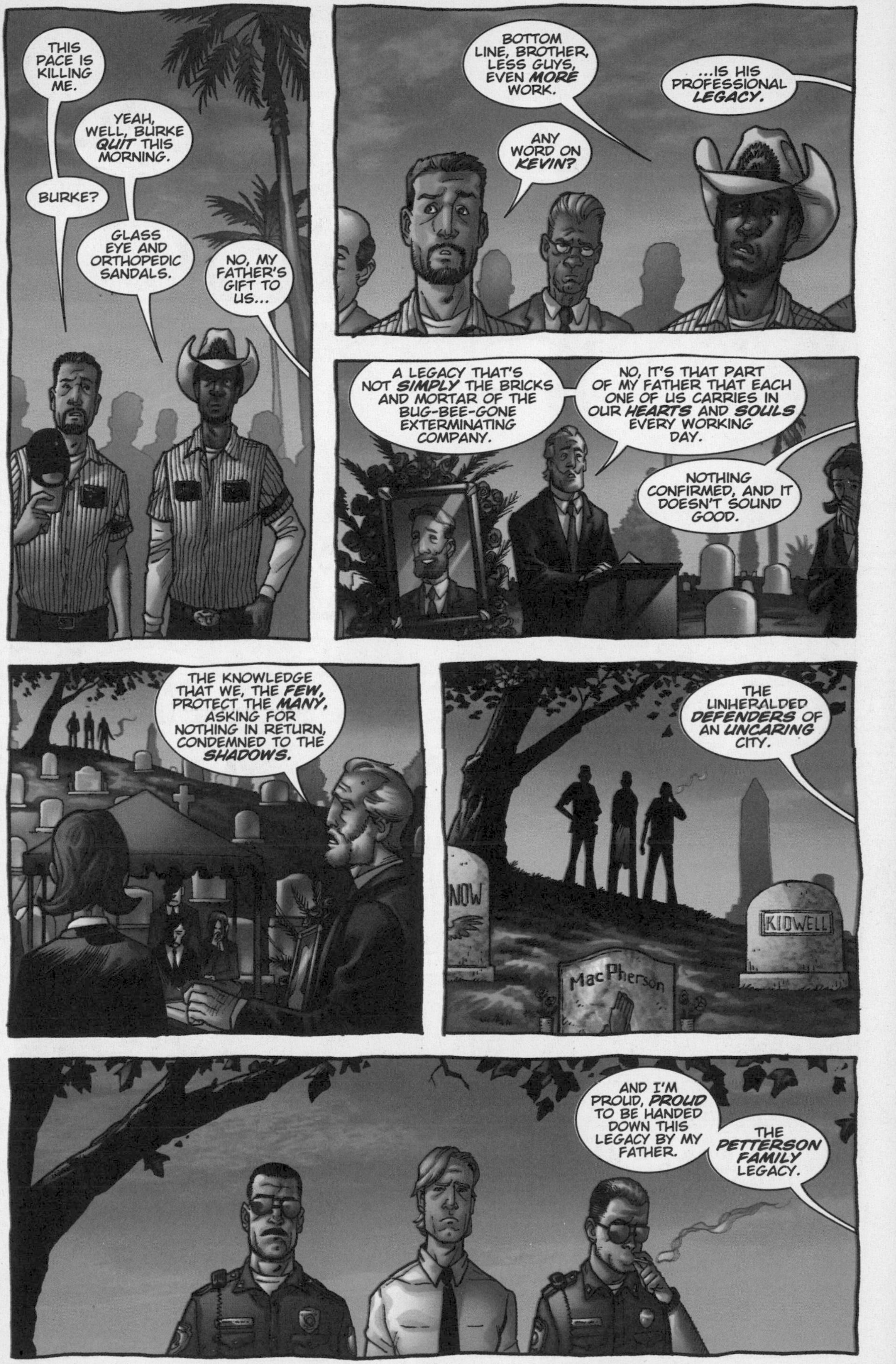
THIS PACE IS KILLING ME.
YEAH, WELL, BURKE QUIT THIS MORNING.
BURKE?
GLASS EYE AND ORTHOPEDIC SANDALS.
NO, MY FATHER'S GIFT TO US...
BOTTOM LINE, BROTHER, LESS GUYS, EVEN MORE WORK.
ANY WORD ON KEVIN?
...IS HIS PROFESSIONAL LEGACY.
A LEGACY THAT'S NOT SIMPLY THE BRICKS AND MORTAR OF THE BUG-BEE-GONE EXTERMINATING COMPANY.
NO, IT'S THAT PART OF MY FATHER THAT EACH ONE OF US CARRIES IN OUR HEARTS AND SOULS EVERY WORKING DAY.
NOTHING CONFIRMED, AND IT DOESN'T SOUND GOOD.
THE KNOWLEDGE THAT WE, THE FEW, PROTECT THE MANY, ASKING FOR NOTHING IN RETURN, CONDEMNED TO THE SHADOWS.
THE UNHERALDED DEFENDERS OF AN UNCARING CITY.
NOW
KIDWELL
MacPherson
AND I'M PROUD, PROUD TO BE HANDED DOWN THIS LEGACY BY MY FATHER.
THE PETTERSON FAMILY LEGACY.

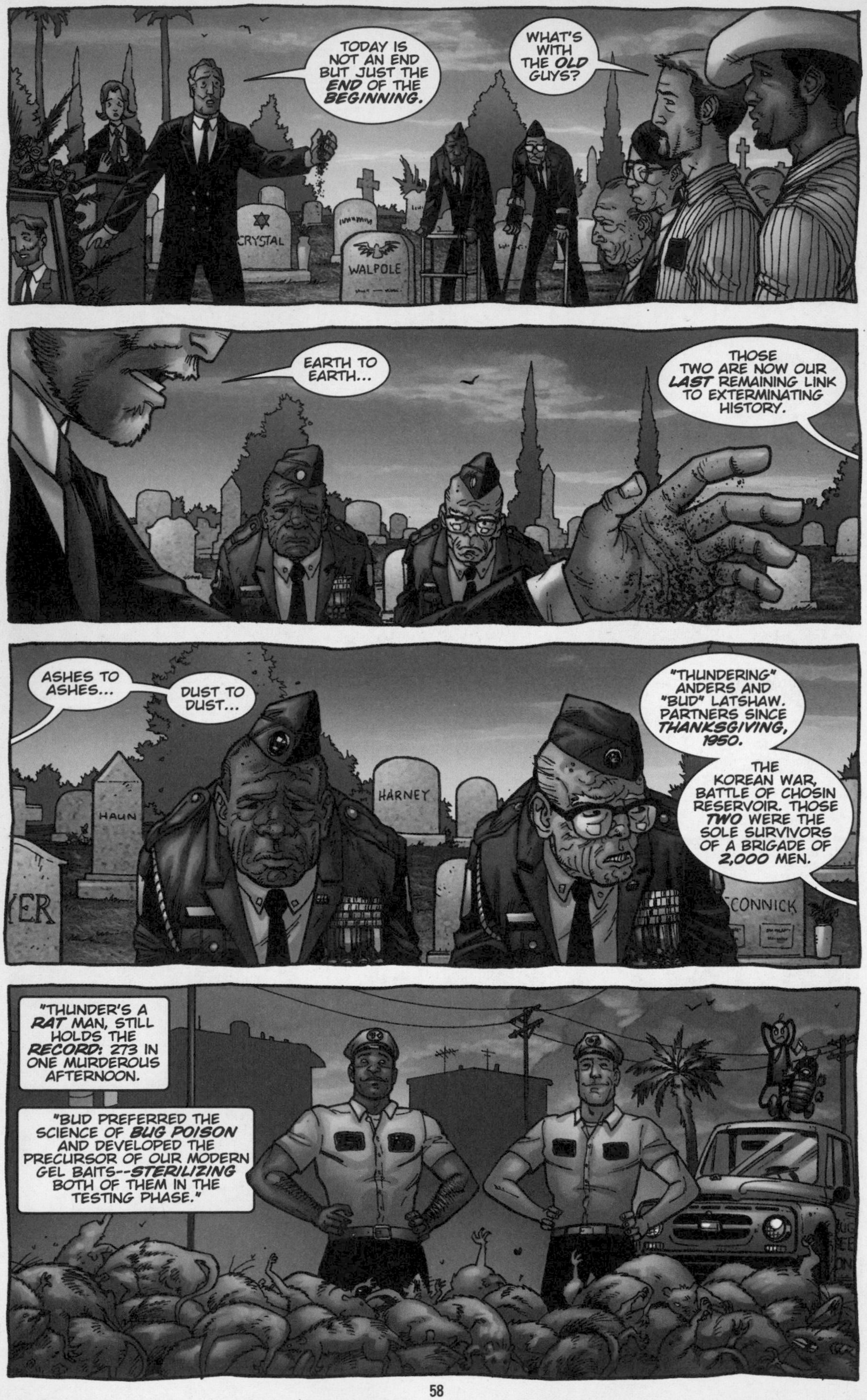
TODAY IS NOT AN END BUT JUST THE END OF THE BEGINNING.
WHAT'S WITH THE OLD GUYS?
CRYSTAL
WALPOLE
EARTH TO EARTH...
THOSE TWO ARE NOW OUR LAST REMAINING LINK TO EXTERMINATING HISTORY.
ASHES TO ASHES...
DUST TO DUST...
"THUNDERING" ANDERS AND "BUD" LATSHAW. PARTNERS SINCE THANKSGIVING, 1950.
THE KOREAN WAR, BATTLE OF CHOSIN RESERVOIR. THOSE TWO WERE THE SOLE SURVIVORS OF A BRIGADE OF 2,000 MEN.
HAUN
HARNEY
YER
CONNICK
"THUNDER'S A RAT MAN, STILL HOLDS THE RECORD: 273 IN ONE MURDEROUS AFTERNOON.
"BUD PREFERRED THE SCIENCE OF BUG POISON AND DEVELOPED THE PRECURSOR OF OUR MODERN GEL BAITS--STERILIZING BOTH OF THEM IN THE TESTING PHASE."

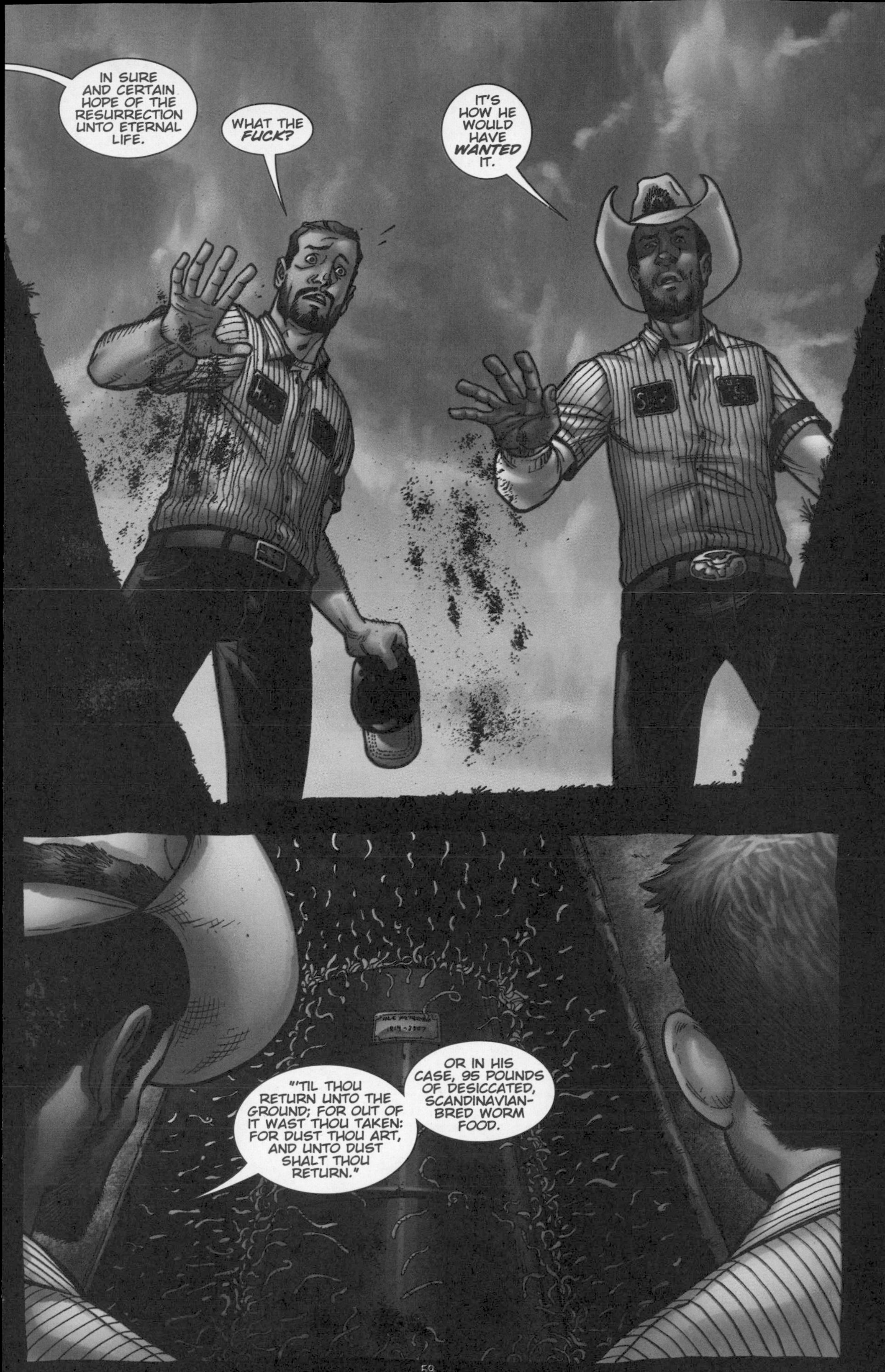
IN SURE AND CERTAIN HOPE OF THE RESURRECTION UNTO ETERNAL LIFE.
WHAT THE FUCK?
IT'S HOW HE WOULD HAVE WANTED IT.
"'TIL THOU RETURN UNTO THE GROUND; FOR OUT OF IT WAST THOU TAKEN: FOR DUST THOU ART, AND UNTO DUST SHALT THOU RETURN."
OR IN HIS CASE, 95 POUNDS OF DESICCATED, SCANDINAVIAN-BRED WORM FOOD.

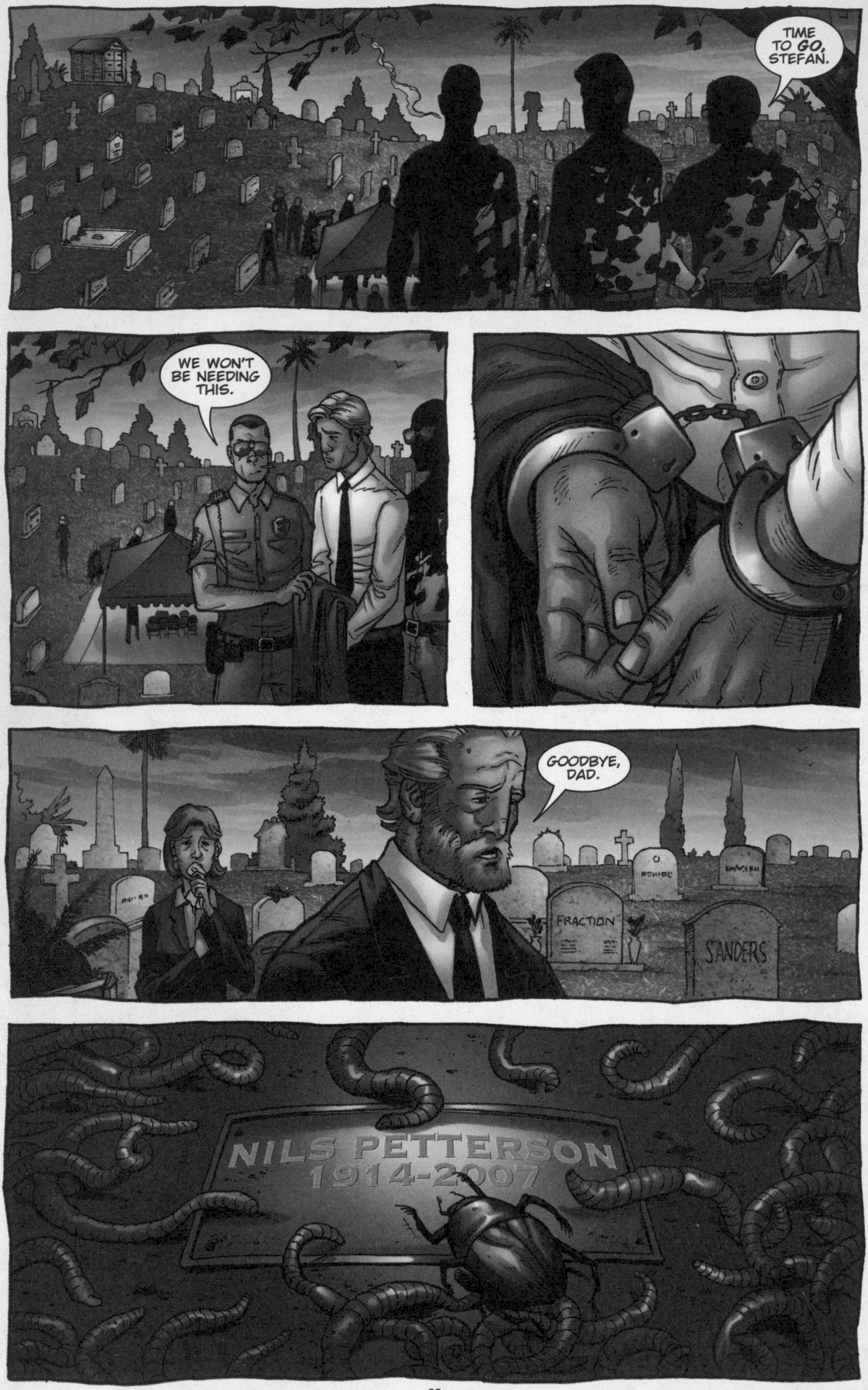
TIME TO GO, STEFAN.
WE WON'T BE NEEDING THIS.
GOODBYE, DAD.
FRACTION
SANDERS
NILS PETTERSON
1914-2007

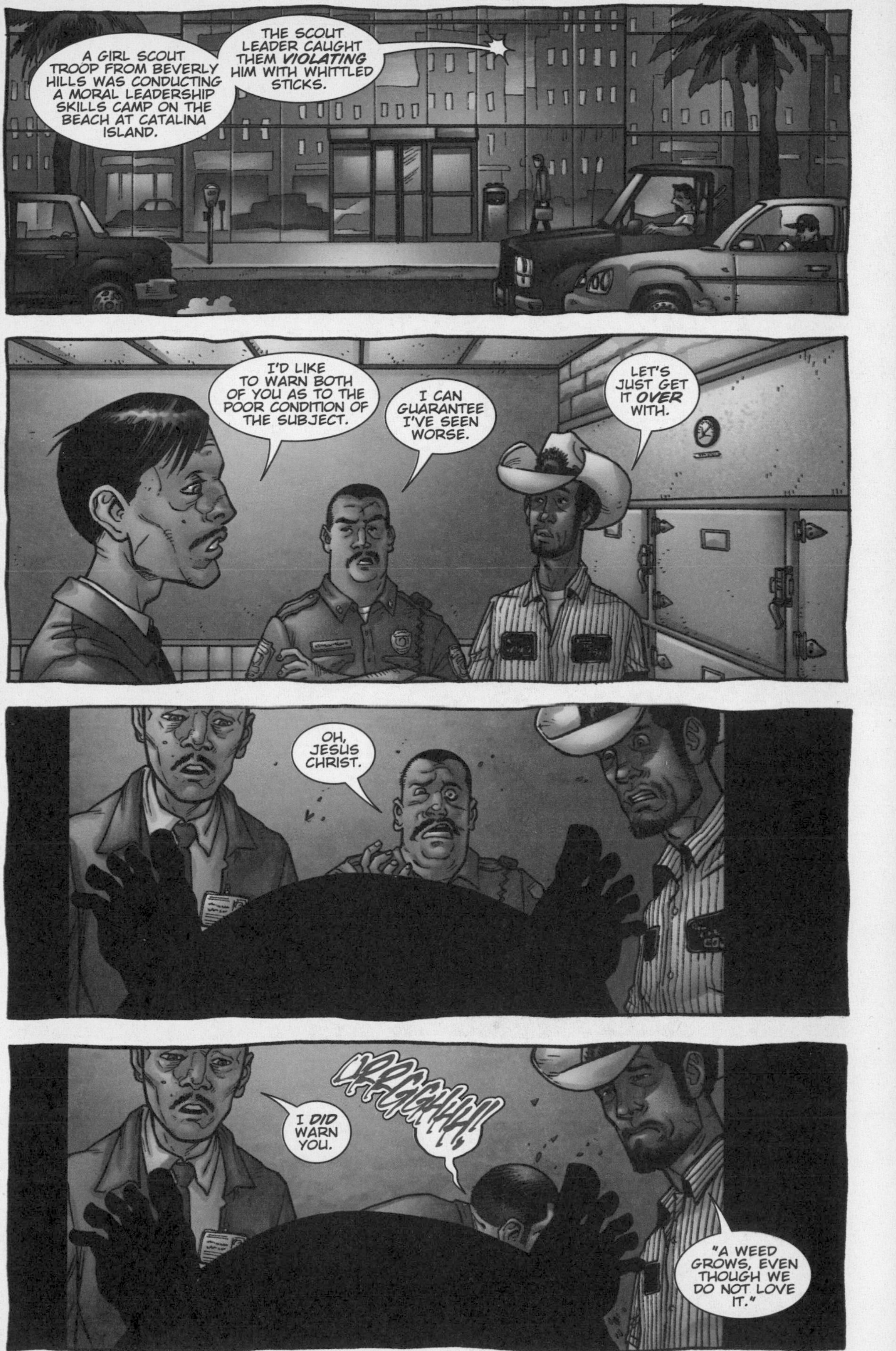
A GIRL SCOUT TROOP FROM BEVERLY HILLS WAS CONDUCTING A MORAL LEADERSHIP SKILLS CAMP ON THE BEACH AT CATALINA ISLAND.
THE SCOUT LEADER CAUGHT THEM *VIOLATING* HIM WITH WHITTLED STICKS.
I'D LIKE TO WARN BOTH OF YOU AS TO THE POOR CONDITION OF THE SUBJECT.
I CAN GUARANTEE I'VE SEEN WORSE.
LET'S JUST GET IT *OVER* WITH.
OH, JESUS CHRIST.
I *DID* WARN YOU.
"A WEED GROWS, EVEN THOUGH WE DO NOT LOVE IT."

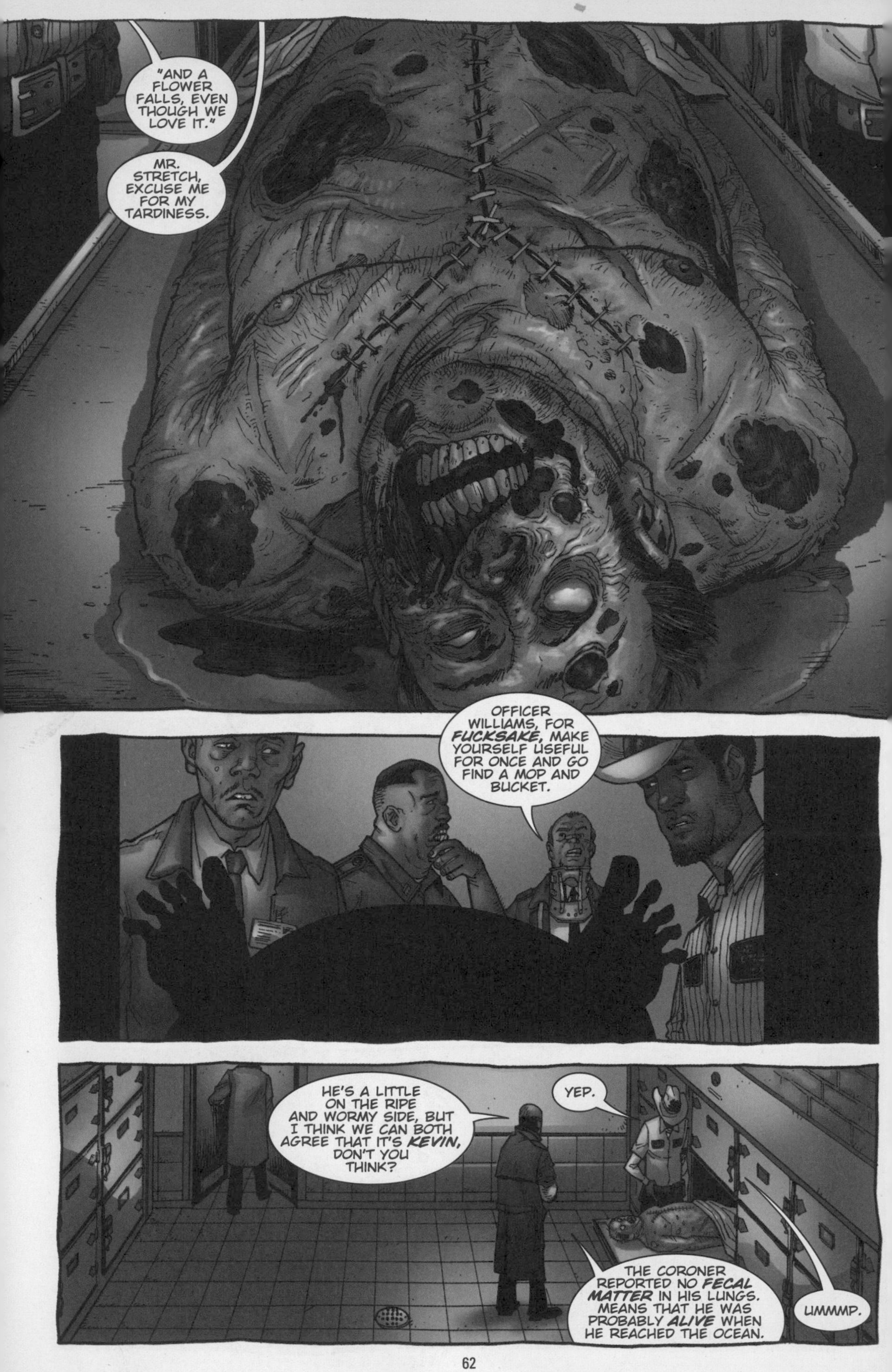
"AND A FLOWER FALLS, EVEN THOUGH WE LOVE IT."
MR. STRETCH, EXCUSE ME FOR MY TARDINESS.
OFFICER WILLIAMS, FOR FUCKSAKE, MAKE YOURSELF USEFUL FOR ONCE AND GO FIND A MOP AND BUCKET.
HE'S A LITTLE ON THE RIPE AND WORMY SIDE, BUT I THINK WE CAN BOTH AGREE THAT IT'S KEVIN, DON'T YOU THINK?
YEP.
THE CORONER REPORTED NO FECAL MATTER IN HIS LUNGS. MEANS THAT HE WAS PROBABLY ALIVE WHEN HE REACHED THE OCEAN.
UMMMP.

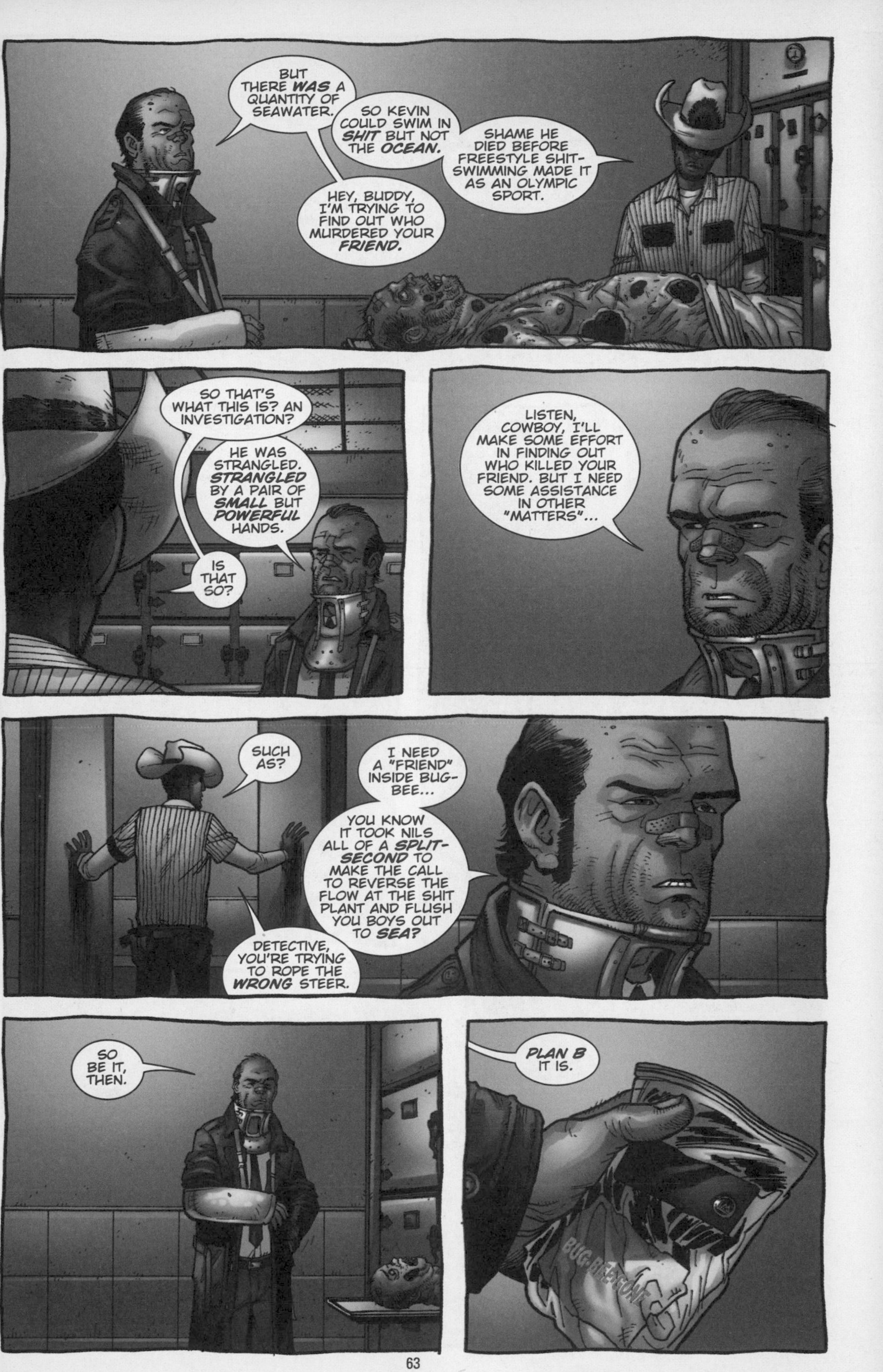

BUT THERE WAS A QUANTITY OF SEAWATER.
SO KEVIN COULD SWIM IN SHIT BUT NOT THE OCEAN.
SHAME HE DIED BEFORE FREESTYLE SHIT-SWIMMING MADE IT AS AN OLYMPIC SPORT.
HEY, BUDDY, I'M TRYING TO FIND OUT WHO MURDERED YOUR FRIEND.
SO THAT'S WHAT THIS IS? AN INVESTIGATION?
HE WAS STRANGLED. STRANGLED BY A PAIR OF SMALL BUT POWERFUL HANDS.
IS THAT SO?
LISTEN, COWBOY, I'LL MAKE SOME EFFORT IN FINDING OUT WHO KILLED YOUR FRIEND. BUT I NEED SOME ASSISTANCE IN OTHER "MATTERS"...
SUCH AS?
I NEED A "FRIEND" INSIDE BUG-BEE...
YOU KNOW IT TOOK NILS ALL OF A SPLIT-SECOND TO MAKE THE CALL TO REVERSE THE FLOW AT THE SHIT PLANT AND FLUSH YOU BOYS OUT TO SEA?
DETECTIVE, YOU'RE TRYING TO ROPE THE WRONG STEER.
SO BE IT, THEN.
PLAN B IT IS.

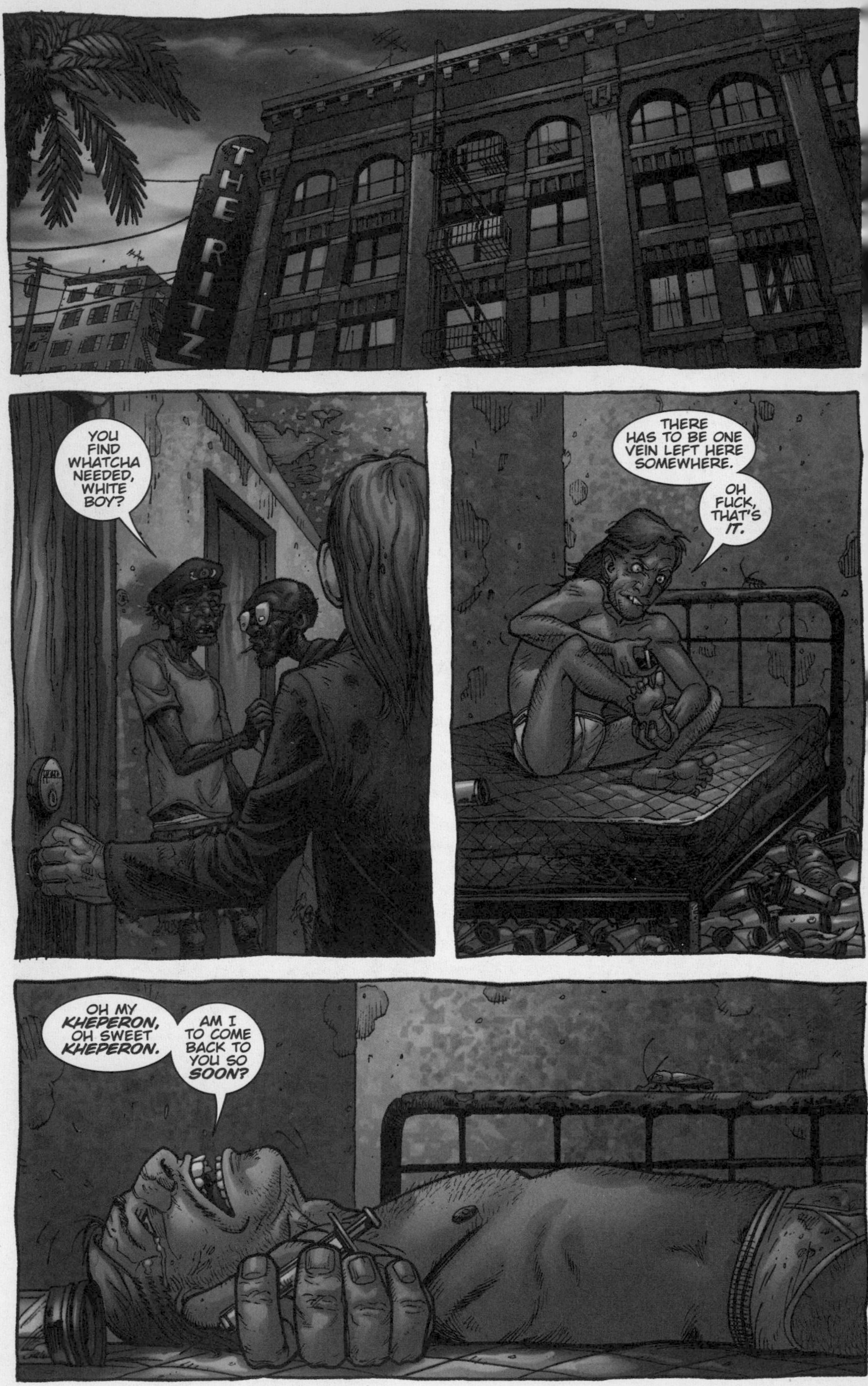
THE RITZ
YOU FIND WHATCHA NEEDED, WHITE BOY?
THERE HAS TO BE ONE VEIN LEFT HERE SOMEWHERE.
OH FUCK, THAT'S *IT.*
OH MY **KHEPERON**, OH SWEET **KHEPERON**.
AM I TO COME BACK TO YOU SO **SOON?**

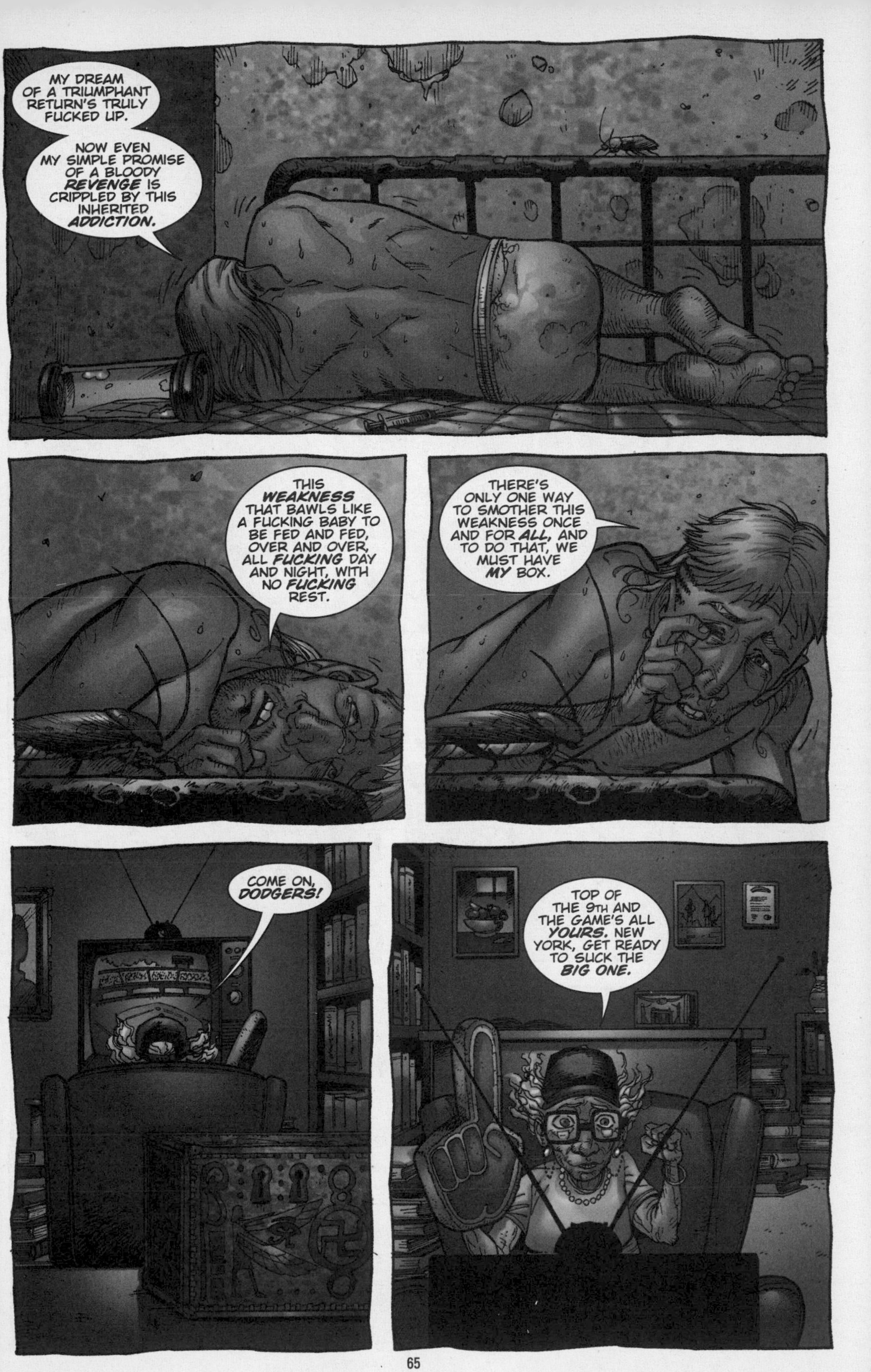
MY DREAM OF A TRIUMPHANT RETURN'S TRULY FUCKED UP.
NOW EVEN MY SIMPLE PROMISE OF A BLOODY *REVENGE* IS CRIPPLED BY THIS INHERITED *ADDICTION*.
THIS *WEAKNESS* THAT BAWLS LIKE A FUCKING BABY TO BE FED AND FED, OVER AND OVER, ALL *FUCKING* DAY AND NIGHT, WITH NO *FUCKING* REST.
THERE'S ONLY ONE WAY TO SMOTHER THIS WEAKNESS ONCE AND FOR *ALL*, AND TO DO THAT, WE MUST HAVE *MY* BOX.
COME ON, *DODGERS!*
TOP OF THE 9TH AND THE GAME'S ALL *YOURS*. NEW YORK, GET READY TO SUCK THE *BIG ONE*.

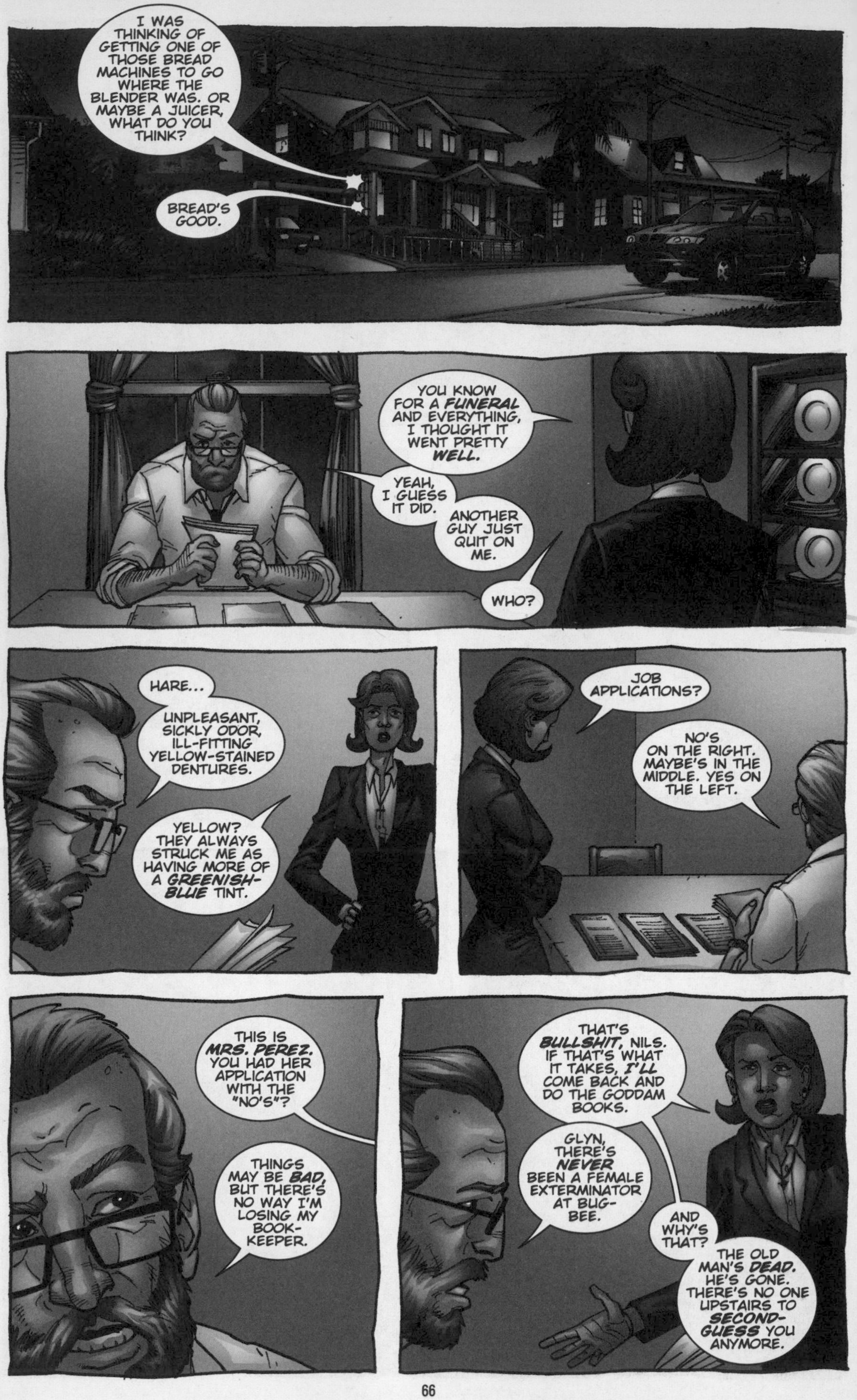
I WAS THINKING OF GETTING ONE OF THOSE BREAD MACHINES TO GO WHERE THE BLENDER WAS. OR MAYBE A JUICER, WHAT DO YOU THINK?
BREAD'S GOOD.
YOU KNOW FOR A FUNERAL AND EVERYTHING, I THOUGHT IT WENT PRETTY WELL.
YEAH, I GUESS IT DID.
ANOTHER GUY JUST QUIT ON ME.
WHO?
HARE...
UNPLEASANT, SICKLY ODOR, ILL-FITTING YELLOW-STAINED DENTURES.
YELLOW? THEY ALWAYS STRUCK ME AS HAVING MORE OF A GREENISH-BLUE TINT.
JOB APPLICATIONS?
NO'S ON THE RIGHT. MAYBE'S IN THE MIDDLE. YES ON THE LEFT.
THIS IS MRS. PEREZ. YOU HAD HER APPLICATION WITH THE "NO'S"?
THINGS MAY BE BAD, BUT THERE'S NO WAY I'M LOSING MY BOOK-KEEPER.
THAT'S BULLSHIT, NILS. IF THAT'S WHAT IT TAKES, I'LL COME BACK AND DO THE GODDAM BOOKS.
GLYN, THERE'S NEVER BEEN A FEMALE EXTERMINATOR AT BUG-BEE.
AND WHY'S THAT?
THE OLD MAN'S DEAD. HE'S GONE. THERE'S NO ONE UPSTAIRS TO SECOND-GUESS YOU ANYMORE.

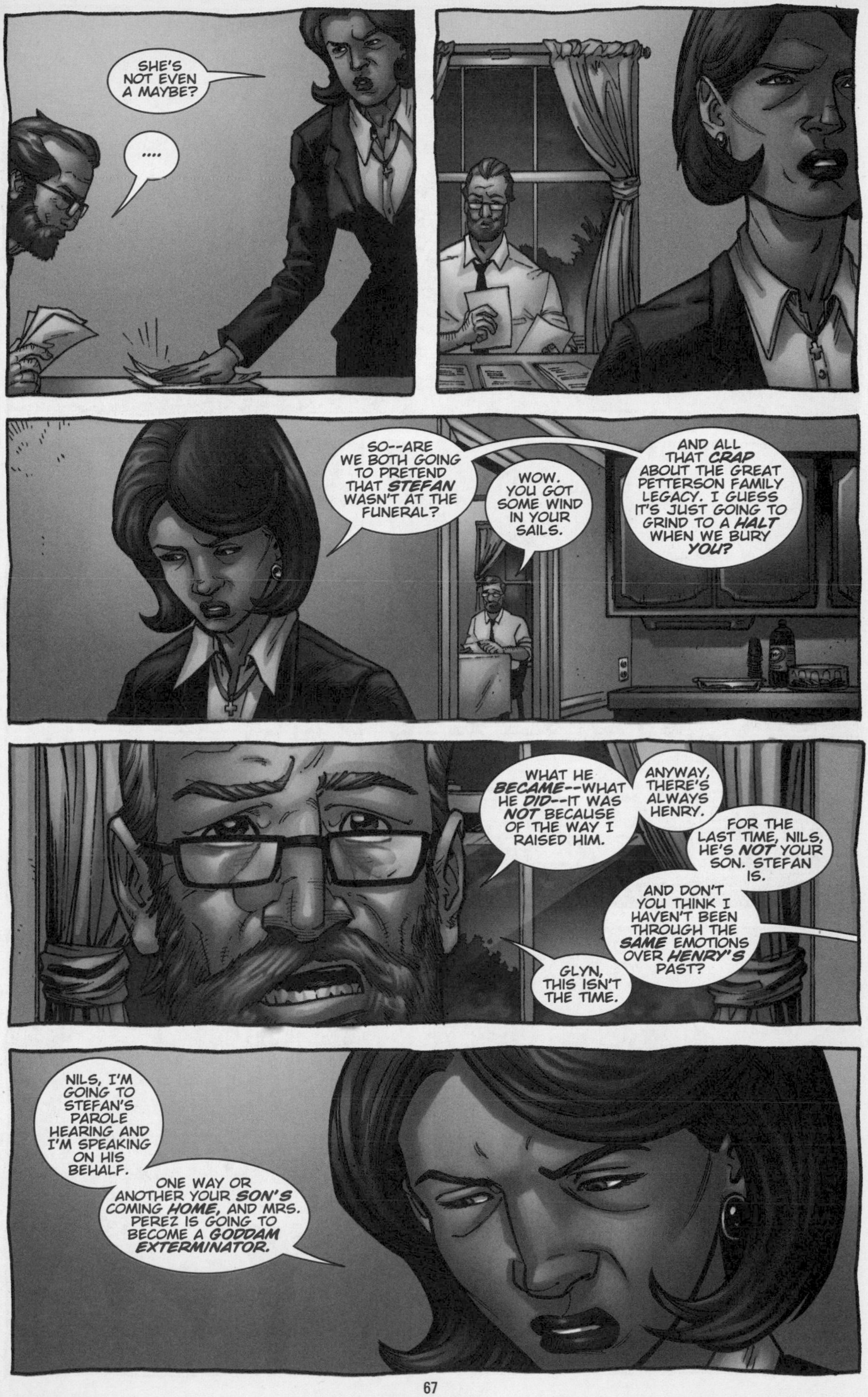
SHE'S NOT EVEN A MAYBE?
....
SO--ARE WE BOTH GOING TO PRETEND THAT STEFAN WASN'T AT THE FUNERAL?
WOW. YOU GOT SOME WIND IN YOUR SAILS.
AND ALL THAT CRAP ABOUT THE GREAT PETTERSON FAMILY LEGACY. I GUESS IT'S JUST GOING TO GRIND TO A HALT WHEN WE BURY YOU?
WHAT HE BECAME--WHAT HE DID--IT WAS NOT BECAUSE OF THE WAY I RAISED HIM.
ANYWAY, THERE'S ALWAYS HENRY.
FOR THE LAST TIME, NILS, HE'S NOT YOUR SON. STEFAN IS.
AND DON'T YOU THINK I HAVEN'T BEEN THROUGH THE SAME EMOTIONS OVER HENRY'S PAST?
GLYN, THIS ISN'T THE TIME.
NILS, I'M GOING TO STEFAN'S PAROLE HEARING AND I'M SPEAKING ON HIS BEHALF.
ONE WAY OR ANOTHER YOUR SON'S COMING HOME, AND MRS. PEREZ IS GOING TO BECOME A GODDAM EXTERMINATOR.

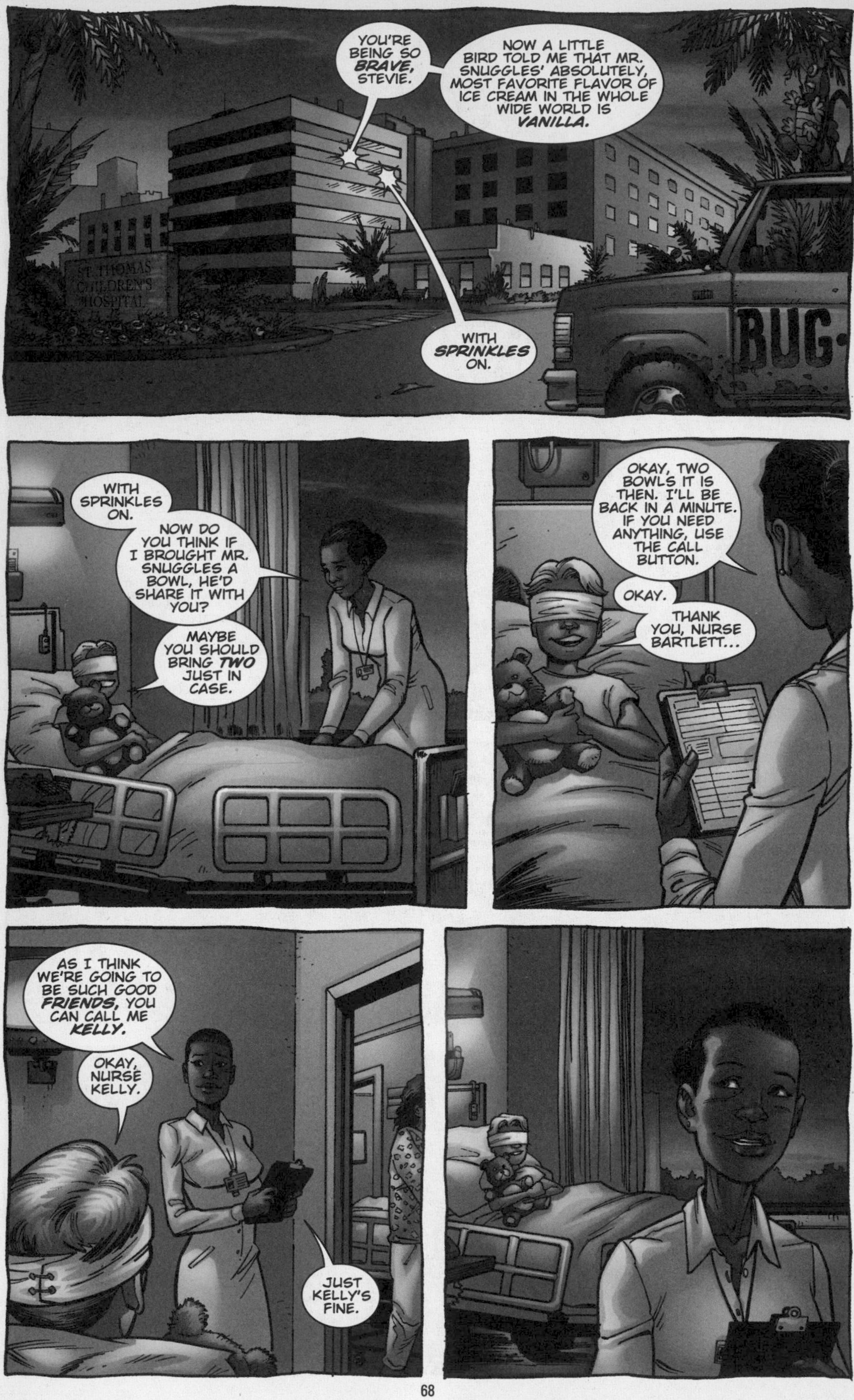
YOU'RE BEING SO BRAVE, STEVIE.
NOW A LITTLE BIRD TOLD ME THAT MR. SNUGGLES' ABSOLUTELY, MOST FAVORITE FLAVOR OF ICE CREAM IN THE WHOLE WIDE WORLD IS VANILLA.
WITH SPRINKLES ON.
ST. THOMAS CHILDREN'S HOSPITAL
BUG-
WITH SPRINKLES ON.
NOW DO YOU THINK IF I BROUGHT MR. SNUGGLES A BOWL, HE'D SHARE IT WITH YOU?
MAYBE YOU SHOULD BRING TWO JUST IN CASE.
OKAY, TWO BOWLS IT IS THEN. I'LL BE BACK IN A MINUTE. IF YOU NEED ANYTHING, USE THE CALL BUTTON.
OKAY.
THANK YOU, NURSE BARTLETT...
AS I THINK WE'RE GOING TO BE SUCH GOOD FRIENDS, YOU CAN CALL ME KELLY.
OKAY, NURSE KELLY.
JUST KELLY'S FINE.

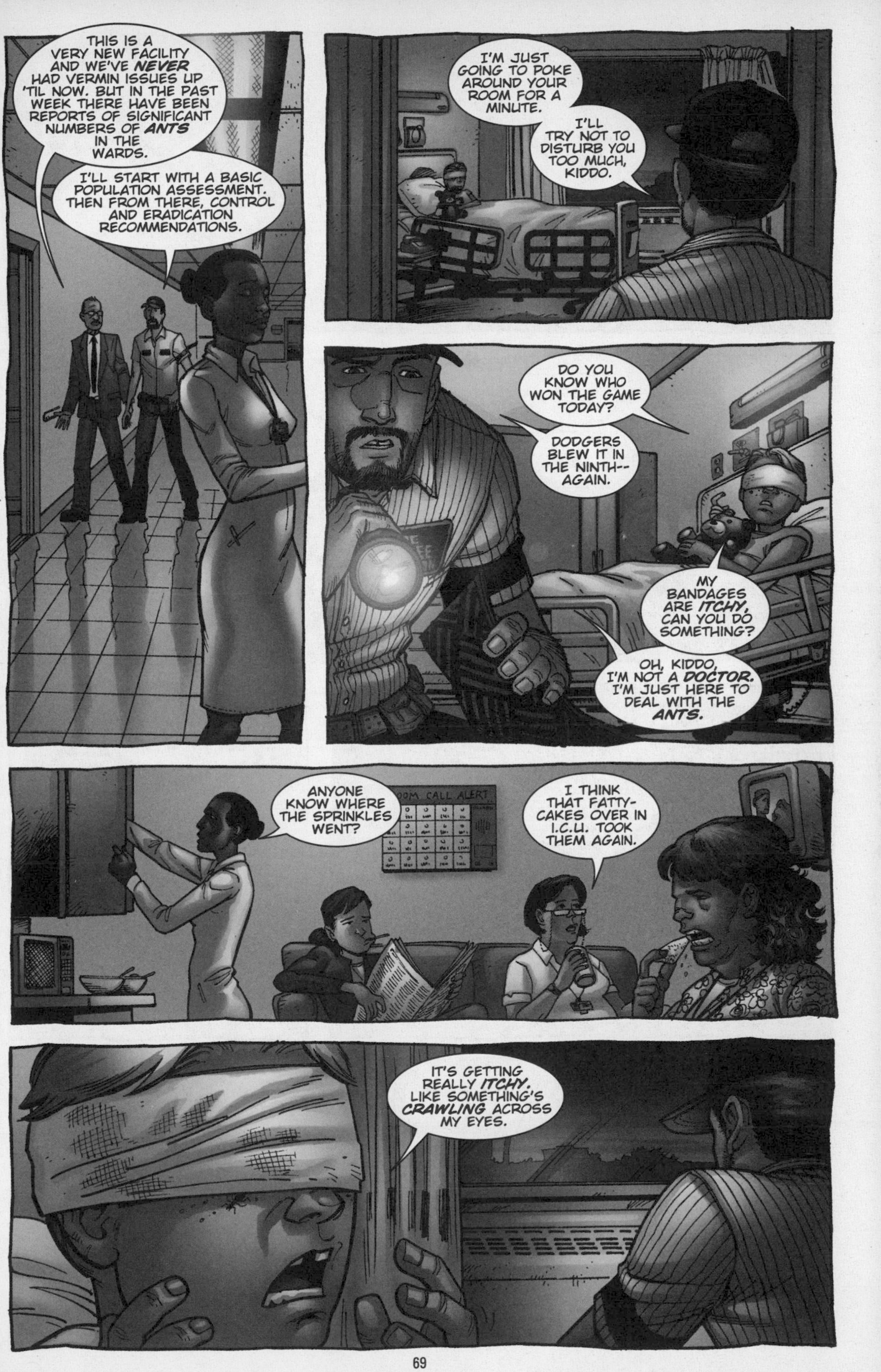
THIS IS A VERY NEW FACILITY AND WE'VE NEVER HAD VERMIN ISSUES UP 'TIL NOW. BUT IN THE PAST WEEK THERE HAVE BEEN REPORTS OF SIGNIFICANT NUMBERS OF ANTS IN THE WARDS.
I'LL START WITH A BASIC POPULATION ASSESSMENT. THEN FROM THERE, CONTROL AND ERADICATION RECOMMENDATIONS.
I'M JUST GOING TO POKE AROUND YOUR ROOM FOR A MINUTE.
I'LL TRY NOT TO DISTURB YOU TOO MUCH, KIDDO.
DO YOU KNOW WHO WON THE GAME TODAY?
DODGERS BLEW IT IN THE NINTH-- AGAIN.
MY BANDAGES ARE ITCHY, CAN YOU DO SOMETHING?
OH, KIDDO, I'M NOT A DOCTOR. I'M JUST HERE TO DEAL WITH THE ANTS.
ANYONE KNOW WHERE THE SPRINKLES WENT?
OOM CALL ALERT
I THINK THAT FATTY-CAKES OVER IN I.C.U. TOOK THEM AGAIN.
IT'S GETTING REALLY ITCHY. LIKE SOMETHING'S CRAWLING ACROSS MY EYES.

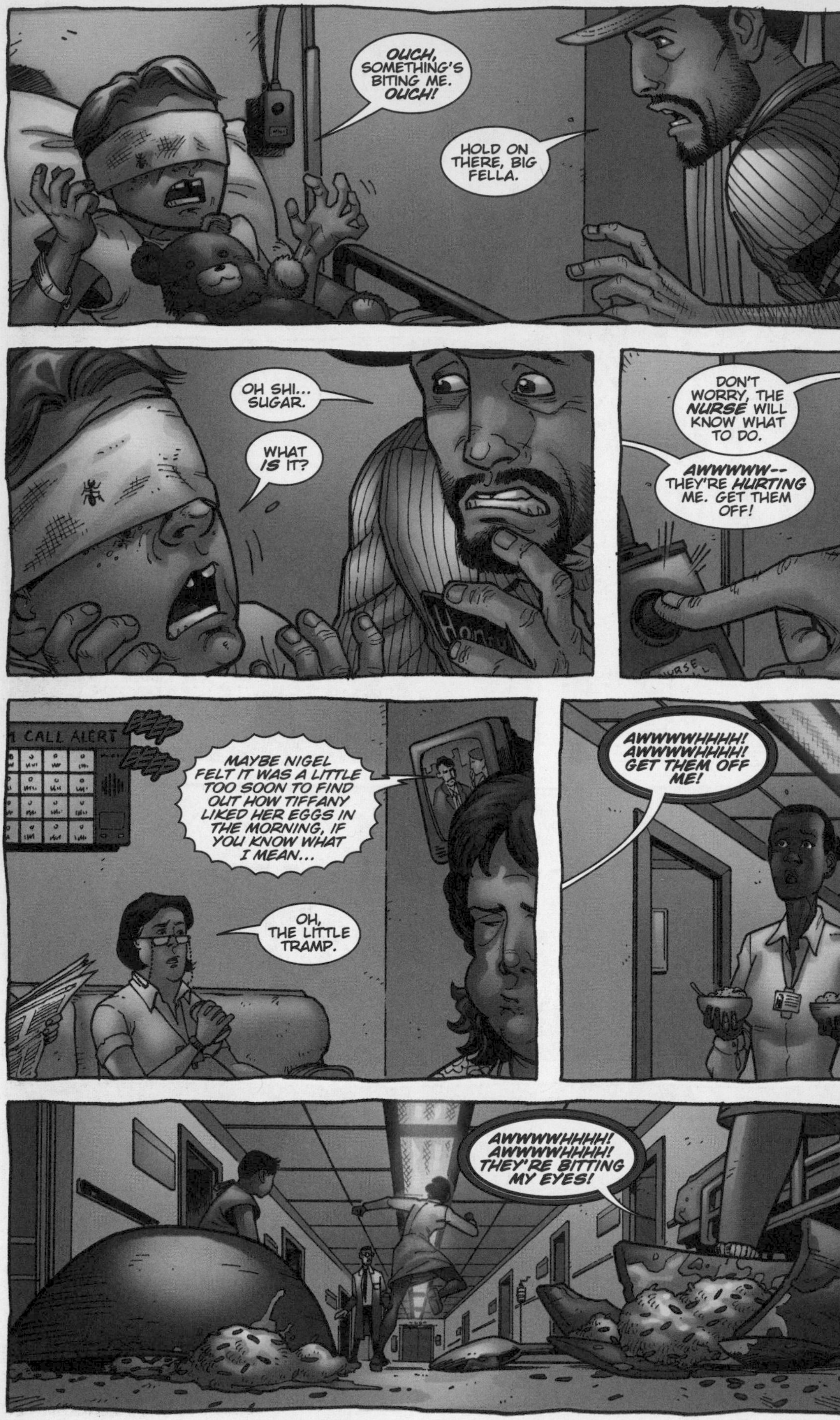
OUCH, SOMETHING'S BITING ME. OUCH!
HOLD ON THERE, BIG FELLA.
OH SHI... SUGAR.
WHAT IS IT?
DON'T WORRY, THE NURSE WILL KNOW WHAT TO DO.
AWWWWW-- THEY'RE HURTING ME. GET THEM OFF!
CALL ALERT
MAYBE NIGEL FELT IT WAS A LITTLE TOO SOON TO FIND OUT HOW TIFFANY LIKED HER EGGS IN THE MORNING, IF YOU KNOW WHAT I MEAN...
OH, THE LITTLE TRAMP.
AWWWWHHHH! AWWWWHHHH! GET THEM OFF ME!
AWWWWHHHH! AWWWWHHHH! THEY'RE BITTING MY EYES!

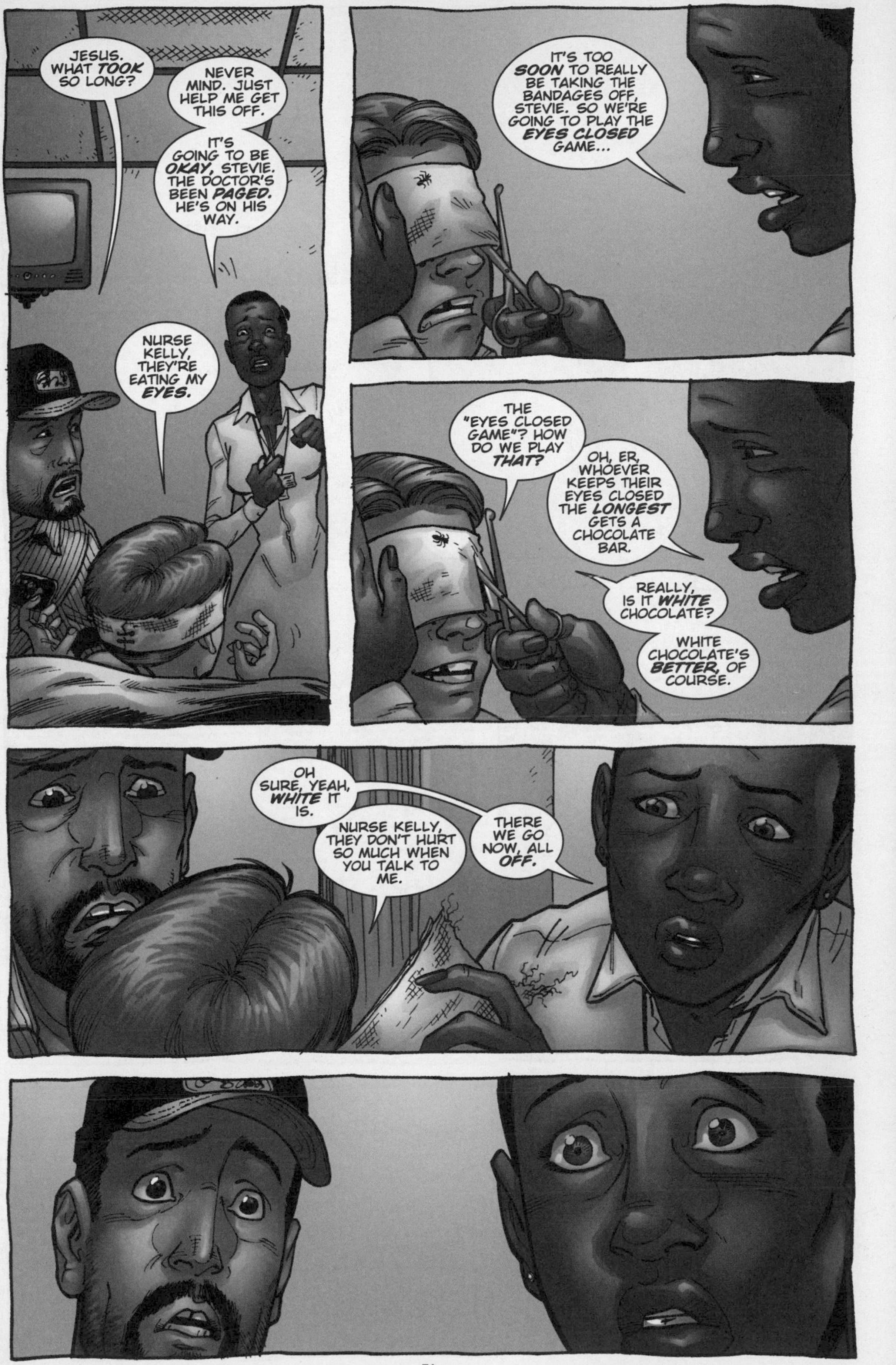

JESUS. WHAT *TOOK* SO LONG?
NEVER MIND. JUST HELP ME GET THIS OFF.
IT'S GOING TO BE *OKAY,* STEVIE. THE DOCTOR'S BEEN *PAGED.* HE'S ON HIS WAY.
NURSE KELLY, THEY'RE EATING MY *EYES.*
IT'S TOO *SOON* TO REALLY BE TAKING THE BANDAGES OFF, STEVIE. SO WE'RE GOING TO PLAY THE *EYES CLOSED* GAME...
THE "EYES CLOSED GAME"? HOW DO WE PLAY *THAT?*
OH, ER, WHOEVER KEEPS THEIR EYES CLOSED THE *LONGEST* GETS A CHOCOLATE BAR.
REALLY, IS IT *WHITE* CHOCOLATE?
WHITE CHOCOLATE'S *BETTER,* OF COURSE.
OH SURE, YEAH, *WHITE* IT IS.
NURSE KELLY, THEY DON'T HURT SO MUCH WHEN YOU TALK TO ME.
THERE WE GO NOW, ALL *OFF.*

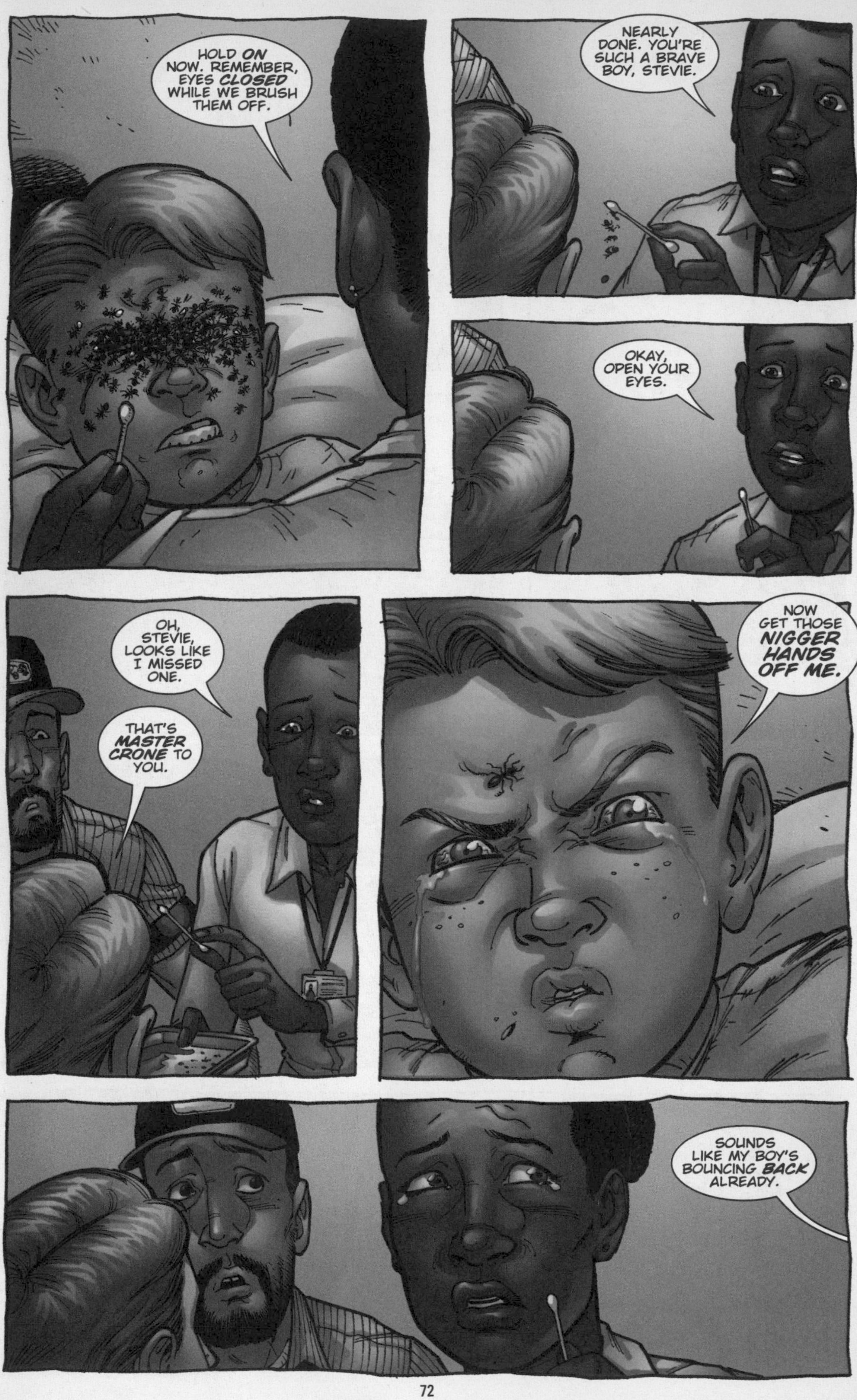
HOLD ON NOW. REMEMBER, EYES CLOSED WHILE WE BRUSH THEM OFF.
NEARLY DONE. YOU'RE SUCH A BRAVE BOY, STEVIE.
OKAY, OPEN YOUR EYES.
OH, STEVIE, LOOKS LIKE I MISSED ONE.
THAT'S MASTER CRONE TO YOU.
NOW GET THOSE NIGGER HANDS OFF ME.
SOUNDS LIKE MY BOY'S BOUNCING BACK ALREADY.

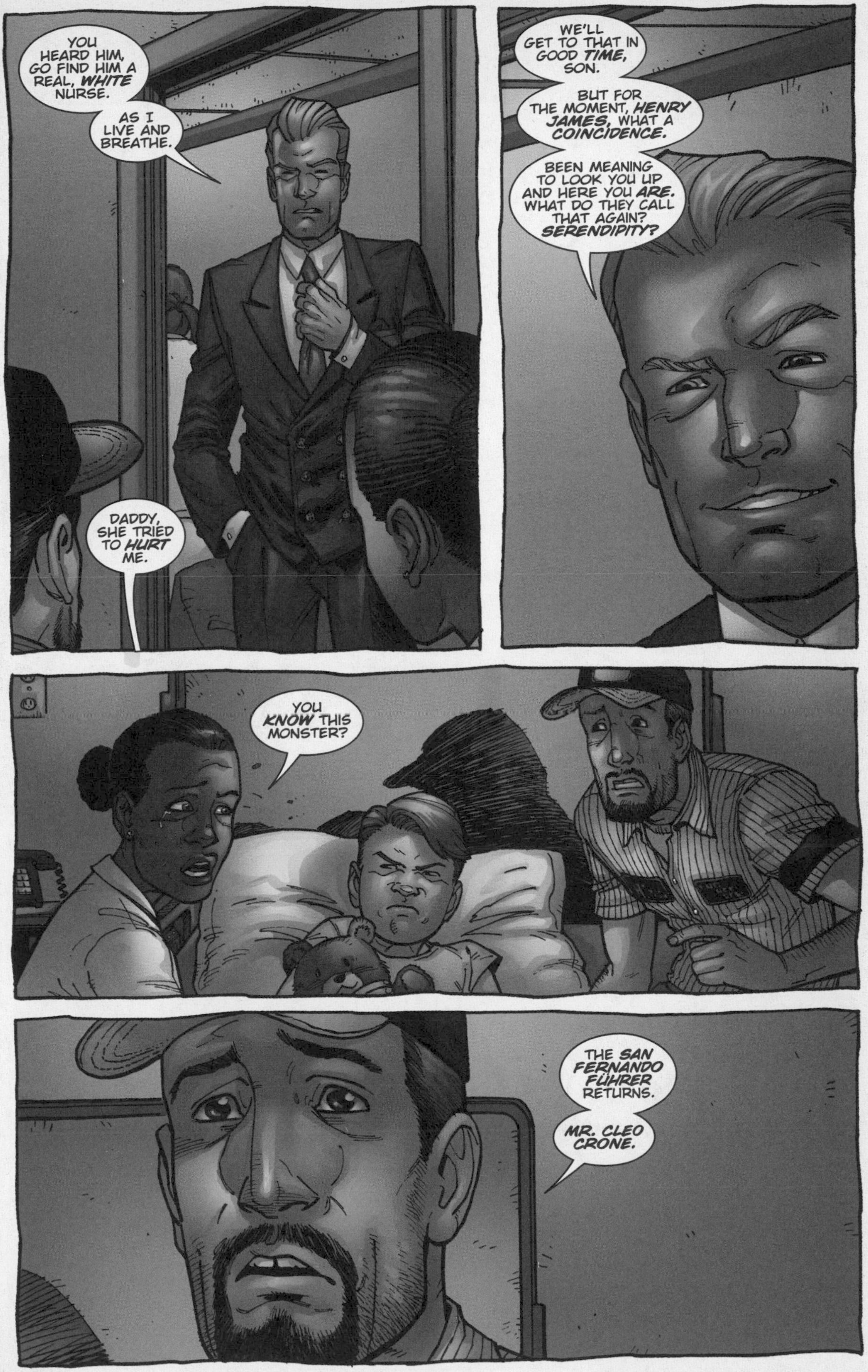

YOU HEARD HIM, GO FIND HIM A REAL, *WHITE* NURSE.
AS I LIVE AND BREATHE.
DADDY, SHE TRIED TO *HURT* ME.
WE'LL GET TO THAT IN GOOD *TIME*, SON.
BUT FOR THE MOMENT, *HENRY JAMES*, WHAT A *COINCIDENCE*.
BEEN MEANING TO LOOK YOU UP AND HERE YOU *ARE*. WHAT DO THEY CALL THAT AGAIN? *SERENDIPITY?*
YOU *KNOW* THIS MONSTER?
THE *SAN FERNANDO FÜHRER* RETURNS.
MR. CLEO CRONE.

CHAPTER FOUR

COVER ART BY PHILIP BOND
INTERIOR PENCILS BY TONY MOORE
INTERIOR INKS BY JOHN LUCAS (pages 75-92)
DAN GREEN (pages 93-96)

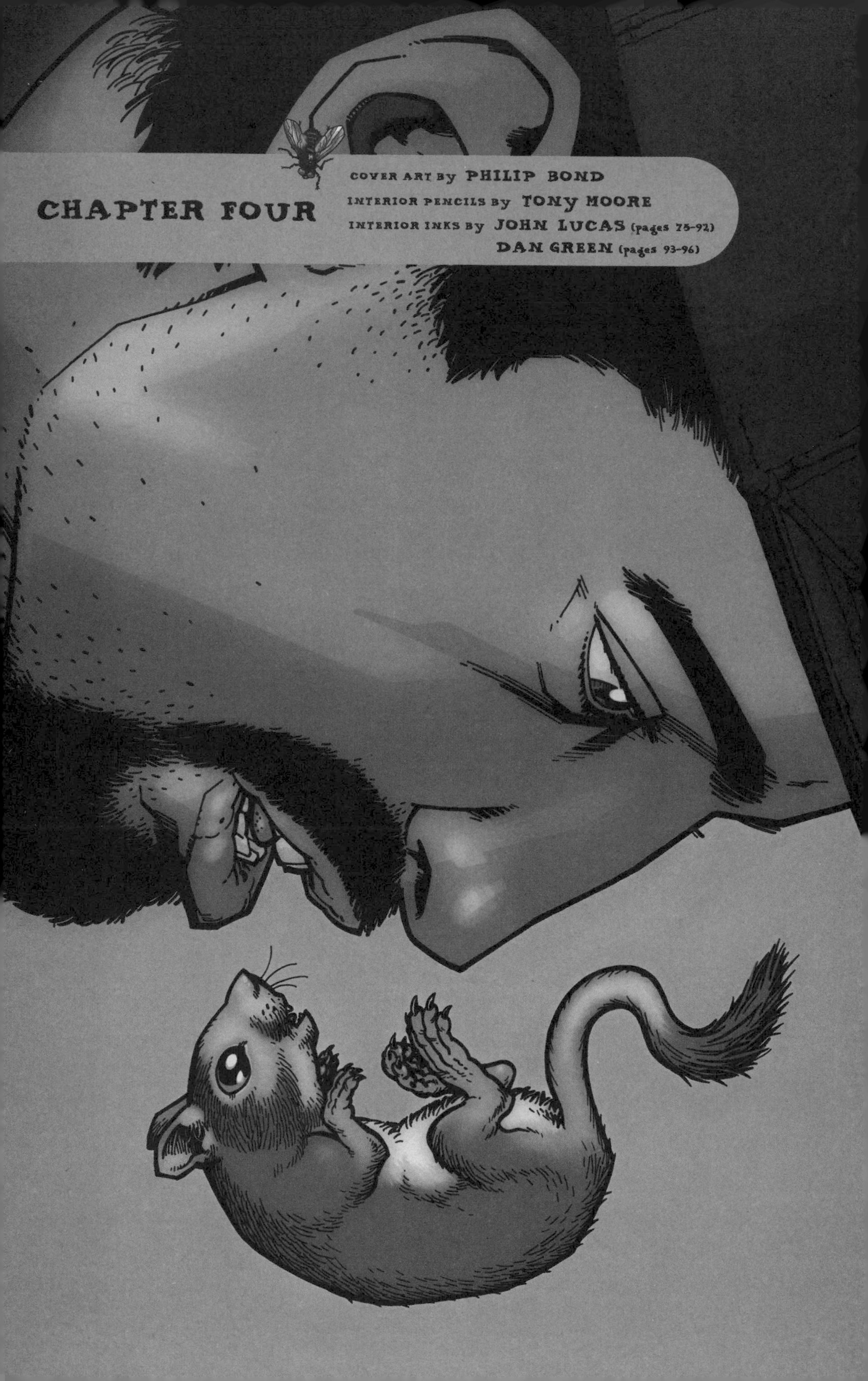

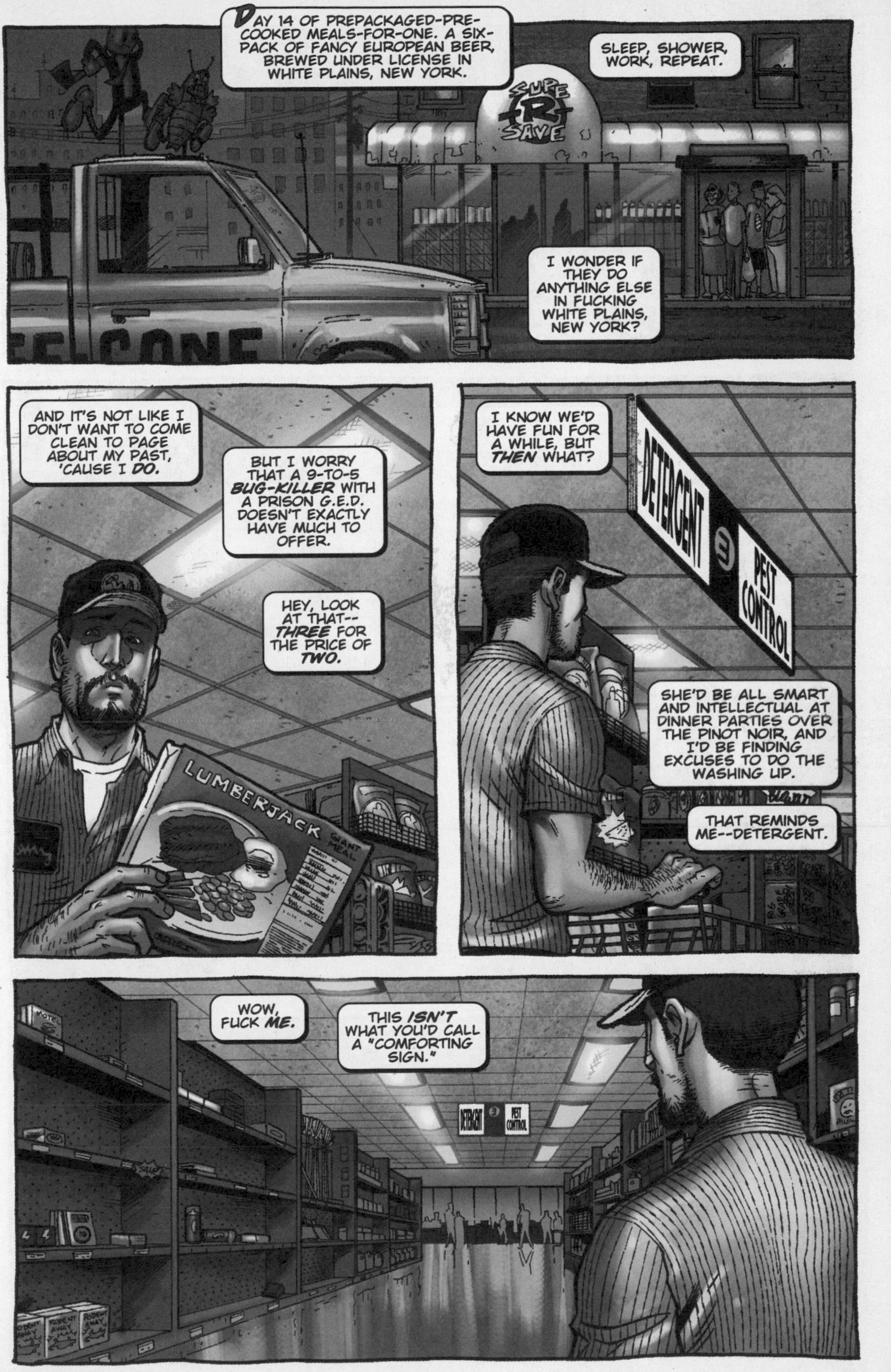
DAY 14 OF PREPACKAGED-PRE-COOKED MEALS-FOR-ONE. A SIX-PACK OF FANCY EUROPEAN BEER, BREWED UNDER LICENSE IN WHITE PLAINS, NEW YORK.
SLEEP, SHOWER, WORK, REPEAT.
SUPE R SAVE
I WONDER IF THEY DO ANYTHING ELSE IN FUCKING WHITE PLAINS, NEW YORK?
AND IT'S NOT LIKE I DON'T WANT TO COME CLEAN TO PAGE ABOUT MY PAST, 'CAUSE I *DO.*
BUT I WORRY THAT A 9-TO-5 ***BUG-KILLER*** WITH A PRISON G.E.D. DOESN'T EXACTLY HAVE MUCH TO OFFER.
HEY, LOOK AT THAT-- ***THREE*** FOR THE PRICE OF ***TWO.***
LUMBERJACK GIANT MEAL
I KNOW WE'D HAVE FUN FOR A WHILE, BUT ***THEN*** WHAT?
DETERGENT
PEST CONTROL
SHE'D BE ALL SMART AND INTELLECTUAL AT DINNER PARTIES OVER THE PINOT NOIR, AND I'D BE FINDING EXCUSES TO DO THE WASHING UP.
THAT REMINDS ME--DETERGENT.
WOW, FUCK ***ME.***
THIS ***ISN'T*** WHAT YOU'D CALL A "COMFORTING SIGN."
DETERGENT
PEST CONTROL

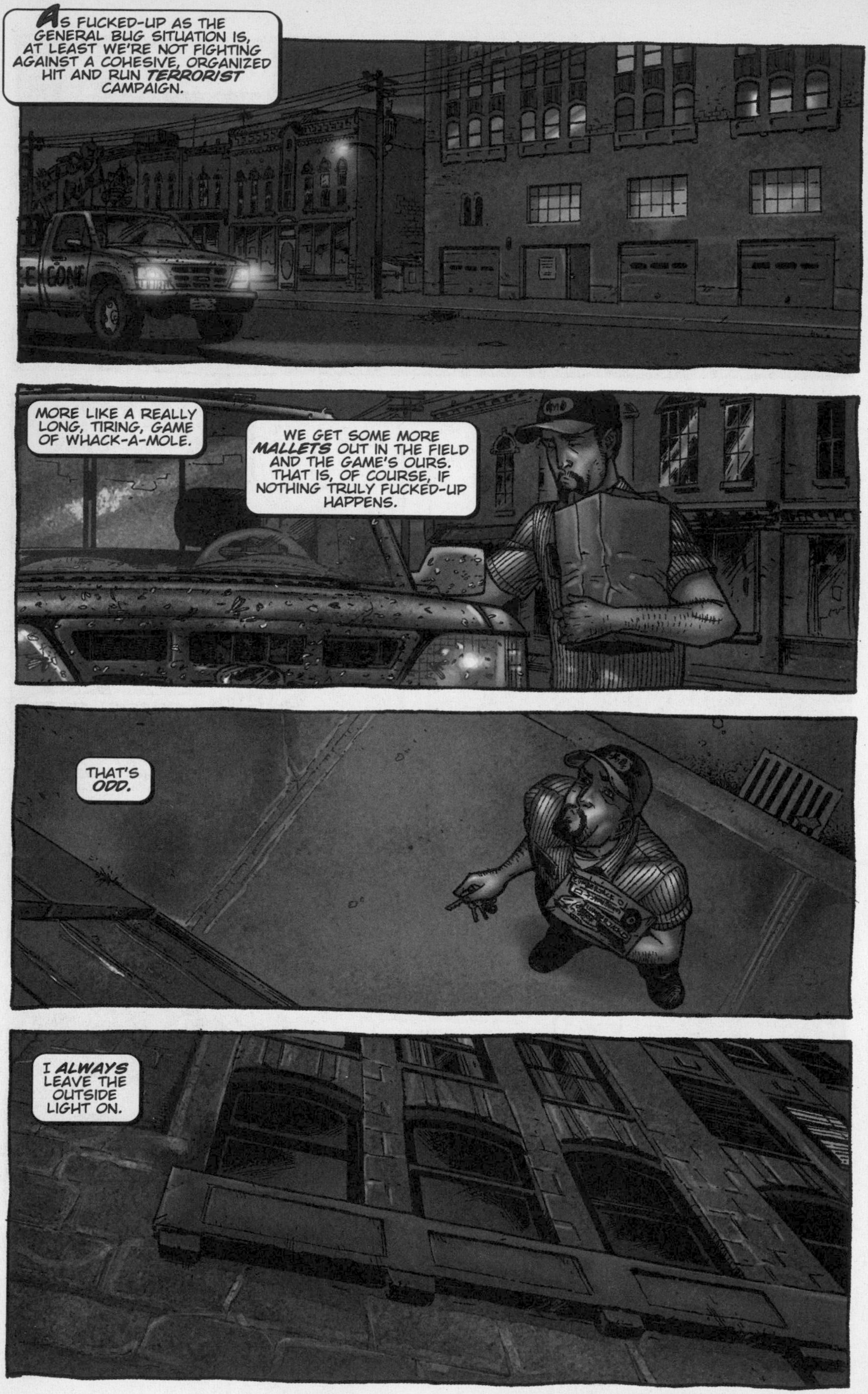
AS FUCKED-UP AS THE GENERAL BUG SITUATION IS, AT LEAST WE'RE NOT FIGHTING AGAINST A COHESIVE, ORGANIZED HIT AND RUN *TERRORIST* CAMPAIGN.
MORE LIKE A REALLY LONG, TIRING, GAME OF WHACK-A-MOLE.
WE GET SOME MORE *MALLETS* OUT IN THE FIELD AND THE GAME'S OURS. THAT IS, OF COURSE, IF NOTHING TRULY FUCKED-UP HAPPENS.
THAT'S *ODD.*
I *ALWAYS* LEAVE THE OUTSIDE LIGHT ON.

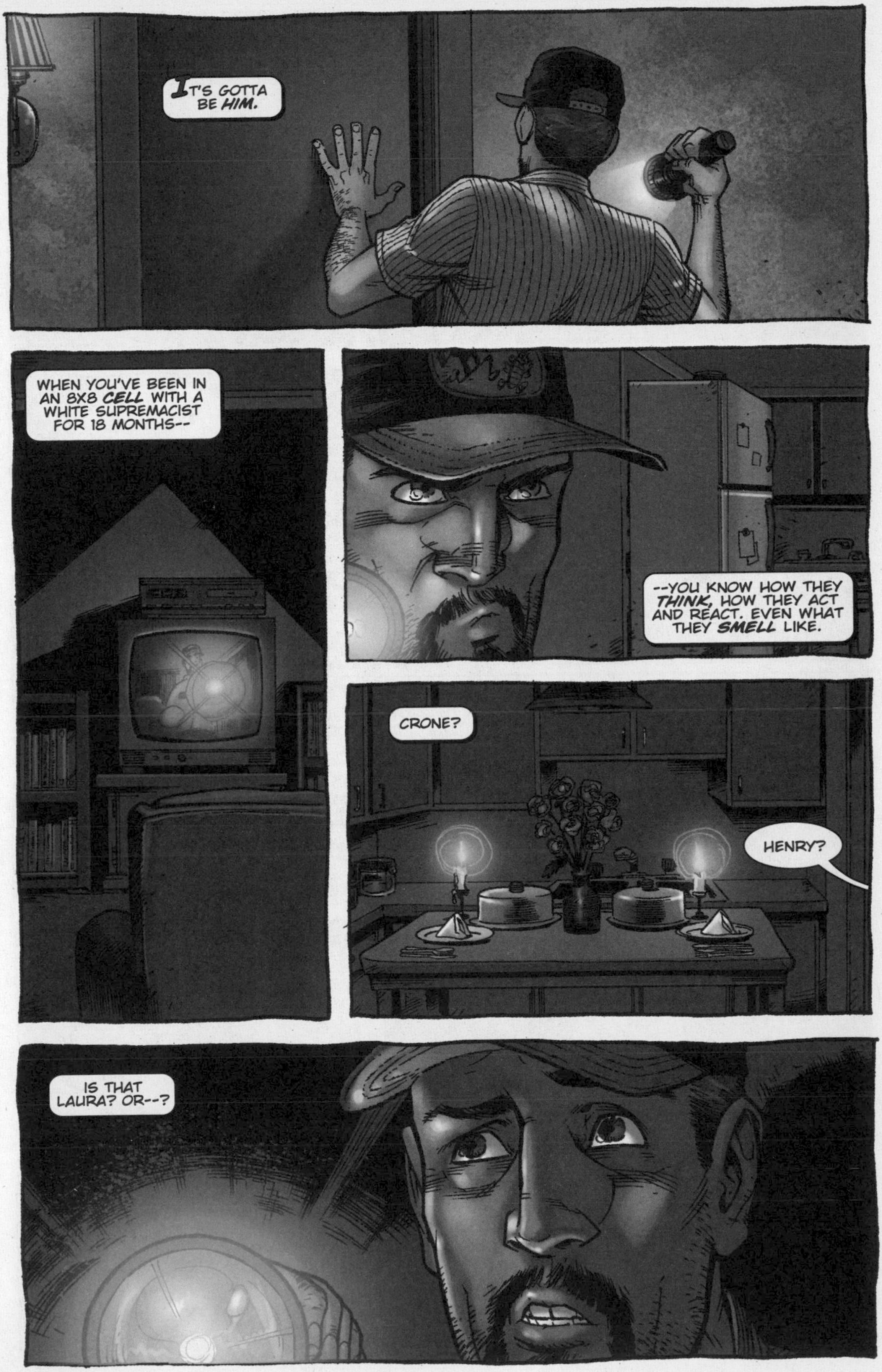
IT'S GOTTA BE HIM.
WHEN YOU'VE BEEN IN AN 8X8 CELL WITH A WHITE SUPREMACIST FOR 18 MONTHS--
--YOU KNOW HOW THEY THINK, HOW THEY ACT AND REACT. EVEN WHAT THEY SMELL LIKE.
CRONE?
HENRY?
IS THAT LAURA? OR--?

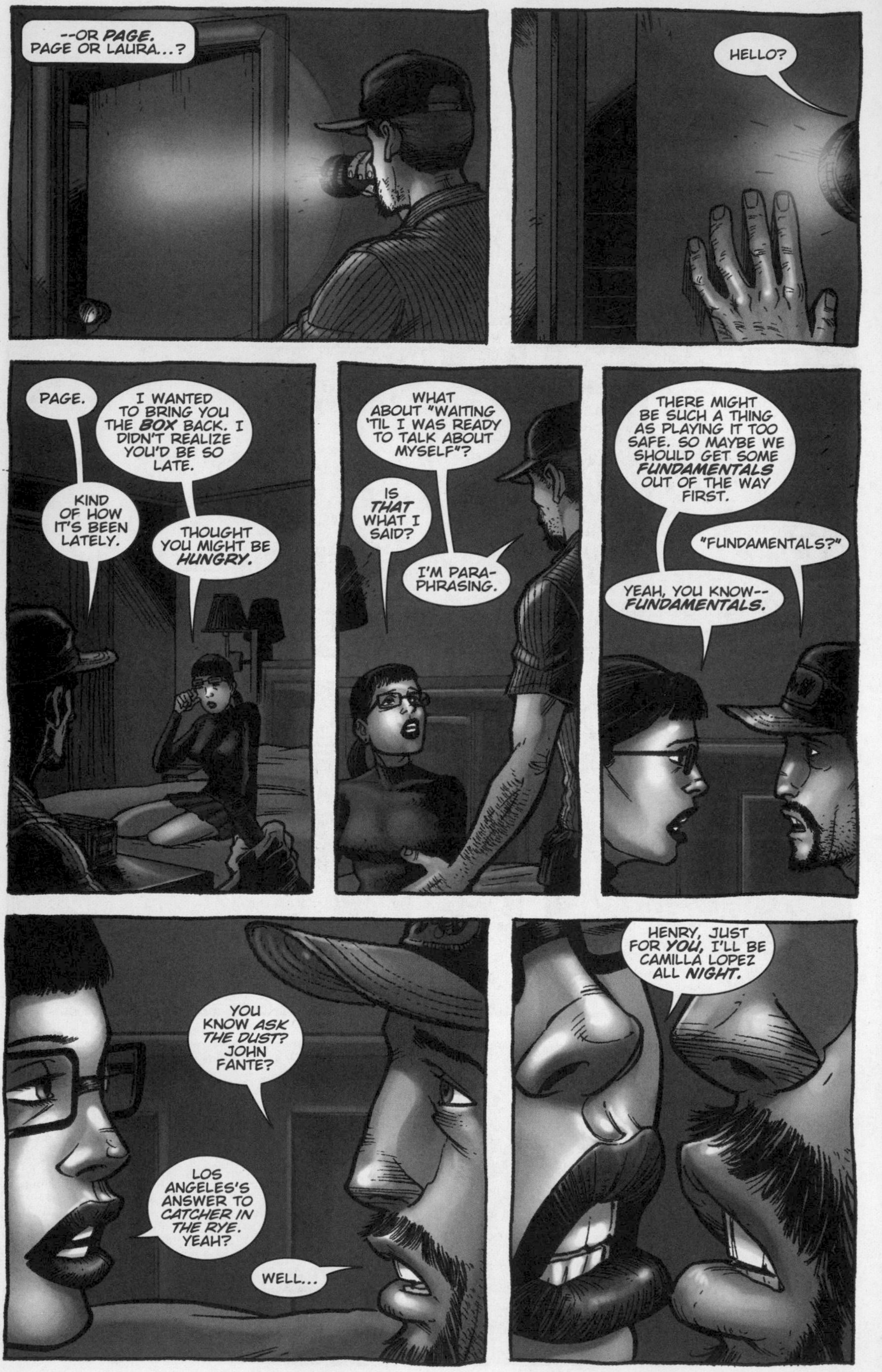
--OR PAGE. PAGE OR LAURA...?
HELLO?
PAGE.
I WANTED TO BRING YOU THE BOX BACK. I DIDN'T REALIZE YOU'D BE SO LATE.
KIND OF HOW IT'S BEEN LATELY.
THOUGHT YOU MIGHT BE HUNGRY.
WHAT ABOUT "WAITING 'TIL I WAS READY TO TALK ABOUT MYSELF"?
IS THAT WHAT I SAID?
I'M PARA-PHRASING.
THERE MIGHT BE SUCH A THING AS PLAYING IT TOO SAFE. SO MAYBE WE SHOULD GET SOME FUNDAMENTALS OUT OF THE WAY FIRST.
"FUNDAMENTALS?"
YEAH, YOU KNOW--FUNDAMENTALS.
YOU KNOW ASK THE DUST? JOHN FANTE?
LOS ANGELES'S ANSWER TO CATCHER IN THE RYE. YEAH?
WELL...
HENRY, JUST FOR YOU, I'LL BE CAMILLA LOPEZ ALL NIGHT.

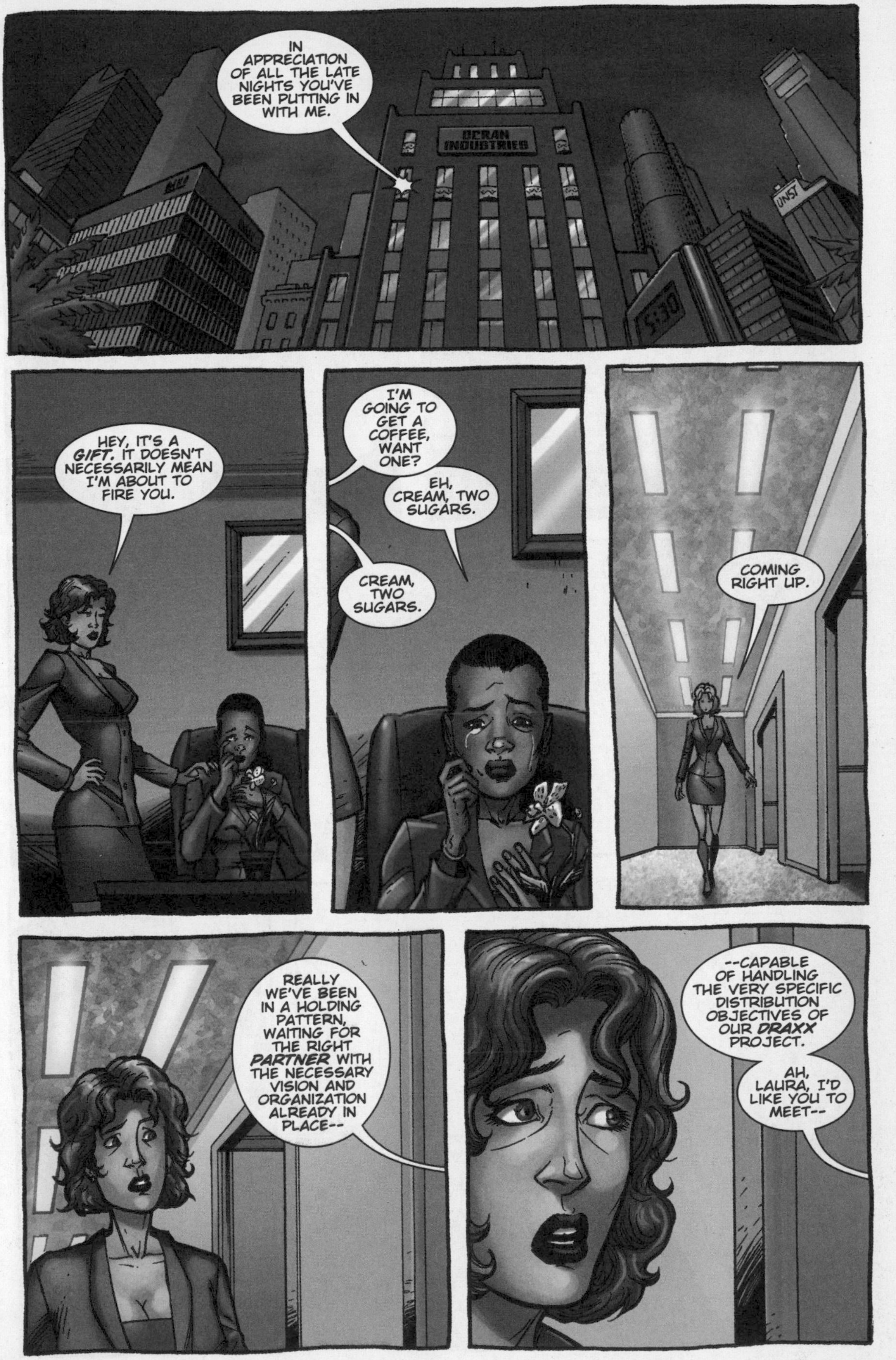
IN APPRECIATION OF ALL THE LATE NIGHTS YOU'VE BEEN PUTTING IN WITH ME.
OCRAN INDUSTRIES
HEY, IT'S A *GIFT*. IT DOESN'T NECESSARILY MEAN I'M ABOUT TO FIRE YOU.
I'M GOING TO GET A COFFEE, WANT ONE?
EH, CREAM, TWO SUGARS.
CREAM, TWO SUGARS.
COMING RIGHT UP.
REALLY WE'VE BEEN IN A HOLDING PATTERN, WAITING FOR THE RIGHT *PARTNER* WITH THE NECESSARY VISION AND ORGANIZATION ALREADY IN PLACE--
--CAPABLE OF HANDLING THE VERY SPECIFIC DISTRIBUTION OBJECTIVES OF OUR *DRAXX* PROJECT.
AH, LAURA, I'D LIKE YOU TO MEET--

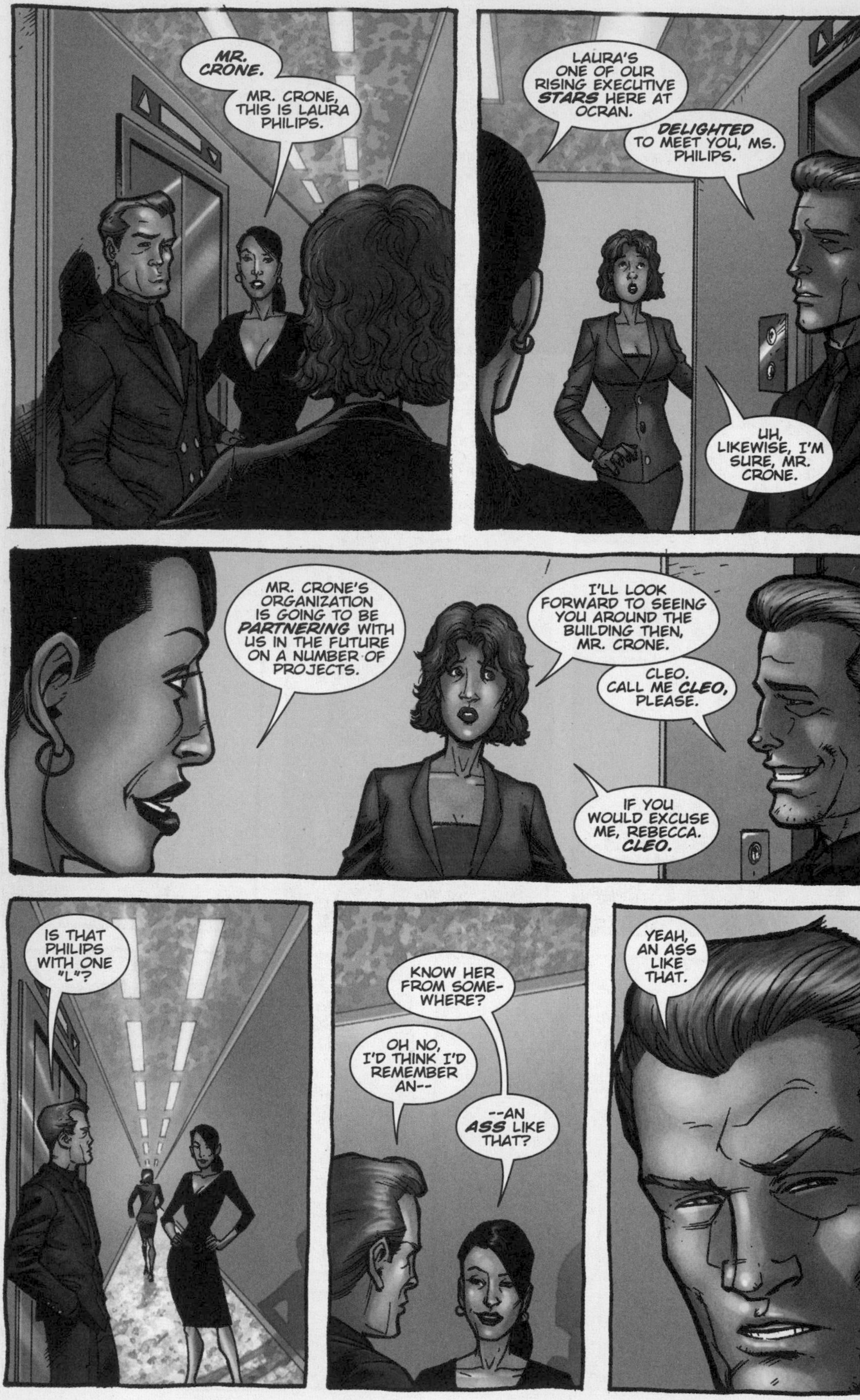
MR. CRONE.
MR. CRONE, THIS IS LAURA PHILIPS.
LAURA'S ONE OF OUR RISING EXECUTIVE STARS HERE AT OCRAN.
DELIGHTED TO MEET YOU, MS. PHILIPS.
UH, LIKEWISE, I'M SURE, MR. CRONE.
MR. CRONE'S ORGANIZATION IS GOING TO BE PARTNERING WITH US IN THE FUTURE ON A NUMBER OF PROJECTS.
I'LL LOOK FORWARD TO SEEING YOU AROUND THE BUILDING THEN, MR. CRONE.
CLEO. CALL ME CLEO, PLEASE.
IF YOU WOULD EXCUSE ME, REBECCA. CLEO.
IS THAT PHILIPS WITH ONE "L"?
KNOW HER FROM SOME-WHERE?
OH NO, I'D THINK I'D REMEMBER AN--
--AN ASS LIKE THAT?
YEAH, AN ASS LIKE THAT.

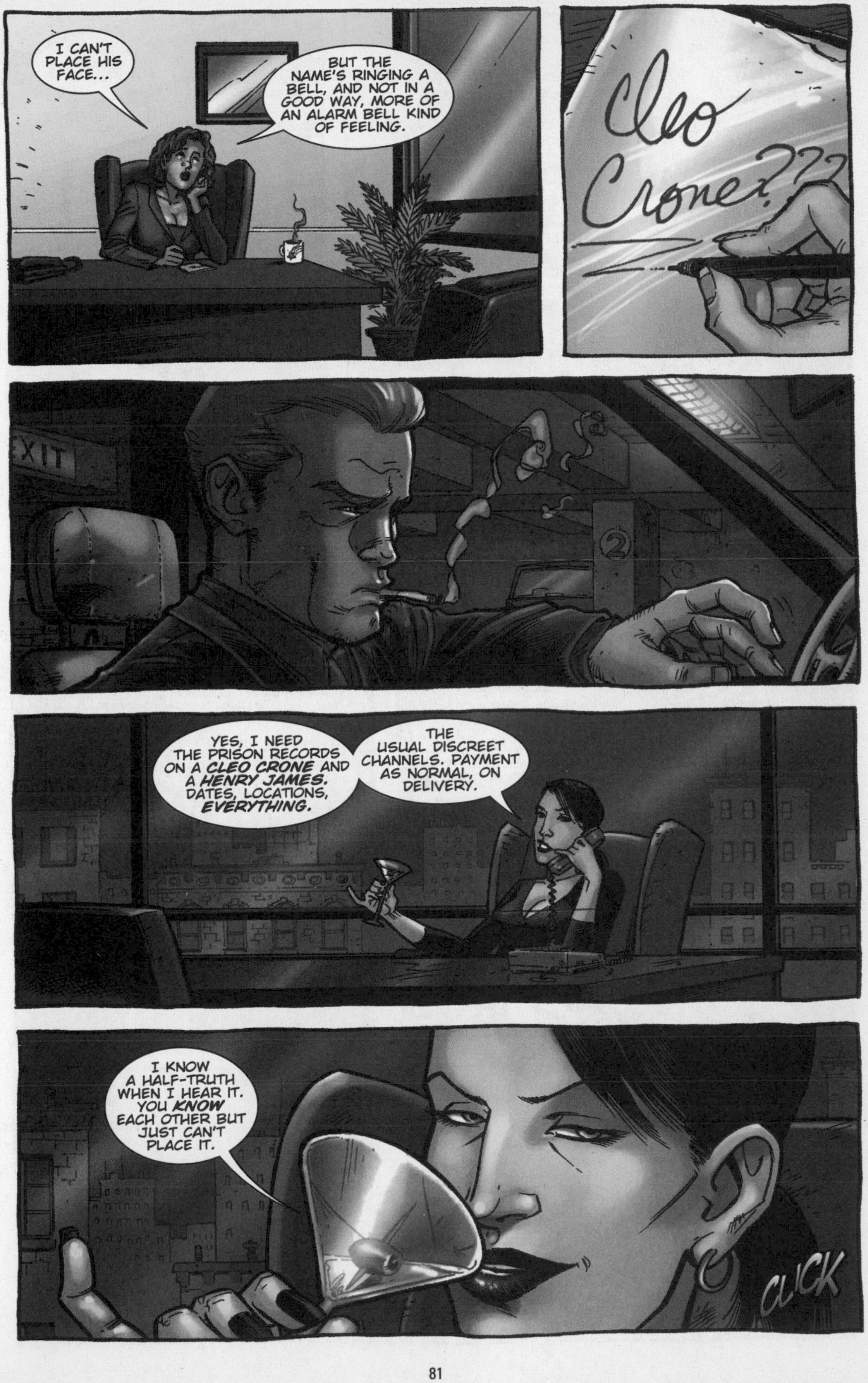
I CAN'T PLACE HIS FACE...
BUT THE NAME'S RINGING A BELL, AND NOT IN A GOOD WAY, MORE OF AN ALARM BELL KIND OF FEELING.
Cleo Crone???
EXIT
YES, I NEED THE PRISON RECORDS ON A CLEO CRONE AND A HENRY JAMES. DATES, LOCATIONS, EVERYTHING.
THE USUAL DISCREET CHANNELS. PAYMENT AS NORMAL, ON DELIVERY.
I KNOW A HALF-TRUTH WHEN I HEAR IT. YOU KNOW EACH OTHER BUT JUST CAN'T PLACE IT.
CLICK

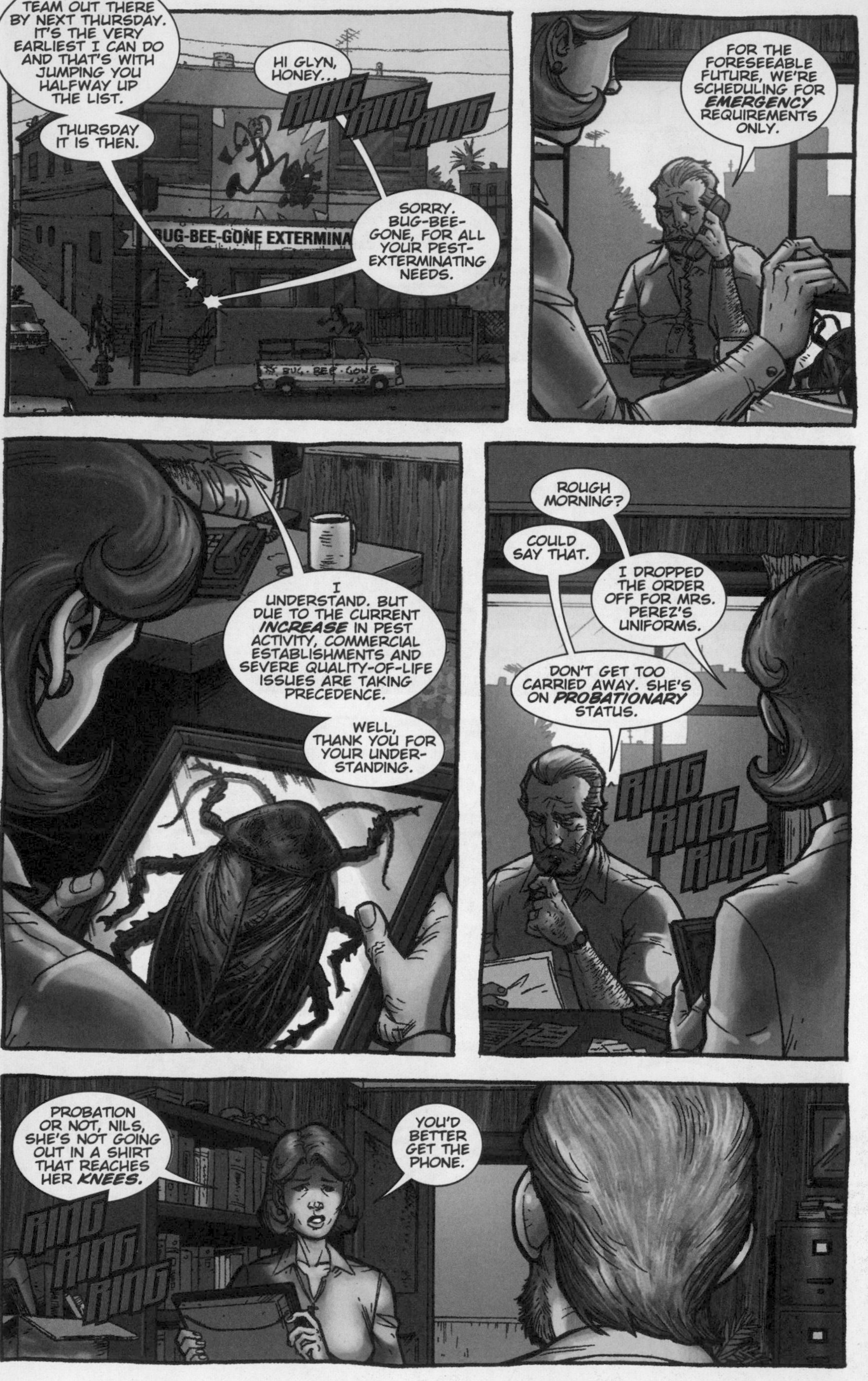

I'LL GET A TEAM OUT THERE BY NEXT THURSDAY. IT'S THE VERY EARLIEST I CAN DO AND THAT'S WITH JUMPING YOU HALFWAY UP THE LIST.
THURSDAY IT IS THEN.
HI GLYN, HONEY...
RING RING RING
BUG-BEE-GONE EXTERMINA
SORRY. BUG-BEE-GONE, FOR ALL YOUR PEST-EXTERMINATING NEEDS.
BUG · BEE · GONE
FOR THE FORESEEABLE FUTURE, WE'RE SCHEDULING FOR EMERGENCY REQUIREMENTS ONLY.
I UNDERSTAND. BUT DUE TO THE CURRENT INCREASE IN PEST ACTIVITY, COMMERCIAL ESTABLISHMENTS AND SEVERE QUALITY-OF-LIFE ISSUES ARE TAKING PRECEDENCE.
WELL, THANK YOU FOR YOUR UNDER-STANDING.
ROUGH MORNING?
COULD SAY THAT.
I DROPPED THE ORDER OFF FOR MRS. PEREZ'S UNIFORMS.
DON'T GET TOO CARRIED AWAY. SHE'S ON PROBATIONARY STATUS.
RING RING RING
PROBATION OR NOT, NILS, SHE'S NOT GOING OUT IN A SHIRT THAT REACHES HER KNEES.
YOU'D BETTER GET THE PHONE.
RING RING RING

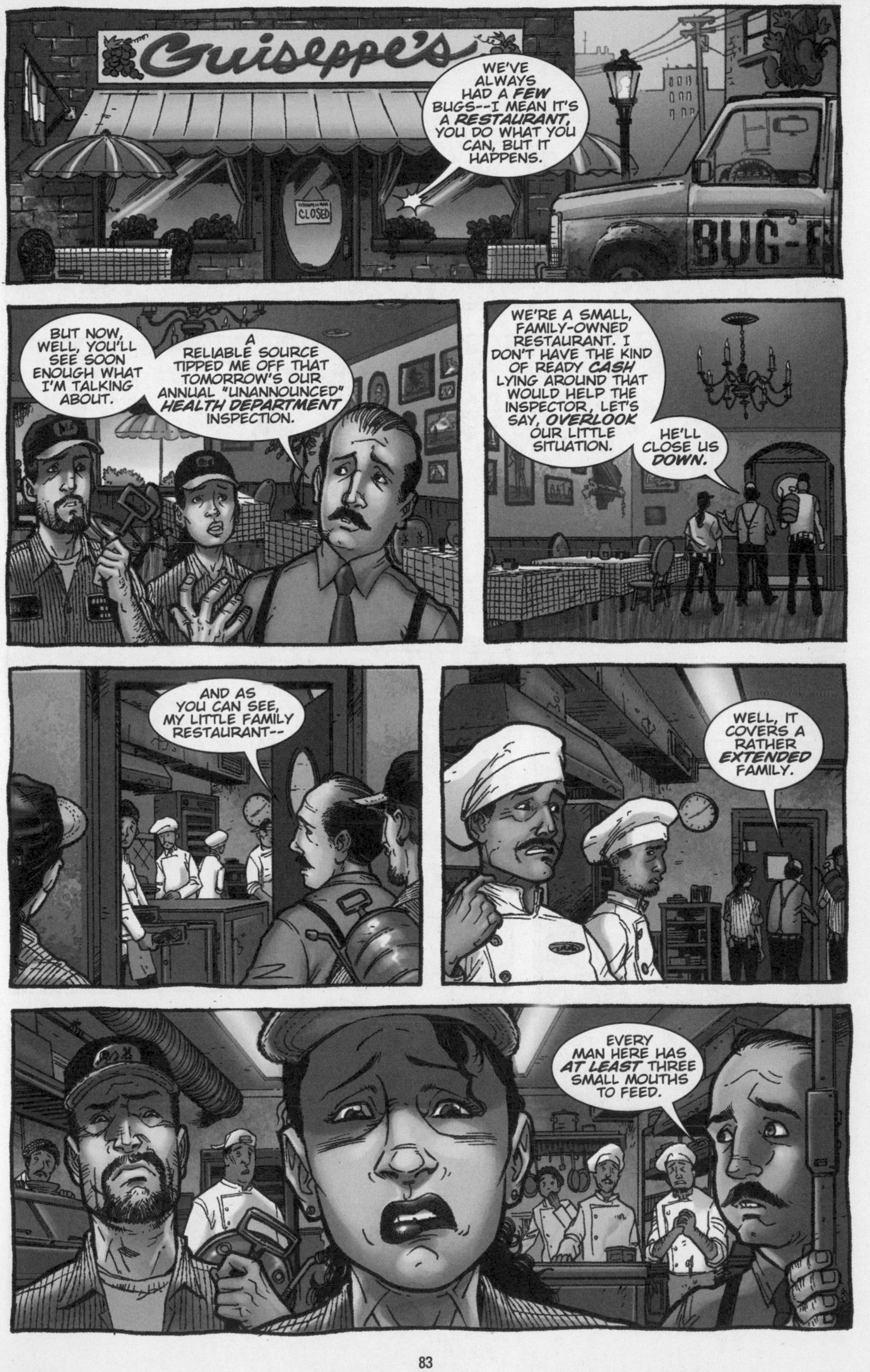
Guiseppe's
WE'VE ALWAYS HAD A FEW BUGS--I MEAN IT'S A RESTAURANT, YOU DO WHAT YOU CAN, BUT IT HAPPENS.
CLOSED
BUG-
BUT NOW, WELL, YOU'LL SEE SOON ENOUGH WHAT I'M TALKING ABOUT.
A RELIABLE SOURCE TIPPED ME OFF THAT TOMORROW'S OUR ANNUAL "UNANNOUNCED" HEALTH DEPARTMENT INSPECTION.
WE'RE A SMALL, FAMILY-OWNED RESTAURANT. I DON'T HAVE THE KIND OF READY CASH LYING AROUND THAT WOULD HELP THE INSPECTOR, LET'S SAY, OVERLOOK OUR LITTLE SITUATION.
HE'LL CLOSE US DOWN.
AND AS YOU CAN SEE, MY LITTLE FAMILY RESTAURANT--
WELL, IT COVERS A RATHER EXTENDED FAMILY.
EVERY MAN HERE HAS AT LEAST THREE SMALL MOUTHS TO FEED.

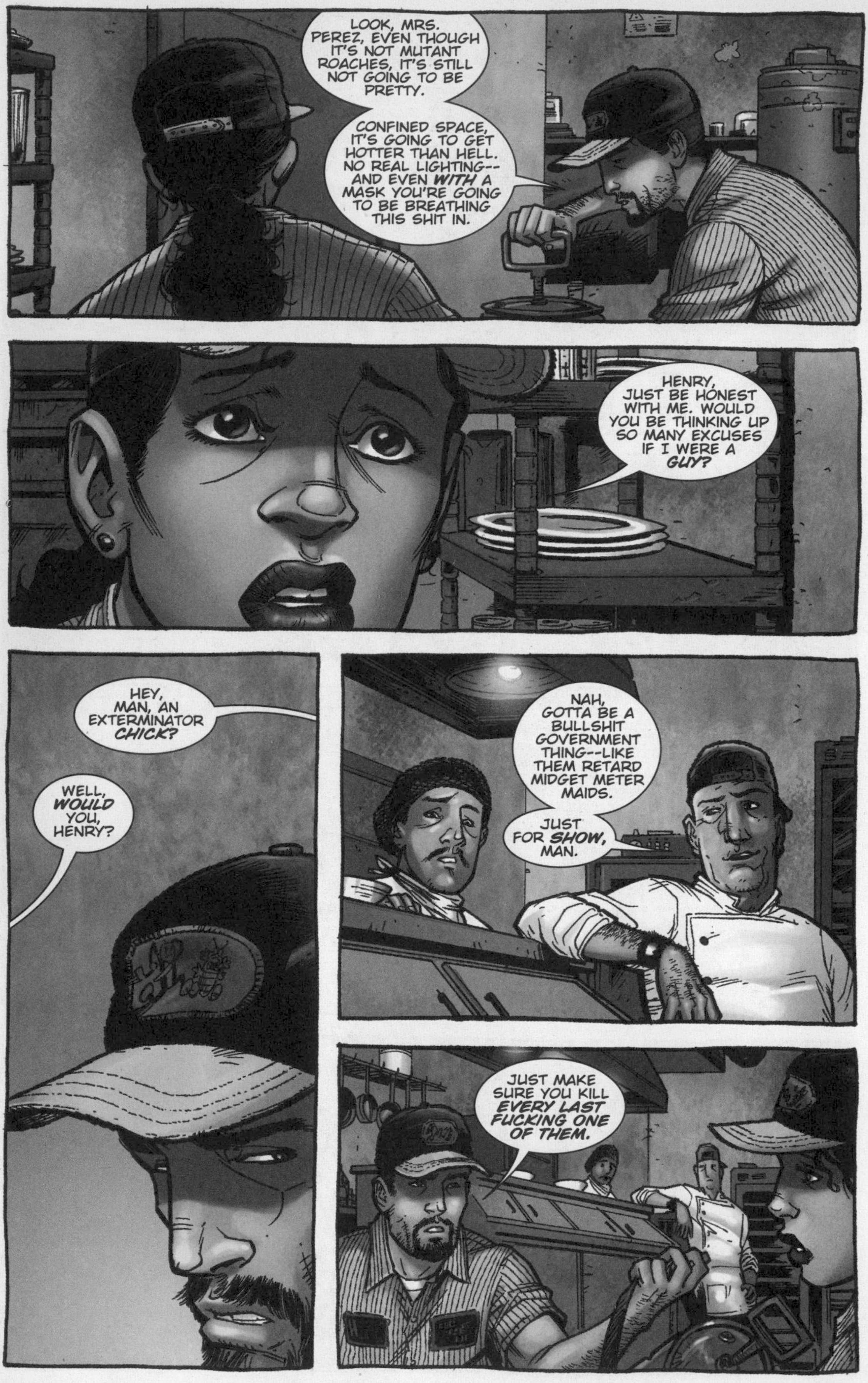
LOOK, MRS. PEREZ, EVEN THOUGH IT'S NOT MUTANT ROACHES, IT'S STILL NOT GOING TO BE PRETTY.
CONFINED SPACE, IT'S GOING TO GET HOTTER THAN HELL. NO REAL LIGHTING-- AND EVEN *WITH* A MASK YOU'RE GOING TO BE BREATHING THIS SHIT IN.
HENRY, JUST BE HONEST WITH ME. WOULD YOU BE THINKING UP SO MANY EXCUSES IF I WERE A *GUY?*
HEY, MAN, AN EXTERMINATOR *CHICK?*
WELL, *WOULD* YOU, HENRY?
NAH, GOTTA BE A BULLSHIT GOVERNMENT THING--LIKE THEM RETARD MIDGET METER MAIDS.
JUST FOR *SHOW,* MAN.
JUST MAKE SURE YOU KILL *EVERY LAST FUCKING ONE OF THEM.*

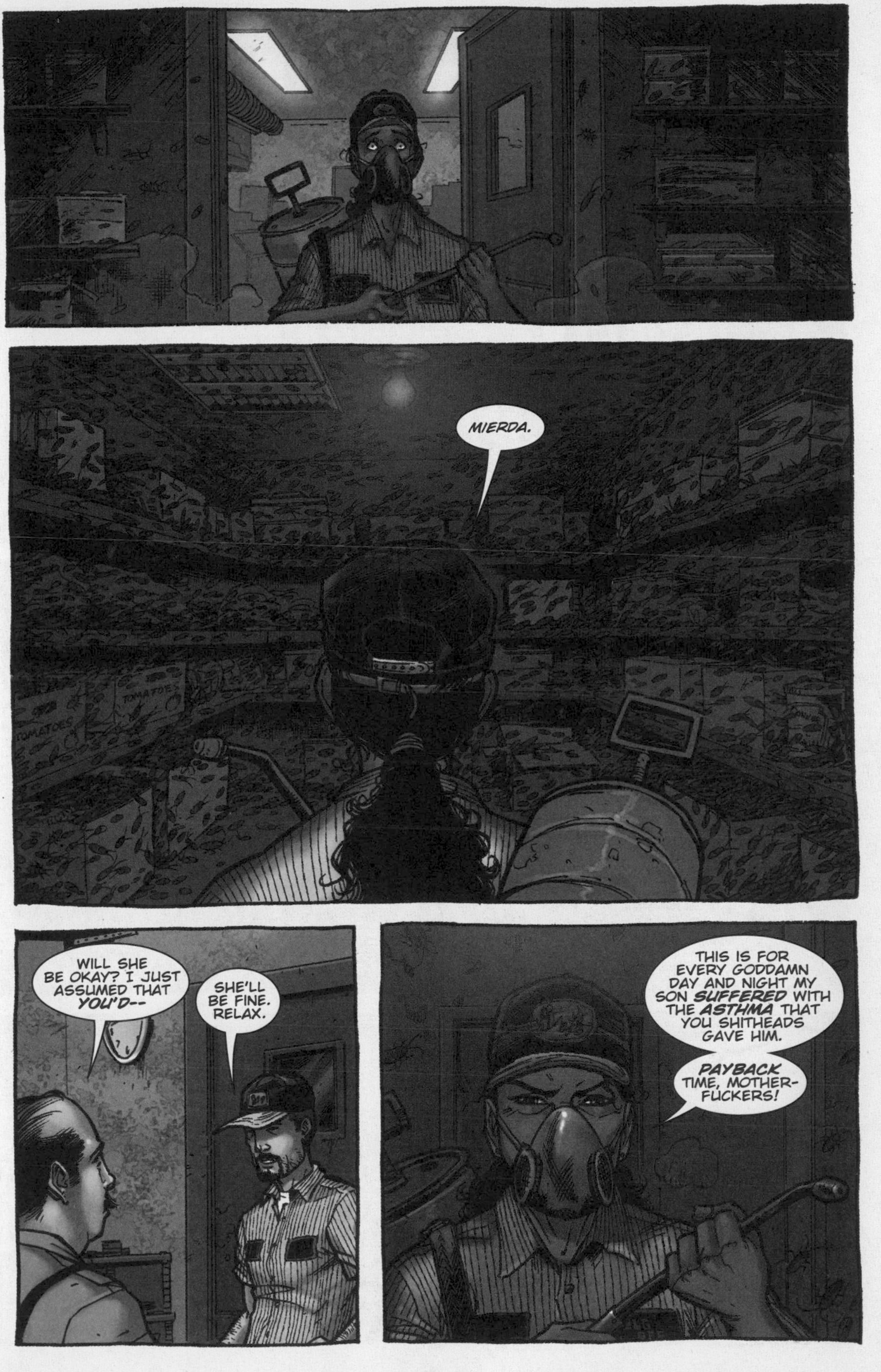
MIERDA.
WILL SHE BE OKAY? I JUST ASSUMED THAT YOU'D--
SHE'LL BE FINE. RELAX.
THIS IS FOR EVERY GODDAMN DAY AND NIGHT MY SON SUFFERED WITH THE ASTHMA THAT YOU SHITHEADS GAVE HIM.
PAYBACK TIME, MOTHER-FUCKERS!

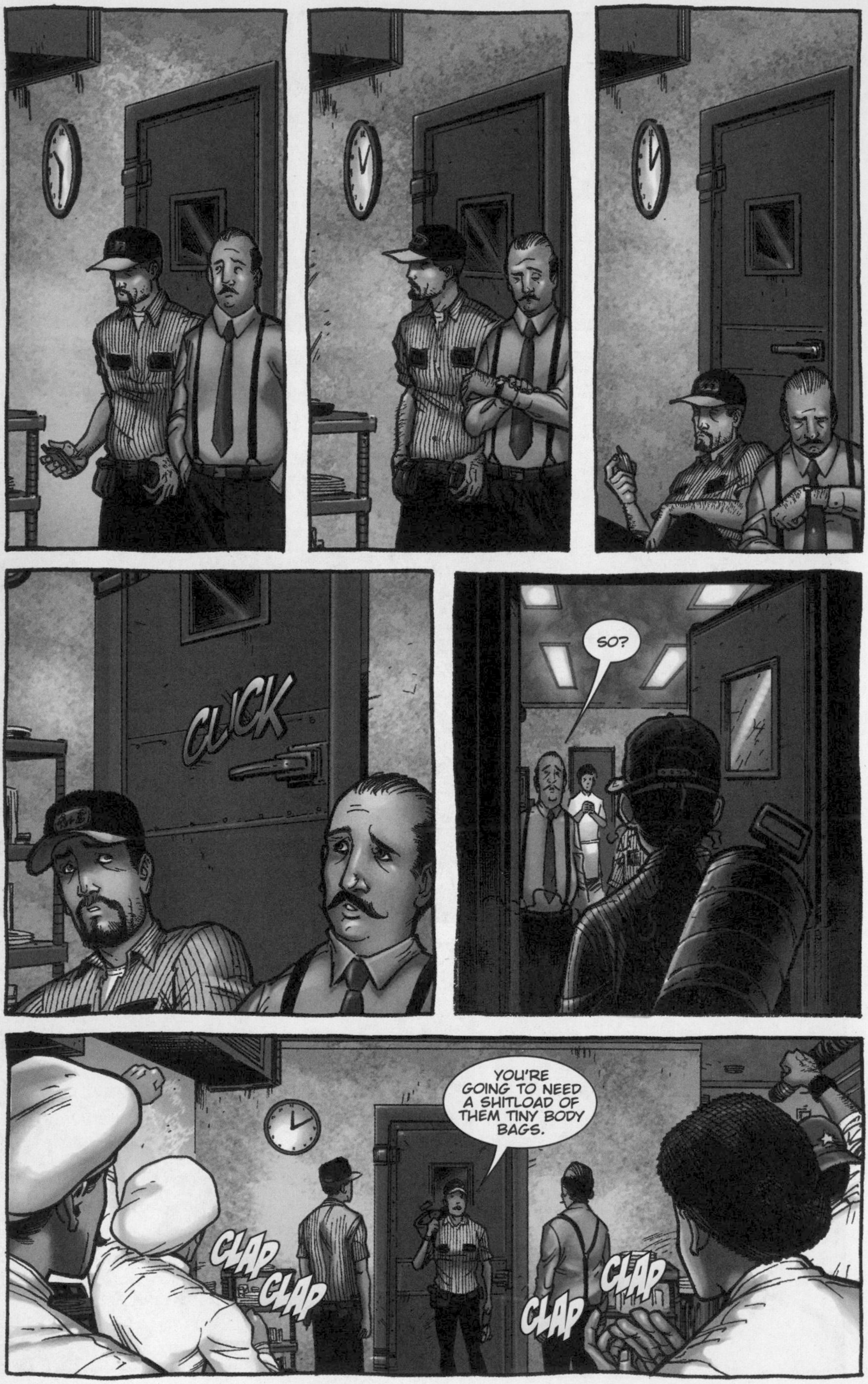
CLICK
SO?
YOU'RE GOING TO NEED A SHITLOAD OF THEM TINY BODY BAGS.
CLAP
CLAP
CLAP
CLAP

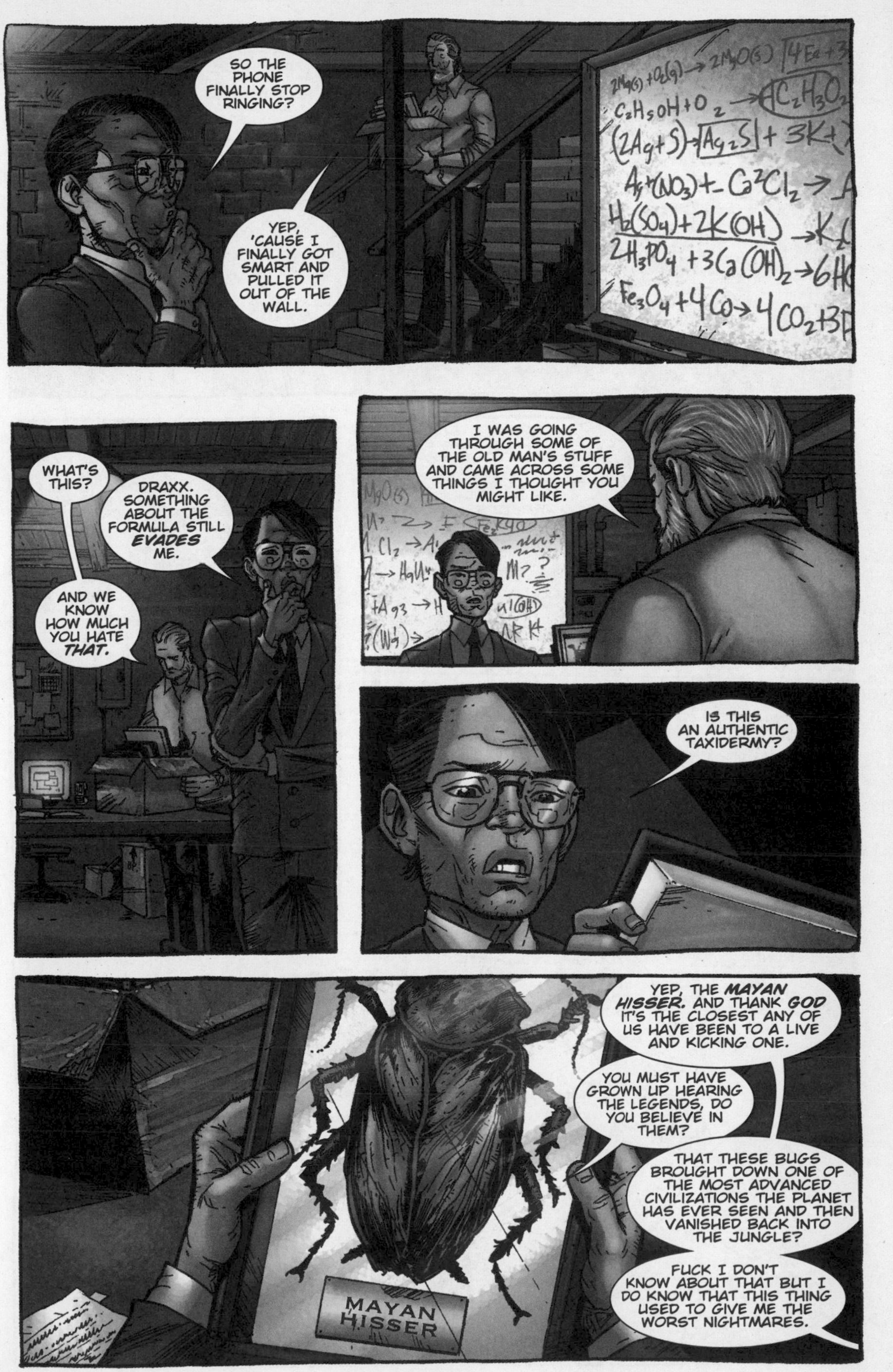

SO THE PHONE FINALLY STOP RINGING?
YEP, 'CAUSE I FINALLY GOT SMART AND PULLED IT OUT OF THE WALL.
WHAT'S THIS?
DRAXX. SOMETHING ABOUT THE FORMULA STILL EVADES ME.
AND WE KNOW HOW MUCH YOU HATE THAT.
I WAS GOING THROUGH SOME OF THE OLD MAN'S STUFF AND CAME ACROSS SOME THINGS I THOUGHT YOU MIGHT LIKE.
IS THIS AN AUTHENTIC TAXIDERMY?
YEP, THE MAYAN HISSER. AND THANK GOD IT'S THE CLOSEST ANY OF US HAVE BEEN TO A LIVE AND KICKING ONE.
YOU MUST HAVE GROWN UP HEARING THE LEGENDS, DO YOU BELIEVE IN THEM?
THAT THESE BUGS BROUGHT DOWN ONE OF THE MOST ADVANCED CIVILIZATIONS THE PLANET HAS EVER SEEN AND THEN VANISHED BACK INTO THE JUNGLE?
FUCK I DON'T KNOW ABOUT THAT BUT I DO KNOW THAT THIS THING USED TO GIVE ME THE WORST NIGHTMARES.
MAYAN HISSER

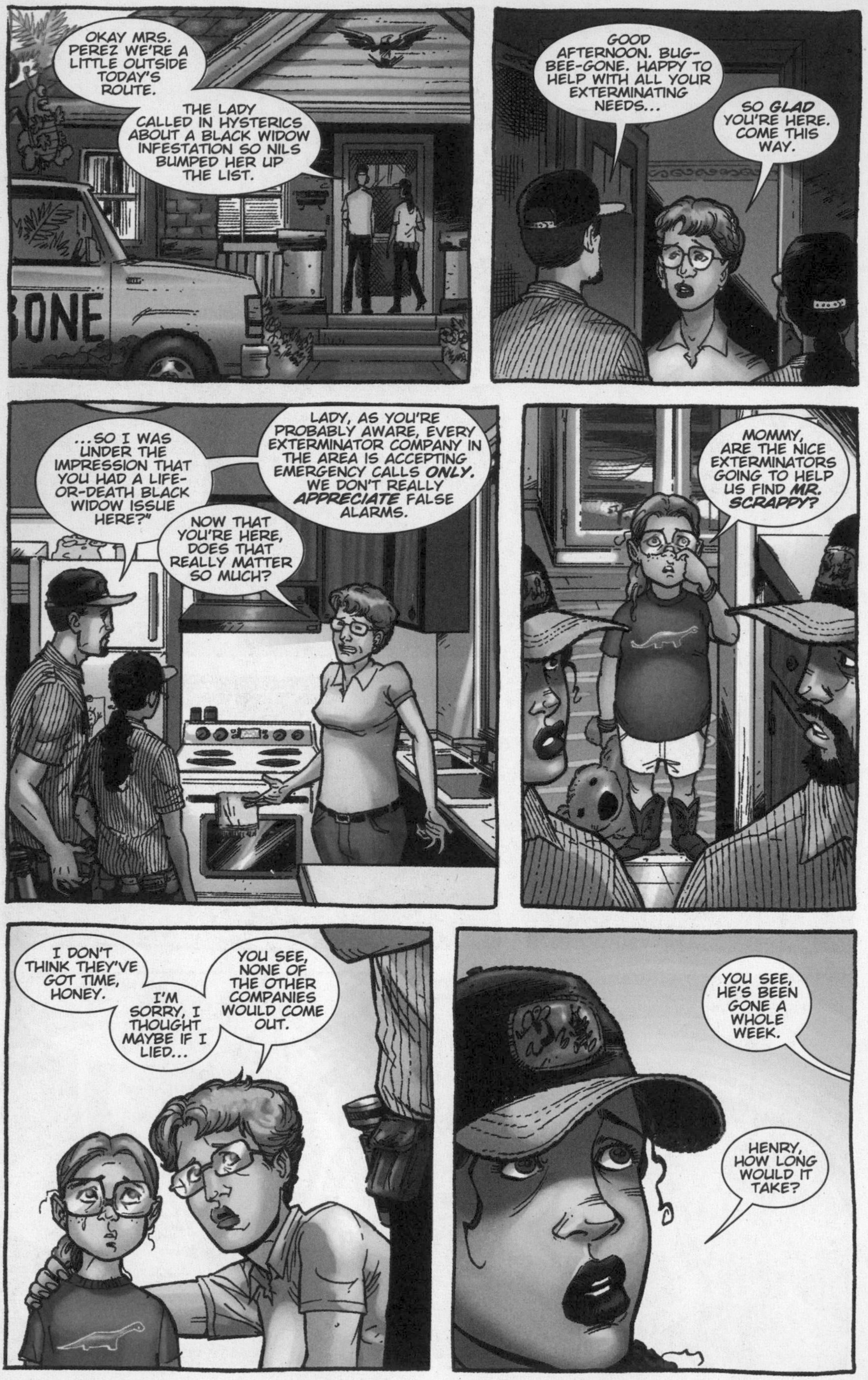
OKAY MRS. PEREZ WE'RE A LITTLE OUTSIDE TODAY'S ROUTE.
THE LADY CALLED IN HYSTERICS ABOUT A BLACK WIDOW INFESTATION SO NILS BUMPED HER UP THE LIST.
BONE
GOOD AFTERNOON. BUG-BEE-GONE. HAPPY TO HELP WITH ALL YOUR EXTERMINATING NEEDS...
SO GLAD YOU'RE HERE. COME THIS WAY.
...SO I WAS UNDER THE IMPRESSION THAT YOU HAD A LIFE-OR-DEATH BLACK WIDOW ISSUE HERE?"
LADY, AS YOU'RE PROBABLY AWARE, EVERY EXTERMINATOR COMPANY IN THE AREA IS ACCEPTING EMERGENCY CALLS ONLY. WE DON'T REALLY APPRECIATE FALSE ALARMS.
NOW THAT YOU'RE HERE, DOES THAT REALLY MATTER SO MUCH?
MOMMY, ARE THE NICE EXTERMINATORS GOING TO HELP US FIND MR. SCRAPPY?
I DON'T THINK THEY'VE GOT TIME, HONEY.
I'M SORRY, I THOUGHT MAYBE IF I LIED...
YOU SEE, NONE OF THE OTHER COMPANIES WOULD COME OUT.
YOU SEE, HE'S BEEN GONE A WHOLE WEEK.
HENRY, HOW LONG WOULD IT TAKE?

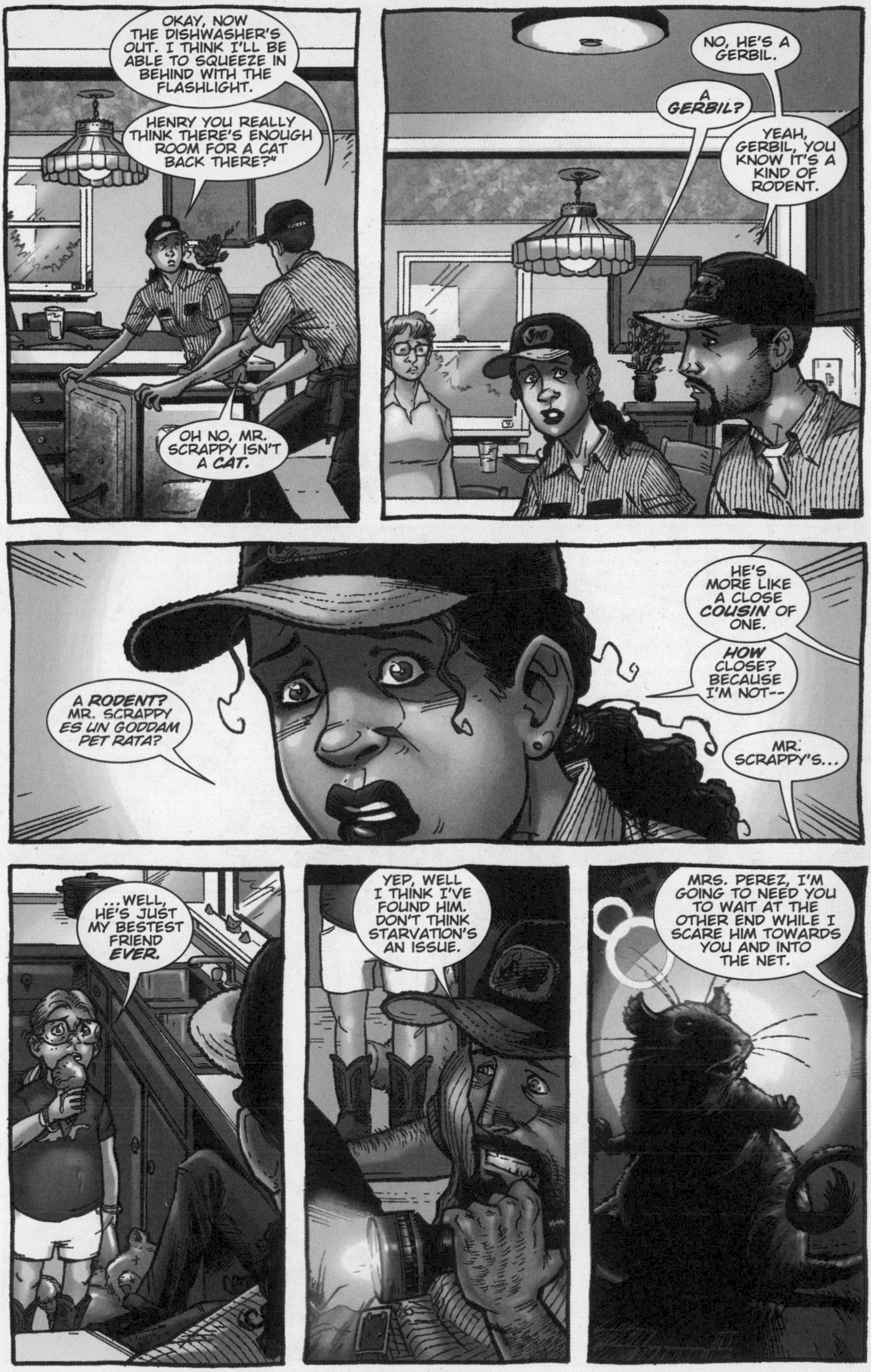
OKAY, NOW THE DISHWASHER'S OUT. I THINK I'LL BE ABLE TO SQUEEZE IN BEHIND WITH THE FLASHLIGHT.
HENRY YOU REALLY THINK THERE'S ENOUGH ROOM FOR A CAT BACK THERE?"
OH NO, MR. SCRAPPY ISN'T A *CAT.*
NO, HE'S A GERBIL.
A *GERBIL?*
YEAH, GERBIL, YOU KNOW IT'S A KIND OF RODENT.
HE'S MORE LIKE A CLOSE *COUSIN* OF ONE.
A *RODENT?* MR. SCRAPPY *ES UN GODDAM PET RATA?*
HOW CLOSE? BECAUSE I'M NOT--
MR. SCRAPPY'S...
...WELL, HE'S JUST MY BESTEST FRIEND *EVER.*
YEP, WELL I THINK I'VE FOUND HIM. DON'T THINK STARVATION'S AN ISSUE.
MRS. PEREZ, I'M GOING TO NEED YOU TO WAIT AT THE OTHER END WHILE I SCARE HIM TOWARDS YOU AND INTO THE NET.

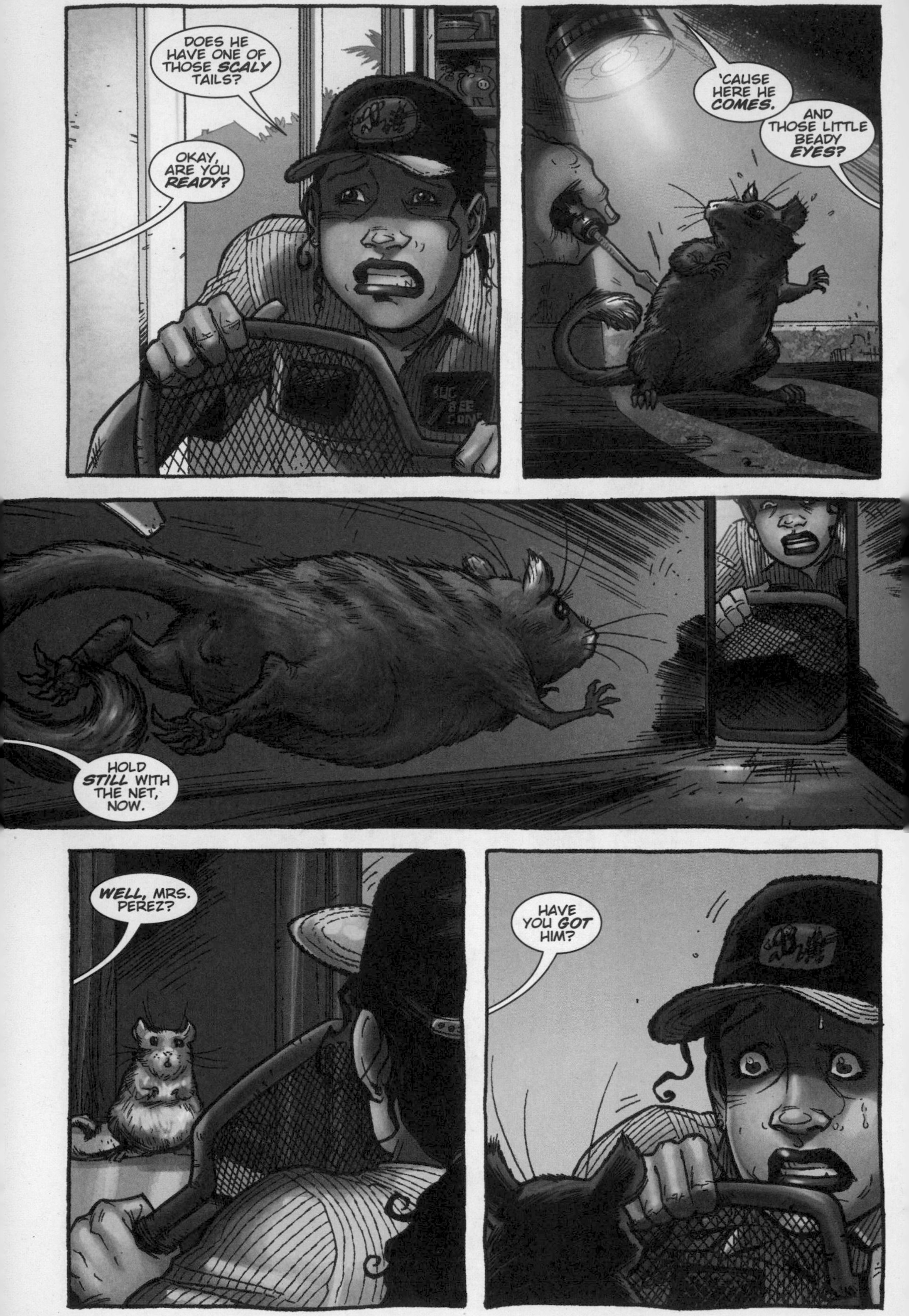
DOES HE HAVE ONE OF THOSE SCALY TAILS?
OKAY, ARE YOU READY?
'CAUSE HERE HE COMES.
AND THOSE LITTLE BEADY EYES?
HOLD STILL WITH THE NET, NOW.
WELL, MRS. PEREZ?
HAVE YOU GOT HIM?

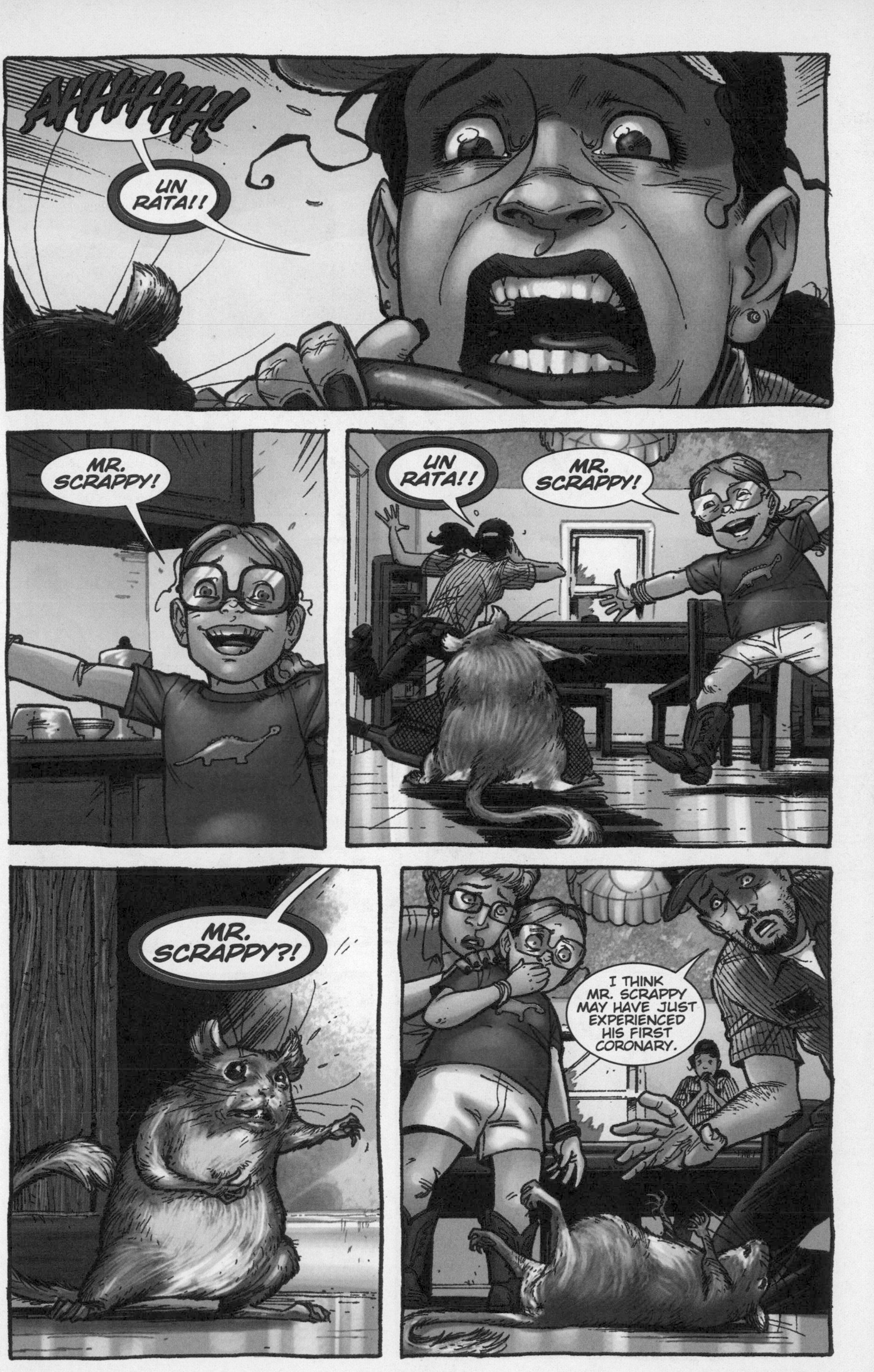
AHHHHHH!
UN RATA!!
MR. SCRAPPY!
UN RATA!!
MR. SCRAPPY!
MR. SCRAPPY?!
I THINK MR. SCRAPPY MAY HAVE JUST EXPERIENCED HIS FIRST CORONARY.

WELL, *YOU'RE* GOING TO NEED TO RESUSCITATE HIM.

LADY WITH ALL DUE RESPECT I GENERALLY DON'T BRING SMALL ANIMALS BACK TO LIFE...I KILL THEM.

MISTER, IS MR SCRAPPY GOING TO BE *OKAY?*

YOU'RE GOING TO NEED TO BLOW HARDER THAN THAT.

HARDER.

OKAY, HARDER IT *IS,* THEN.

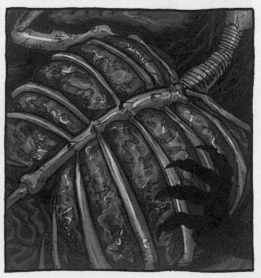

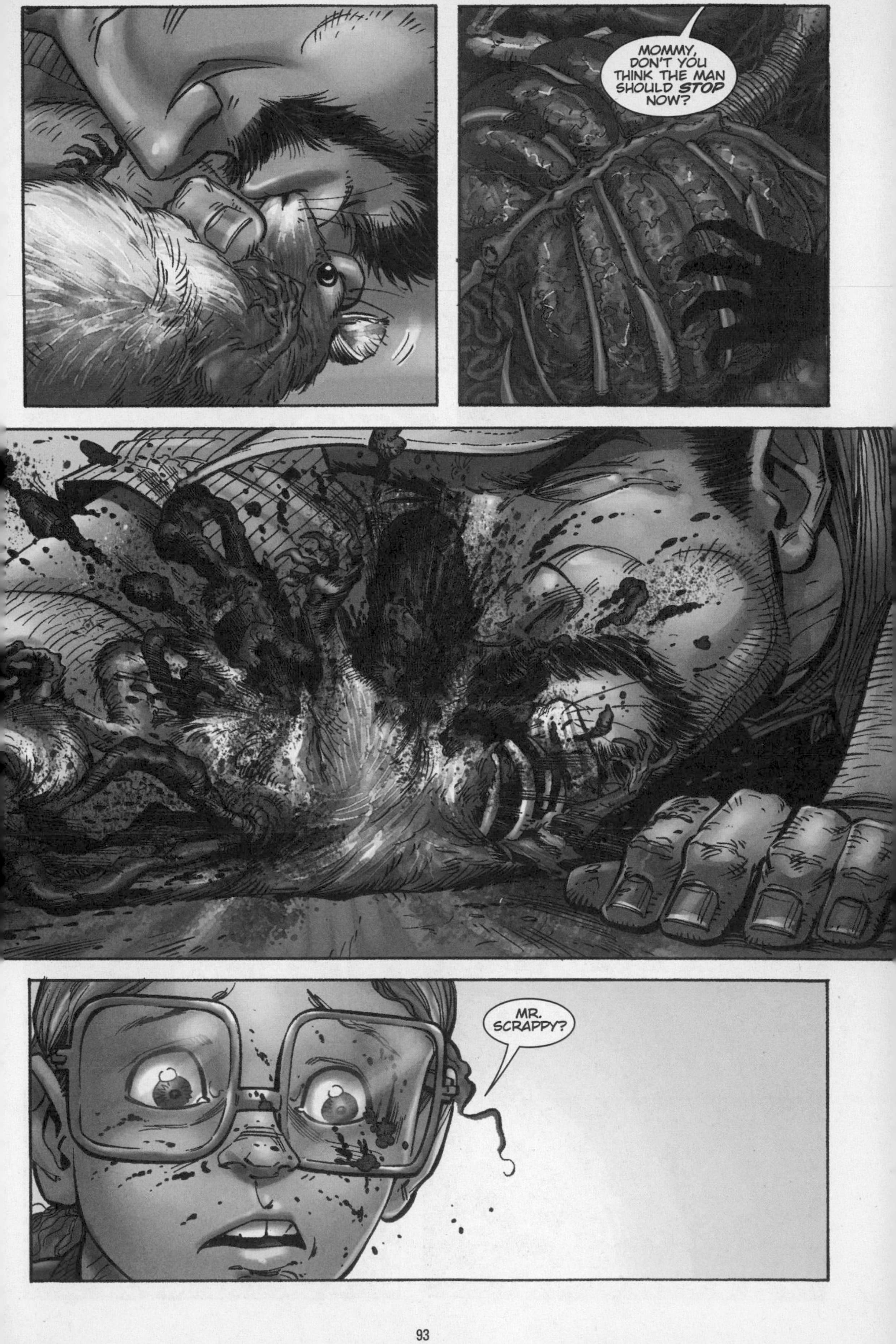
MOMMY, DON'T YOU THINK THE MAN SHOULD STOP NOW?
MR. SCRAPPY?

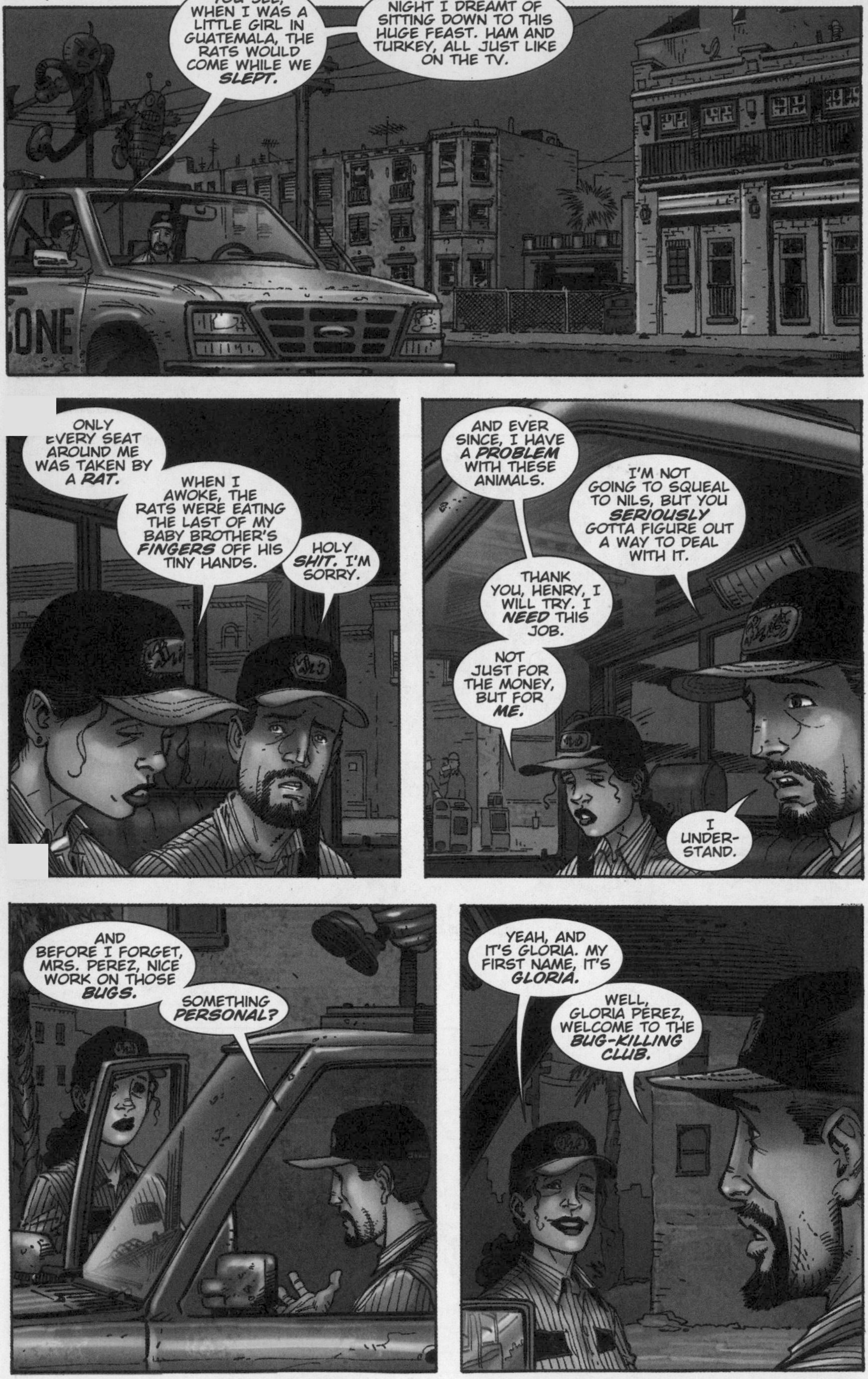
YOU SEE, WHEN I WAS A LITTLE GIRL IN GUATEMALA, THE RATS WOULD COME WHILE WE SLEPT.
ONE NIGHT I DREAMT OF SITTING DOWN TO THIS HUGE FEAST. HAM AND TURKEY, ALL JUST LIKE ON THE TV.
ONE
ONLY EVERY SEAT AROUND ME WAS TAKEN BY A RAT.
WHEN I AWOKE, THE RATS WERE EATING THE LAST OF MY BABY BROTHER'S FINGERS OFF HIS TINY HANDS.
HOLY SHIT. I'M SORRY.
AND EVER SINCE, I HAVE A PROBLEM WITH THESE ANIMALS.
I'M NOT GOING TO SQUEAL TO NILS, BUT YOU SERIOUSLY GOTTA FIGURE OUT A WAY TO DEAL WITH IT.
THANK YOU, HENRY, I WILL TRY. I NEED THIS JOB.
NOT JUST FOR THE MONEY, BUT FOR ME.
I UNDER-STAND.
AND BEFORE I FORGET, MRS. PEREZ, NICE WORK ON THOSE BUGS.
SOMETHING PERSONAL?
YEAH, AND IT'S GLORIA. MY FIRST NAME, IT'S GLORIA.
WELL, GLORIA PÉREZ, WELCOME TO THE BUG-KILLING CLUB.

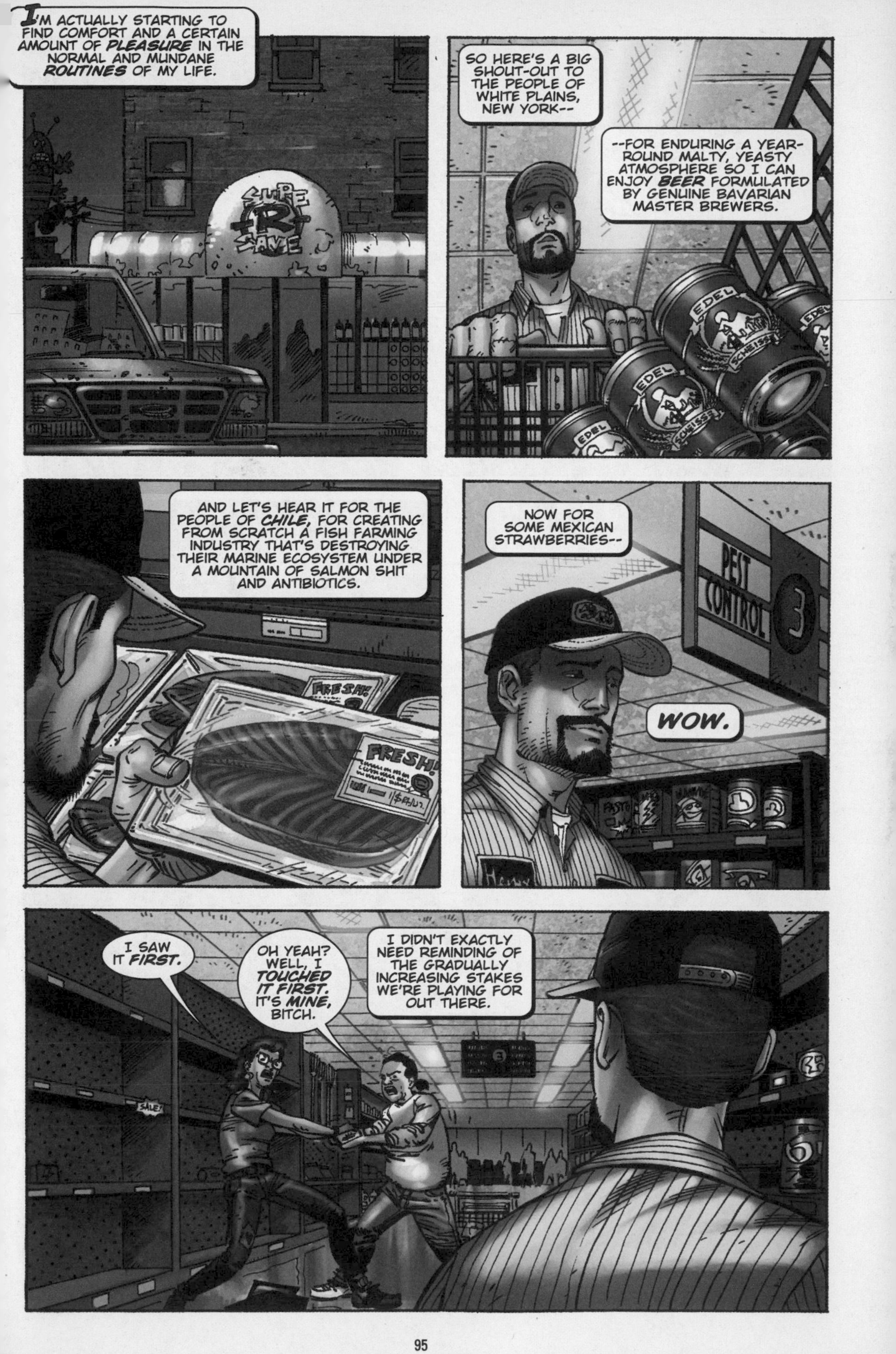
I'M ACTUALLY STARTING TO FIND COMFORT AND A CERTAIN AMOUNT OF PLEASURE IN THE NORMAL AND MUNDANE ROUTINES OF MY LIFE.
SURE R SAVE
SO HERE'S A BIG SHOUT-OUT TO THE PEOPLE OF WHITE PLAINS, NEW YORK--
--FOR ENDURING A YEAR-ROUND MALTY, YEASTY ATMOSPHERE SO I CAN ENJOY BEER FORMULATED BY GENUINE BAVARIAN MASTER BREWERS.
EDEL SCHEISSE
AND LET'S HEAR IT FOR THE PEOPLE OF CHILE, FOR CREATING FROM SCRATCH A FISH FARMING INDUSTRY THAT'S DESTROYING THEIR MARINE ECOSYSTEM UNDER A MOUNTAIN OF SALMON SHIT AND ANTIBIOTICS.
FRESH!
NOW FOR SOME MEXICAN STRAWBERRIES--
PEST CONTROL 3
WOW.
I SAW IT FIRST.
OH YEAH? WELL, I TOUCHED IT FIRST. IT'S MINE, BITCH.
I DIDN'T EXACTLY NEED REMINDING OF THE GRADUALLY INCREASING STAKES WE'RE PLAYING FOR OUT THERE.
SALE!

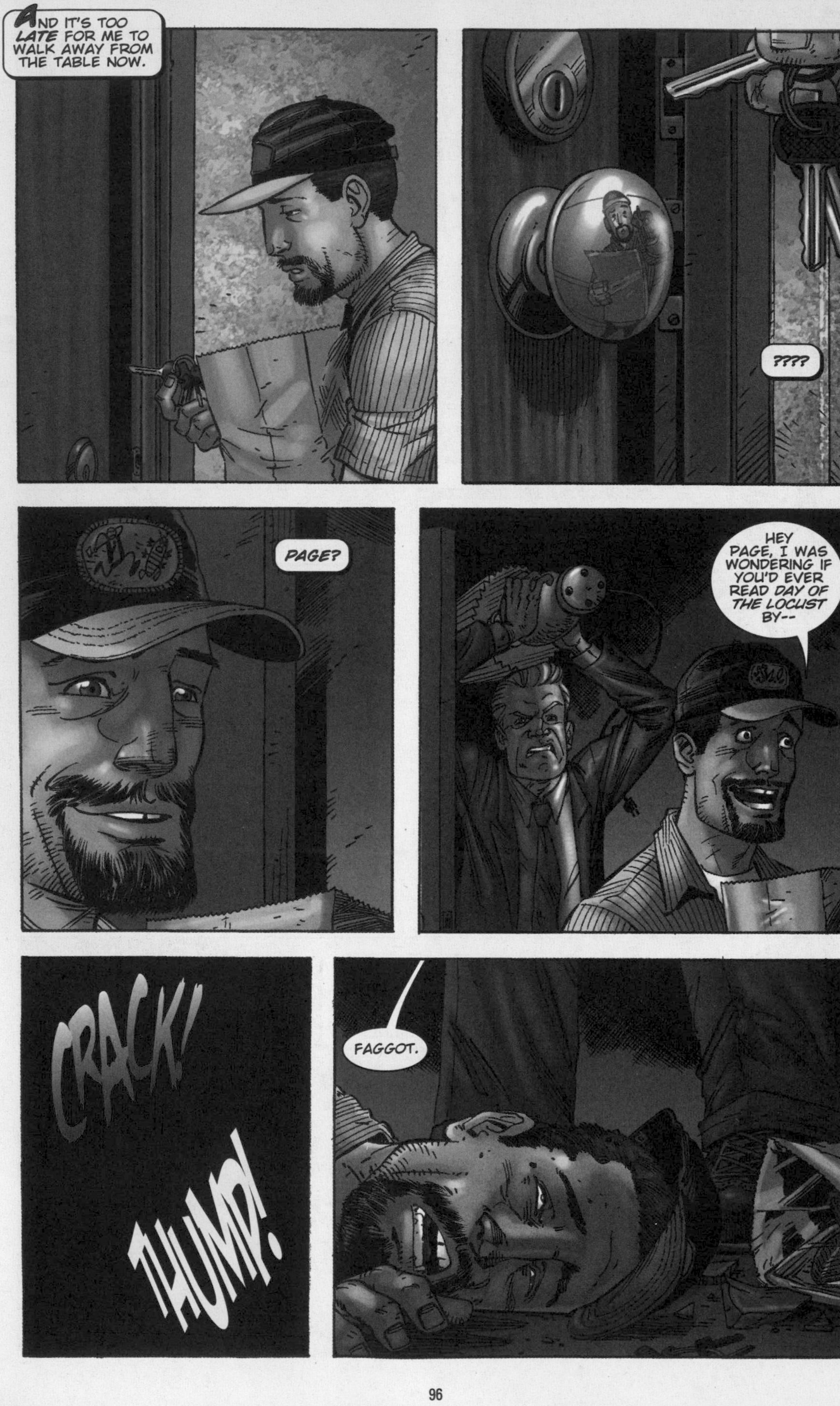
AND IT'S TOO LATE FOR ME TO WALK AWAY FROM THE TABLE NOW.
????
PAGE?
HEY PAGE, I WAS WONDERING IF YOU'D EVER READ DAY OF THE LOCUST BY--
CRACK!
THUMP!
FAGGOT.

COVER ART BY PHILIP BOND
INTERIOR ART BY JOHN LUCAS

CHAPTER FIVE

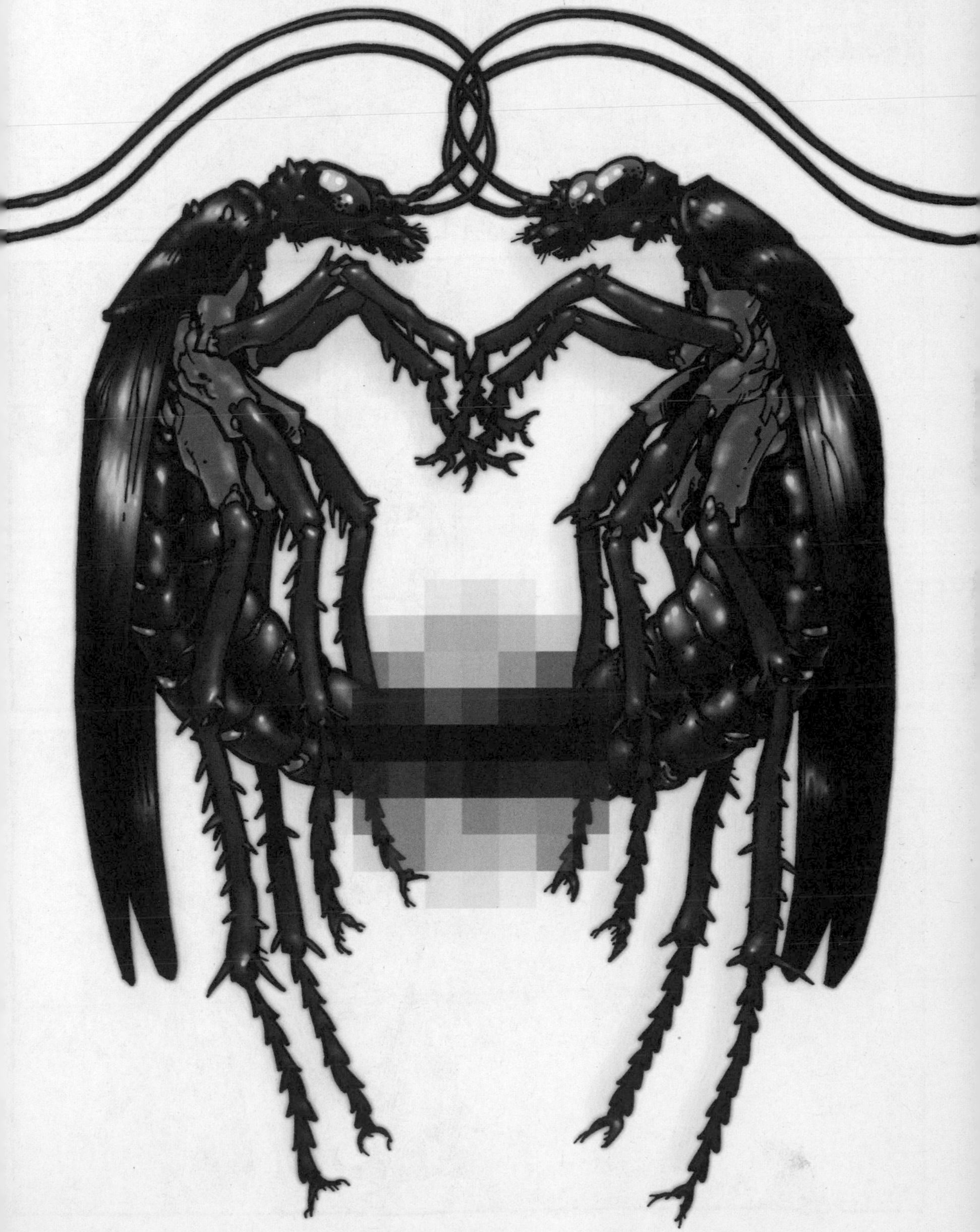

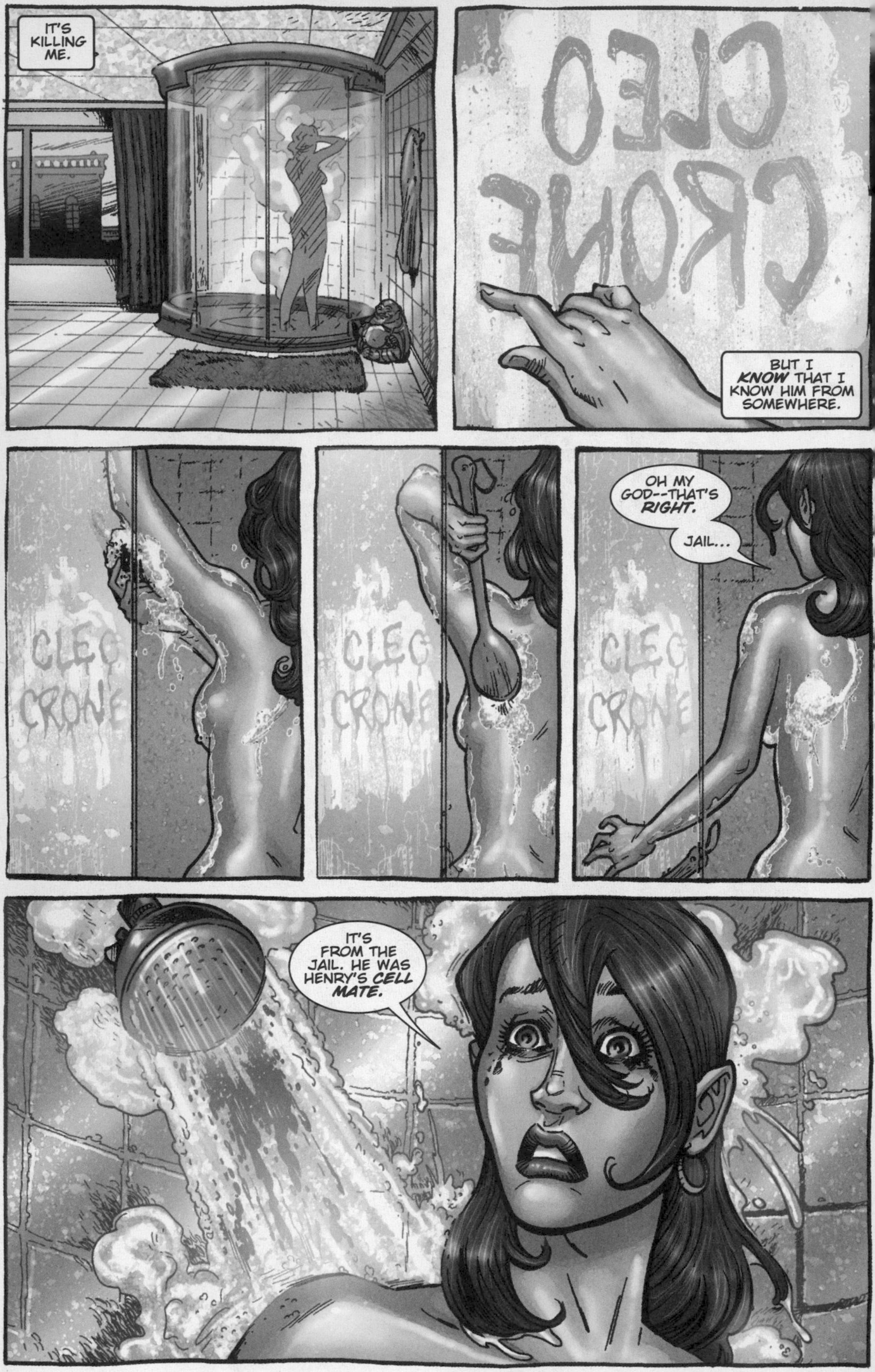
IT'S KILLING ME.
CLEO CRONE
BUT I *KNOW* THAT I KNOW HIM FROM SOMEWHERE.
CLEO CRONE
CLEO CRONE
OH MY GOD--THAT'S *RIGHT.*
JAIL...
CLEO CRONE
IT'S FROM THE JAIL. HE WAS HENRY'S *CELL MATE.*

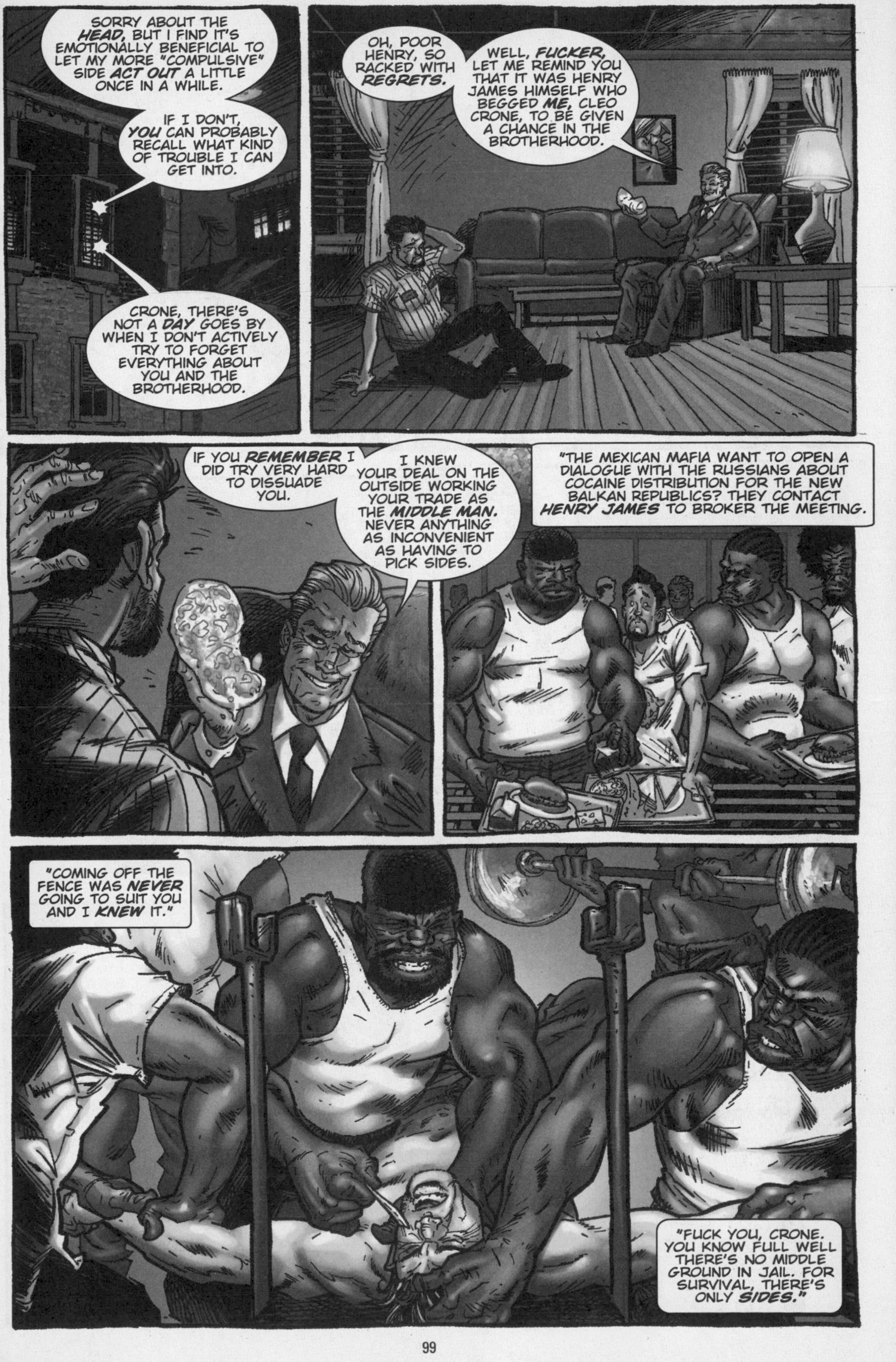
SORRY ABOUT THE HEAD, BUT I FIND IT'S EMOTIONALLY BENEFICIAL TO LET MY MORE "COMPULSIVE" SIDE ACT OUT A LITTLE ONCE IN A WHILE.
IF I DON'T, YOU CAN PROBABLY RECALL WHAT KIND OF TROUBLE I CAN GET INTO.
CRONE, THERE'S NOT A DAY GOES BY WHEN I DON'T ACTIVELY TRY TO FORGET EVERYTHING ABOUT YOU AND THE BROTHERHOOD.
OH, POOR HENRY, SO RACKED WITH REGRETS.
WELL, FUCKER, LET ME REMIND YOU THAT IT WAS HENRY JAMES HIMSELF WHO BEGGED ME, CLEO CRONE, TO BE GIVEN A CHANCE IN THE BROTHERHOOD.
IF YOU REMEMBER I DID TRY VERY HARD TO DISSUADE YOU.
I KNEW YOUR DEAL ON THE OUTSIDE WORKING YOUR TRADE AS THE MIDDLE MAN. NEVER ANYTHING AS INCONVENIENT AS HAVING TO PICK SIDES.
"THE MEXICAN MAFIA WANT TO OPEN A DIALOGUE WITH THE RUSSIANS ABOUT COCAINE DISTRIBUTION FOR THE NEW BALKAN REPUBLICS? THEY CONTACT HENRY JAMES TO BROKER THE MEETING.
"COMING OFF THE FENCE WAS NEVER GOING TO SUIT YOU AND I KNEW IT."
"FUCK YOU, CRONE. YOU KNOW FULL WELL THERE'S NO MIDDLE GROUND IN JAIL. FOR SURVIVAL, THERE'S ONLY SIDES."

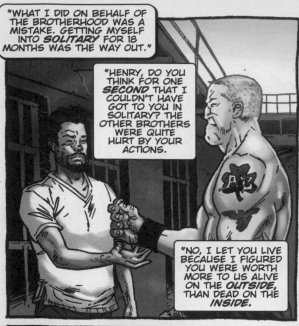

"WHAT I DID ON BEHALF OF THE BROTHERHOOD WAS A MISTAKE. GETTING MYSELF INTO *SOLITARY* FOR 18 MONTHS WAS THE WAY OUT."

"HENRY, DO YOU THINK FOR ONE *SECOND* THAT I COULDN'T HAVE GOT TO YOU IN SOLITARY? THE OTHER BROTHERS WERE QUITE HURT BY YOUR ACTIONS.

"NO, I LET YOU LIVE BECAUSE I FIGURED YOU WERE WORTH MORE TO US ALIVE ON THE *OUTSIDE*, THAN DEAD ON THE *INSIDE*.

AND NOW I'M CASHING IN. YOU SEE, THE BROTHERHOOD'S ABOUT TO START A NEW, MORE *GLORIOUS* CHAPTER--AND *YOU'RE* GOING TO BE HELPING ME.

SINCE OUR INCEPTION WE'VE BEEN ACTING LOCALLY AND, QUITE HONESTLY, HAVING NEXT TO ZERO FUCKING EFFECT GLOBALLY.

WELL THE *GRASS ROOTS* ARE DEAD. YOU WANT POWER, YOU DON'T PUT UP YOUR OWN CANDIDATES TO GET LEFT-WING MEDIA CONSPIRACY ROCKS THROWN AT THEM.

NO, YOU *PURCHASE* AND *SUBVERT* EXISTING POLITICIANS AND YOU DO IT GRADUALLY, SUBLIMINALLY PULLING THE POLITICAL CENTER AROUND TO YOUR WAY OF THINKING.

YOU'RE INSANE.

THAT'S PROBABLY WHAT THEY SAID ABOUT THE RELIGIOUS RIGHT 20 YEARS AGO.

WELL, YOU NEED MONEY. EVEN POLITICIANS WON'T SPEW HATE ON A *BUDGET*.

CORRECT, AND WE'RE GOING TO NEED CONSIDERABLY MORE THAN OUR JACKBOOTED THUGS CAN RAISE GOING DOOR TO DOOR SELLING COOKIES.

THAT'S WHERE *YOU* COME IN.

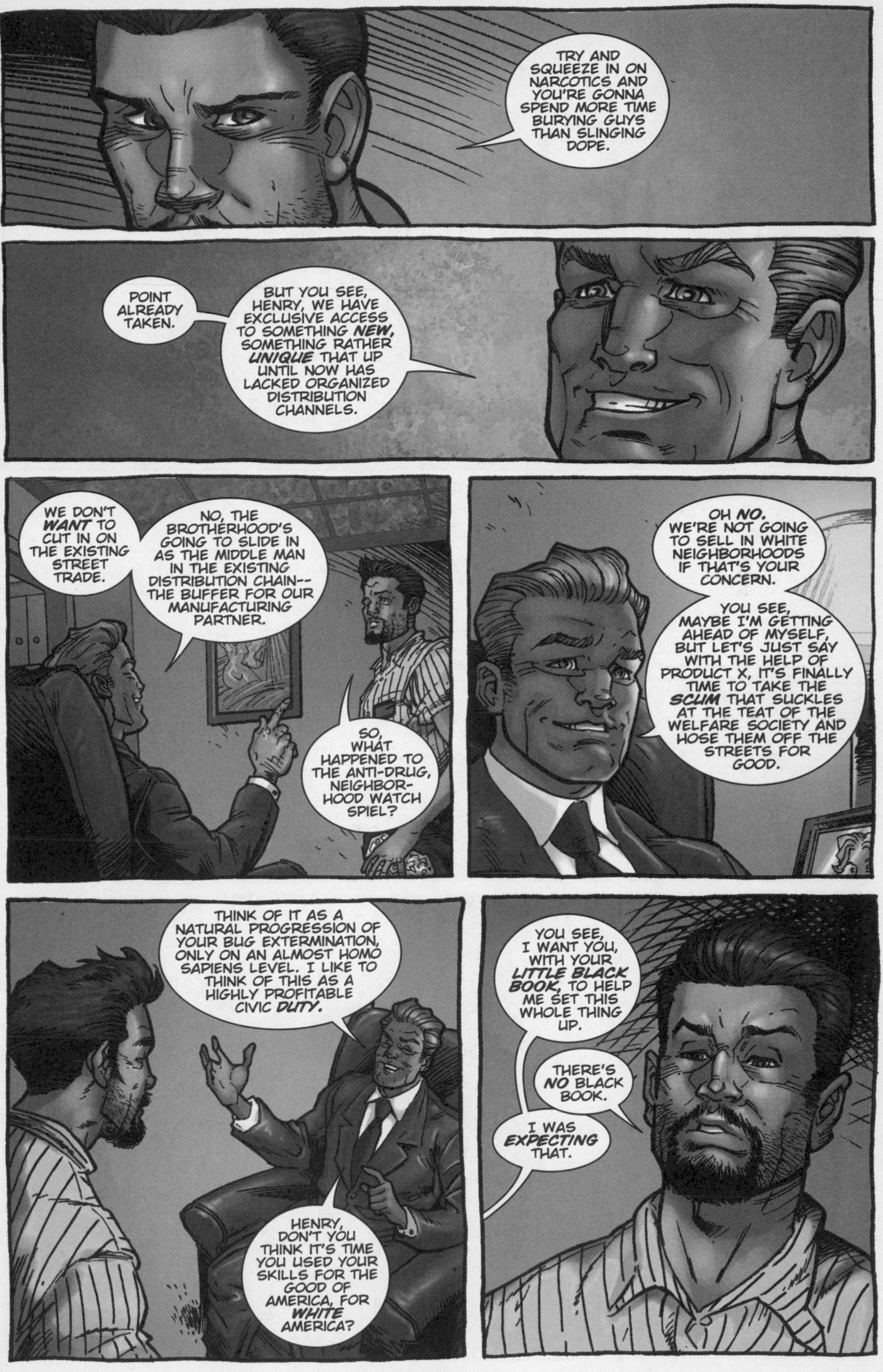
TRY AND SQUEEZE IN ON NARCOTICS AND YOU'RE GONNA SPEND MORE TIME BURYING GUYS THAN SLINGING DOPE.
POINT ALREADY TAKEN.
BUT YOU SEE, HENRY, WE HAVE EXCLUSIVE ACCESS TO SOMETHING NEW, SOMETHING RATHER UNIQUE THAT UP UNTIL NOW HAS LACKED ORGANIZED DISTRIBUTION CHANNELS.
WE DON'T WANT TO CUT IN ON THE EXISTING STREET TRADE.
NO, THE BROTHERHOOD'S GOING TO SLIDE IN AS THE MIDDLE MAN IN THE EXISTING DISTRIBUTION CHAIN-- THE BUFFER FOR OUR MANUFACTURING PARTNER.
SO, WHAT HAPPENED TO THE ANTI-DRUG, NEIGHBOR-HOOD WATCH SPIEL?
OH NO. WE'RE NOT GOING TO SELL IN WHITE NEIGHBORHOODS IF THAT'S YOUR CONCERN.
YOU SEE, MAYBE I'M GETTING AHEAD OF MYSELF, BUT LET'S JUST SAY WITH THE HELP OF PRODUCT X, IT'S FINALLY TIME TO TAKE THE SCUM THAT SUCKLES AT THE TEAT OF THE WELFARE SOCIETY AND HOSE THEM OFF THE STREETS FOR GOOD.
THINK OF IT AS A NATURAL PROGRESSION OF YOUR BUG EXTERMINATION, ONLY ON AN ALMOST HOMO SAPIENS LEVEL. I LIKE TO THINK OF THIS AS A HIGHLY PROFITABLE CIVIC DUTY.
HENRY, DON'T YOU THINK IT'S TIME YOU USED YOUR SKILLS FOR THE GOOD OF AMERICA, FOR WHITE AMERICA?
YOU SEE, I WANT YOU, WITH YOUR LITTLE BLACK BOOK, TO HELP ME SET THIS WHOLE THING UP.
THERE'S NO BLACK BOOK.
I WAS EXPECTING THAT.

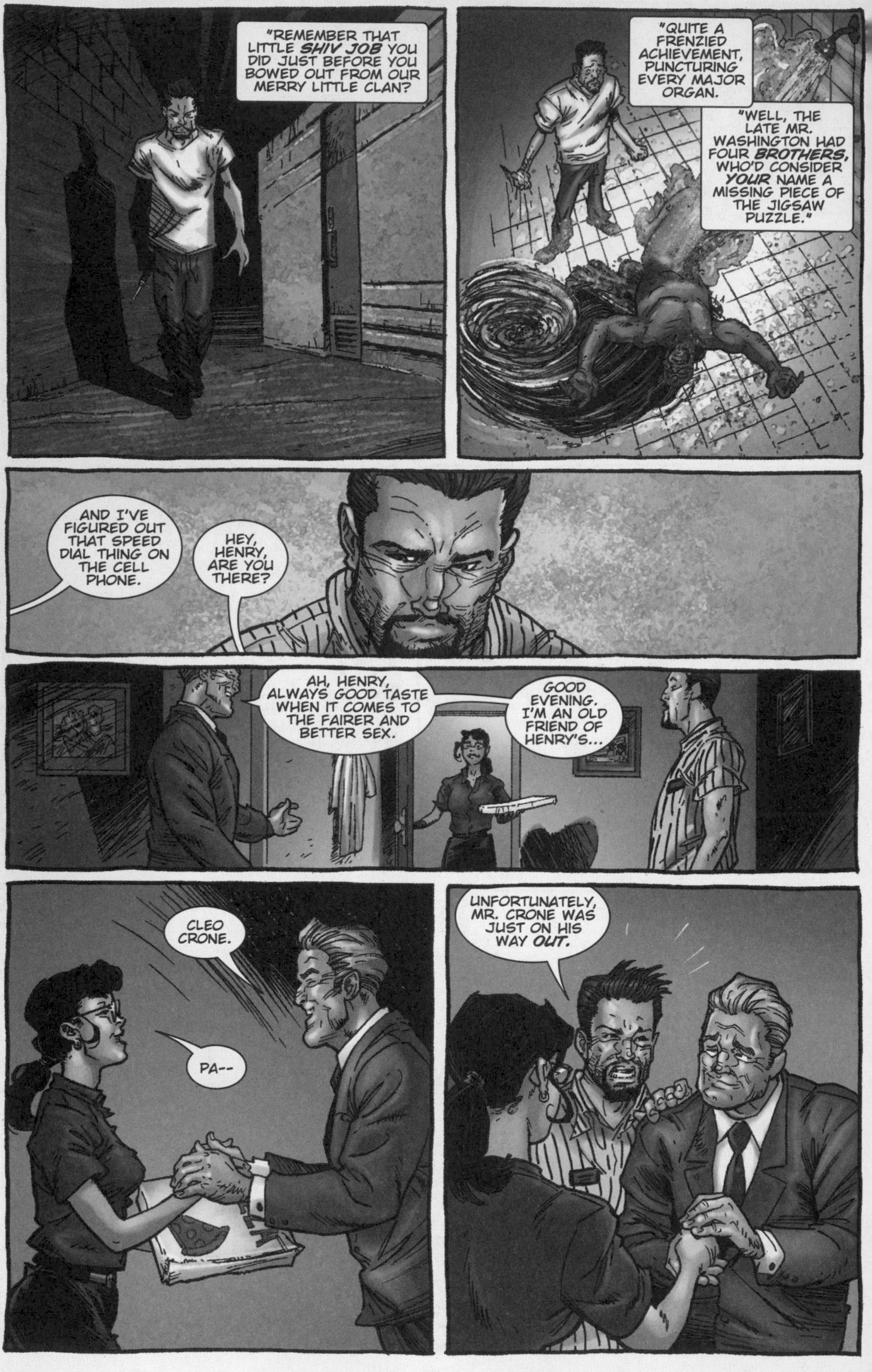
"REMEMBER THAT LITTLE SHIV JOB YOU DID JUST BEFORE YOU BOWED OUT FROM OUR MERRY LITTLE CLAN?
"QUITE A FRENZIED ACHIEVEMENT, PUNCTURING EVERY MAJOR ORGAN.
"WELL, THE LATE MR. WASHINGTON HAD FOUR BROTHERS, WHO'D CONSIDER YOUR NAME A MISSING PIECE OF THE JIGSAW PUZZLE."
AND I'VE FIGURED OUT THAT SPEED DIAL THING ON THE CELL PHONE.
HEY, HENRY, ARE YOU THERE?
AH, HENRY, ALWAYS GOOD TASTE WHEN IT COMES TO THE FAIRER AND BETTER SEX.
GOOD EVENING. I'M AN OLD FRIEND OF HENRY'S...
CLEO CRONE.
PA--
UNFORTUNATELY, MR. CRONE WAS JUST ON HIS WAY OUT.

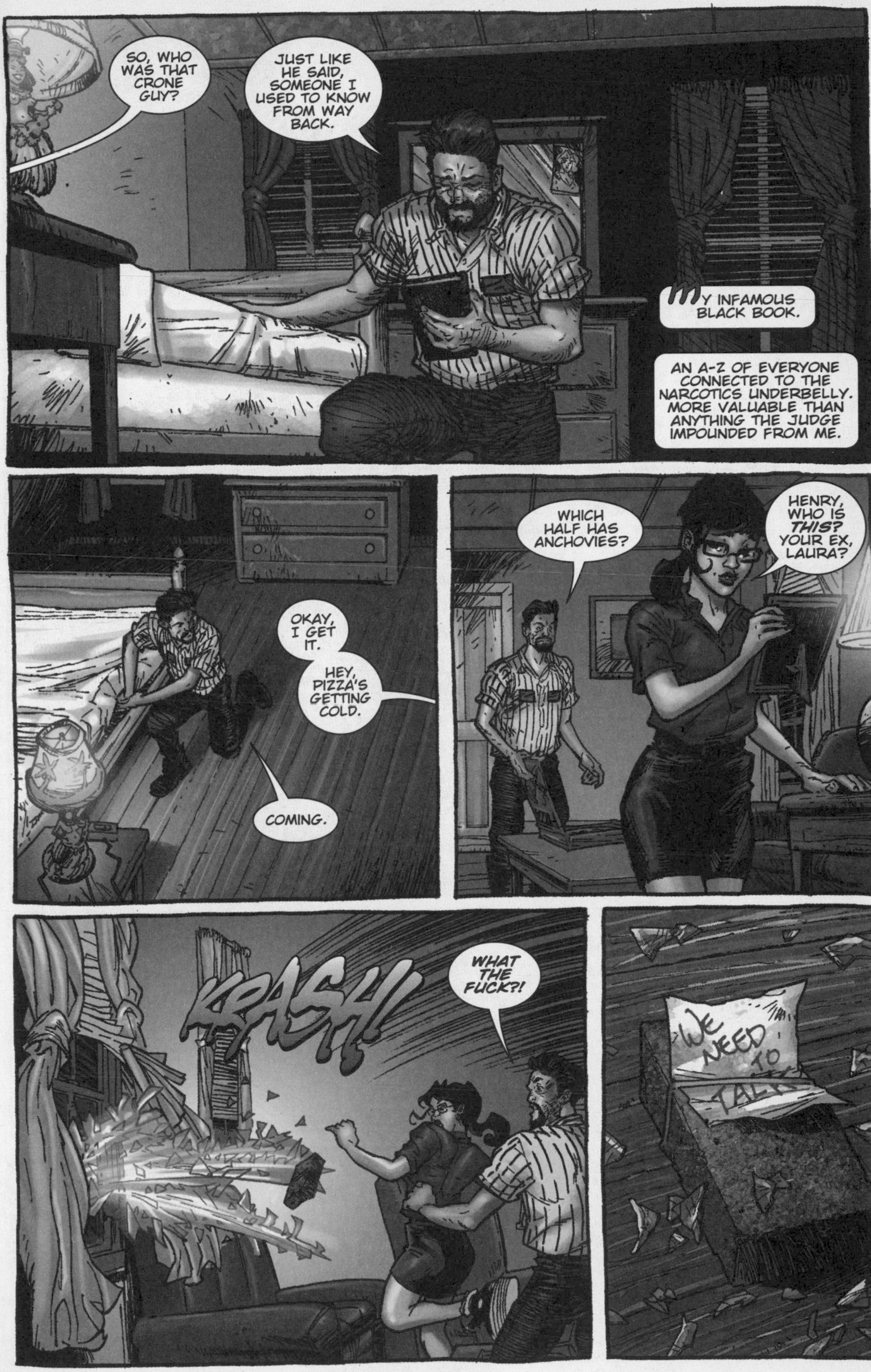
SO, WHO WAS THAT CRONE GUY?
JUST LIKE HE SAID, SOMEONE I USED TO KNOW FROM WAY BACK.
MY INFAMOUS BLACK BOOK.
AN A-Z OF EVERYONE CONNECTED TO THE NARCOTICS UNDERBELLY. MORE VALUABLE THAN ANYTHING THE JUDGE IMPOUNDED FROM ME.
OKAY, I GET IT.
HEY, PIZZA'S GETTING COLD.
COMING.
WHICH HALF HAS ANCHOVIES?
HENRY, WHO IS *THIS?* YOUR EX, LAURA?
KRASH!
WHAT THE FUCK?!
WE NEED TO TALK

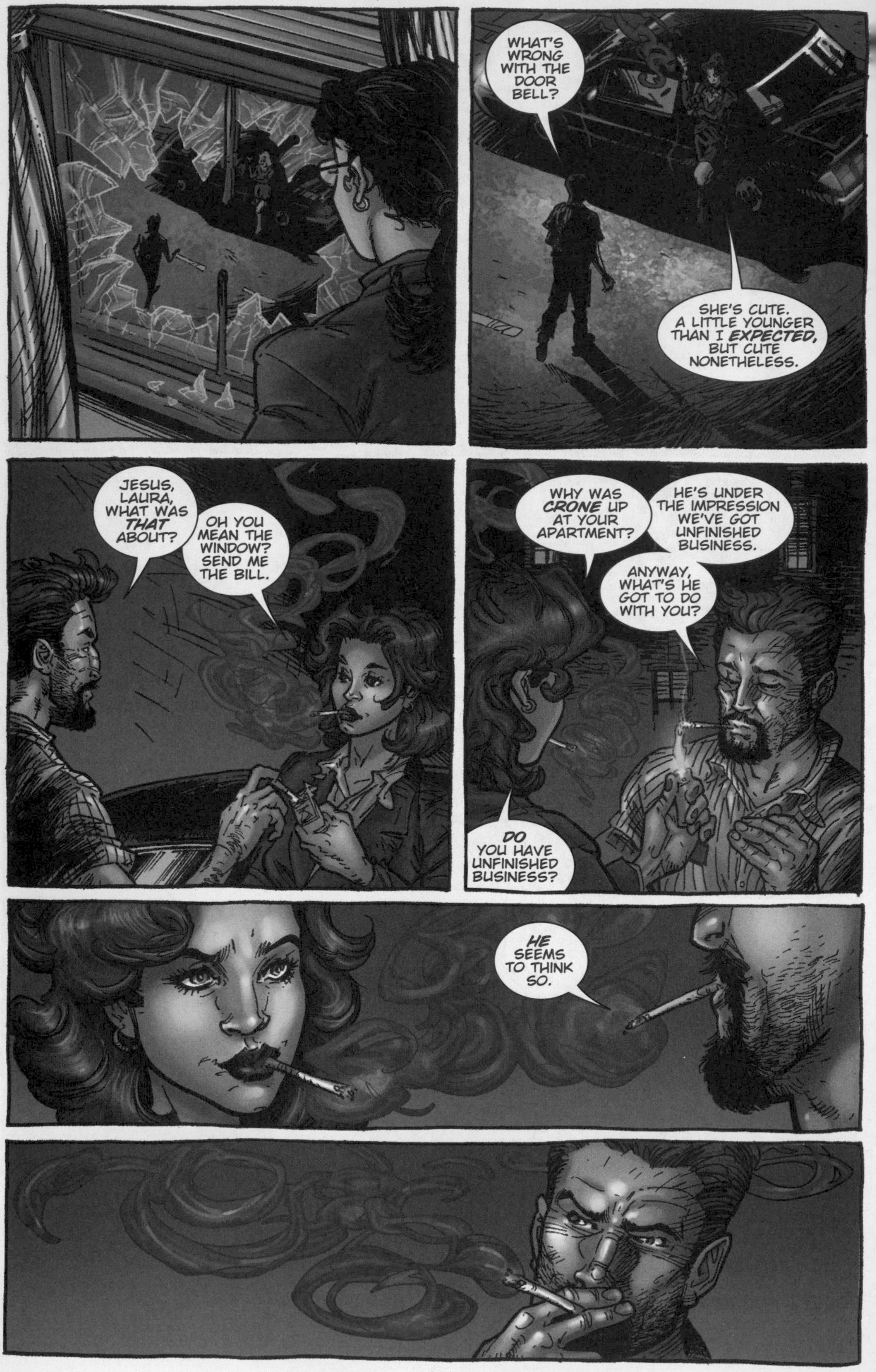
WHAT'S WRONG WITH THE DOOR BELL?
SHE'S CUTE. A LITTLE YOUNGER THAN I EXPECTED, BUT CUTE NONETHELESS.
JESUS, LAURA, WHAT WAS THAT ABOUT?
OH YOU MEAN THE WINDOW? SEND ME THE BILL.
WHY WAS CRONE UP AT YOUR APARTMENT?
HE'S UNDER THE IMPRESSION WE'VE GOT UNFINISHED BUSINESS.
ANYWAY, WHAT'S HE GOT TO DO WITH YOU?
DO YOU HAVE UNFINISHED BUSINESS?
HE SEEMS TO THINK SO.

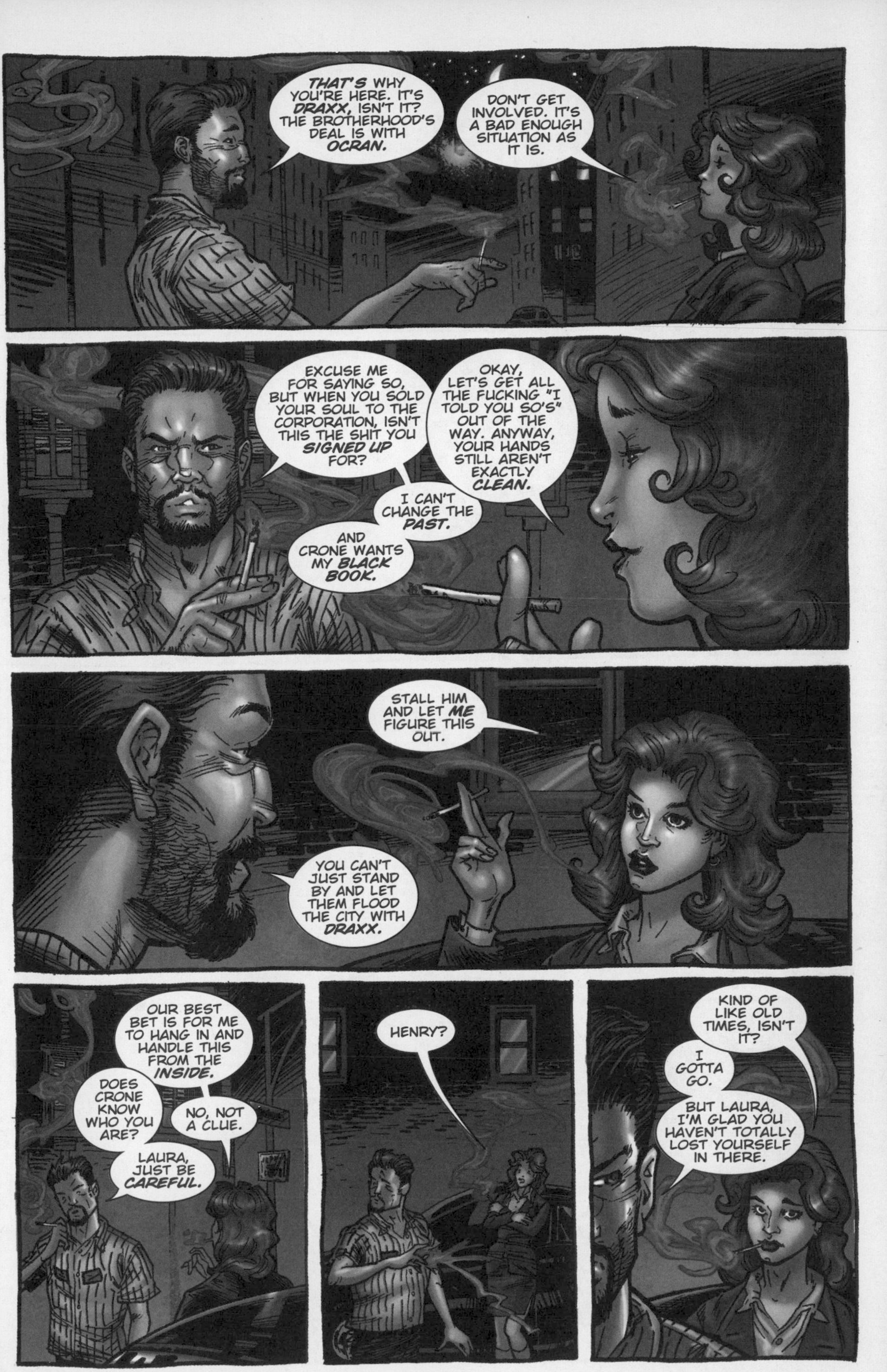
THAT'S WHY YOU'RE HERE. IT'S DRAXX, ISN'T IT? THE BROTHERHOOD'S DEAL IS WITH OCRAN.
DON'T GET INVOLVED. IT'S A BAD ENOUGH SITUATION AS IT IS.
EXCUSE ME FOR SAYING SO, BUT WHEN YOU SOLD YOUR SOUL TO THE CORPORATION, ISN'T THIS THE SHIT YOU SIGNED UP FOR?
OKAY, LET'S GET ALL THE FUCKING "I TOLD YOU SO'S" OUT OF THE WAY. ANYWAY, YOUR HANDS STILL AREN'T EXACTLY CLEAN.
I CAN'T CHANGE THE PAST.
AND CRONE WANTS MY BLACK BOOK.
STALL HIM AND LET ME FIGURE THIS OUT.
YOU CAN'T JUST STAND BY AND LET THEM FLOOD THE CITY WITH DRAXX.
OUR BEST BET IS FOR ME TO HANG IN AND HANDLE THIS FROM THE INSIDE.
DOES CRONE KNOW WHO YOU ARE?
NO, NOT A CLUE.
LAURA, JUST BE CAREFUL.
HENRY?
KIND OF LIKE OLD TIMES, ISN'T IT?
I GOTTA GO.
BUT LAURA, I'M GLAD YOU HAVEN'T TOTALLY LOST YOURSELF IN THERE.

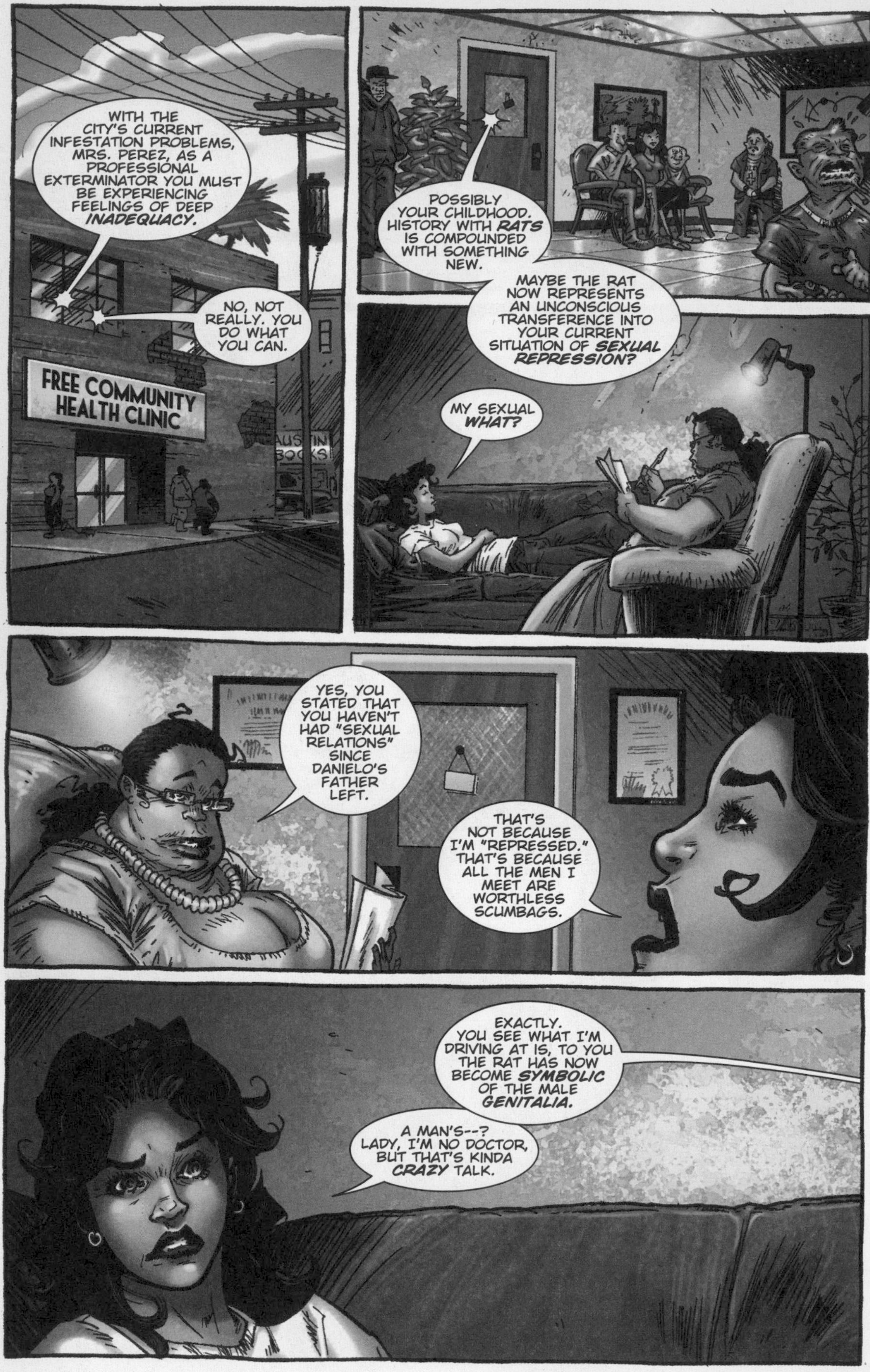
WITH THE CITY'S CURRENT INFESTATION PROBLEMS, MRS. PEREZ, AS A PROFESSIONAL EXTERMINATOR YOU MUST BE EXPERIENCING FEELINGS OF DEEP INADEQUACY.
NO, NOT REALLY. YOU DO WHAT YOU CAN.
FREE COMMUNITY HEALTH CLINIC
POSSIBLY YOUR CHILDHOOD. HISTORY WITH RATS IS COMPOUNDED WITH SOMETHING NEW.
MAYBE THE RAT NOW REPRESENTS AN UNCONSCIOUS TRANSFERENCE INTO YOUR CURRENT SITUATION OF SEXUAL REPRESSION?
MY SEXUAL WHAT?
YES, YOU STATED THAT YOU HAVEN'T HAD "SEXUAL RELATIONS" SINCE DANIELO'S FATHER LEFT.
THAT'S NOT BECAUSE I'M "REPRESSED." THAT'S BECAUSE ALL THE MEN I MEET ARE WORTHLESS SCUMBAGS.
EXACTLY. YOU SEE WHAT I'M DRIVING AT IS, TO YOU THE RAT HAS NOW BECOME SYMBOLIC OF THE MALE GENITALIA.
A MAN'S--? LADY, I'M NO DOCTOR, BUT THAT'S KINDA CRAZY TALK.

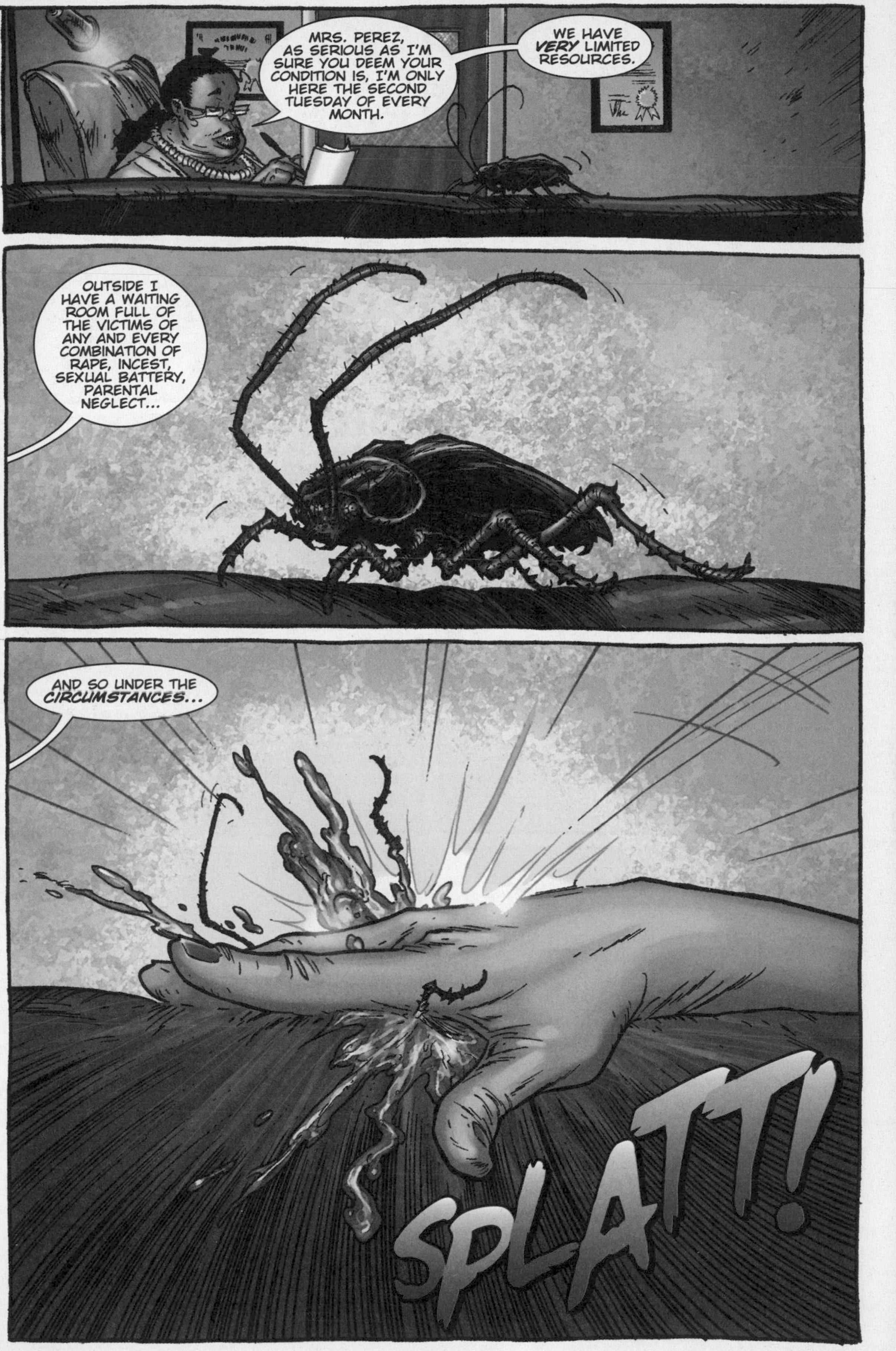
MRS. PEREZ, AS SERIOUS AS I'M SURE YOU DEEM YOUR CONDITION IS, I'M ONLY HERE THE SECOND TUESDAY OF EVERY MONTH.
WE HAVE VERY LIMITED RESOURCES.
OUTSIDE I HAVE A WAITING ROOM FULL OF THE VICTIMS OF ANY AND EVERY COMBINATION OF RAPE, INCEST, SEXUAL BATTERY, PARENTAL NEGLECT...
AND SO UNDER THE CIRCUMSTANCES...
SPLATT!

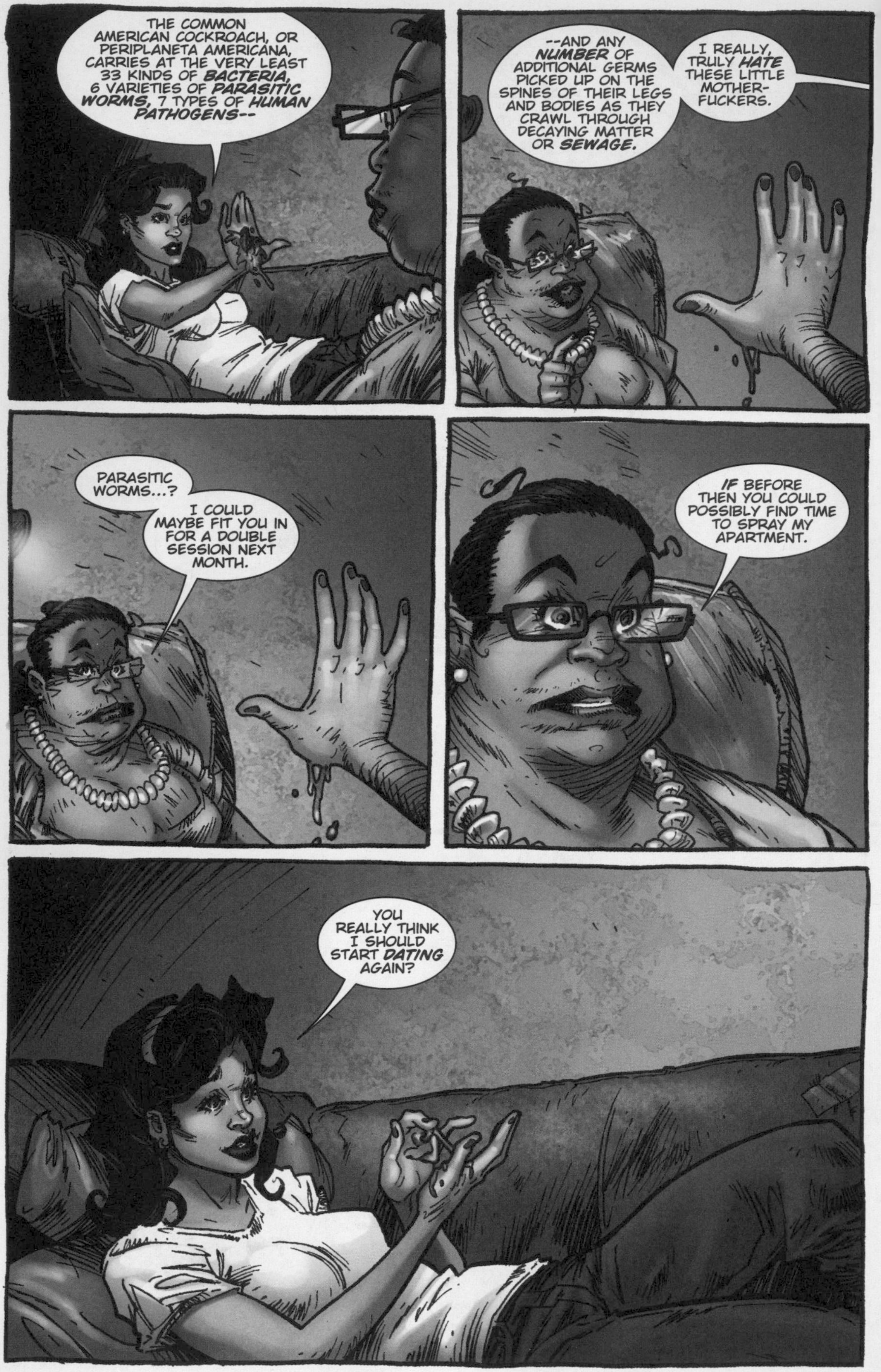
THE COMMON AMERICAN COCKROACH, OR PERIPLANETA AMERICANA, CARRIES AT THE VERY LEAST 33 KINDS OF BACTERIA, 6 VARIETIES OF PARASITIC WORMS, 7 TYPES OF HUMAN PATHOGENS--
--AND ANY NUMBER OF ADDITIONAL GERMS PICKED UP ON THE SPINES OF THEIR LEGS AND BODIES AS THEY CRAWL THROUGH DECAYING MATTER OR SEWAGE.
I REALLY, TRULY HATE THESE LITTLE MOTHER-FUCKERS.
PARASITIC WORMS...?
I COULD MAYBE FIT YOU IN FOR A DOUBLE SESSION NEXT MONTH.
IF BEFORE THEN YOU COULD POSSIBLY FIND TIME TO SPRAY MY APARTMENT.
YOU REALLY THINK I SHOULD START DATING AGAIN?

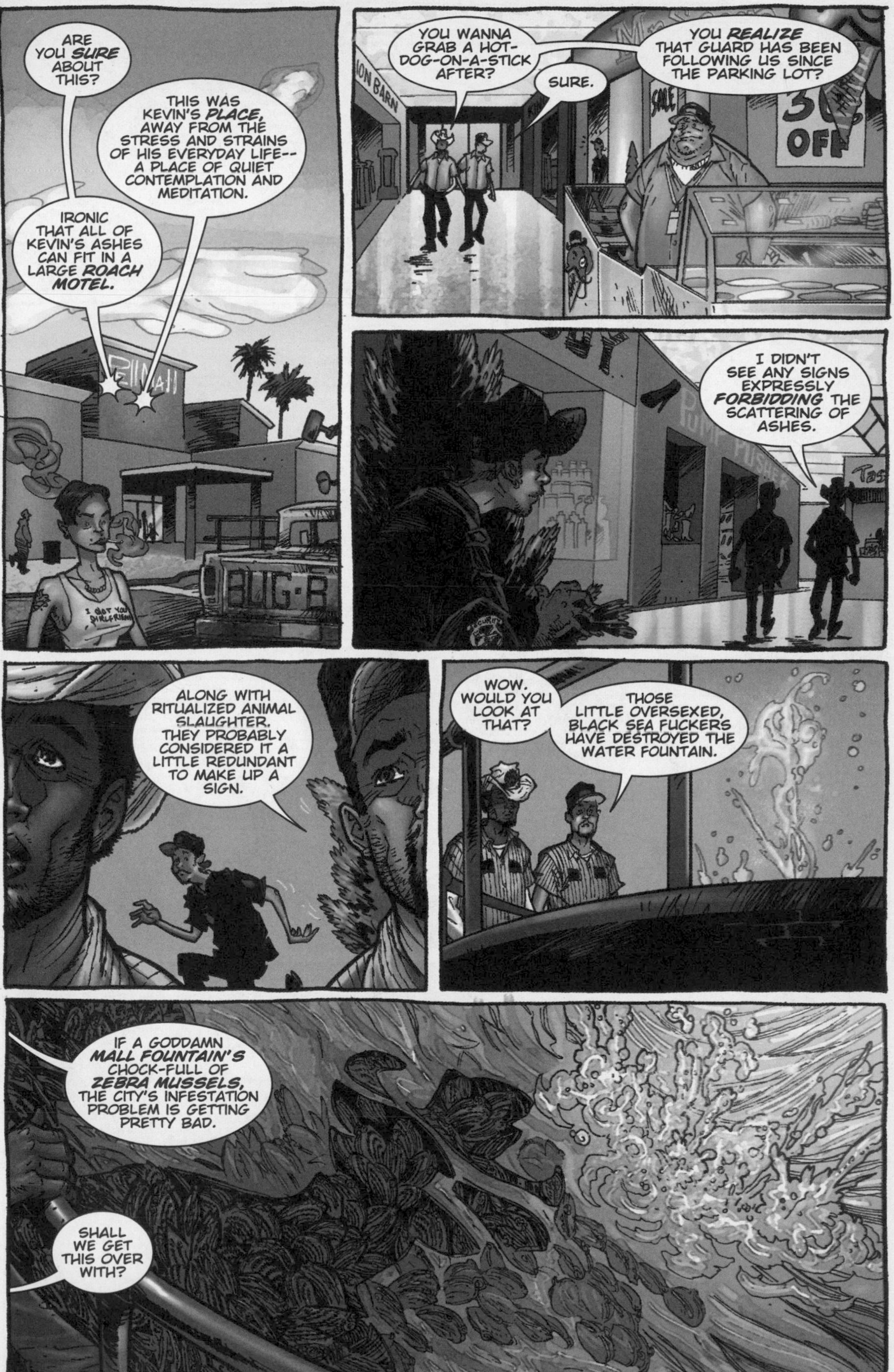
ARE YOU SURE ABOUT THIS?
THIS WAS KEVIN'S PLACE, AWAY FROM THE STRESS AND STRAINS OF HIS EVERYDAY LIFE-- A PLACE OF QUIET CONTEMPLATION AND MEDITATION.
IRONIC THAT ALL OF KEVIN'S ASHES CAN FIT IN A LARGE ROACH MOTEL.
BUG-B
YOU WANNA GRAB A HOT-DOG-ON-A-STICK AFTER?
SURE.
YOU REALIZE THAT GUARD HAS BEEN FOLLOWING US SINCE THE PARKING LOT?
30 OFF
I DIDN'T SEE ANY SIGNS EXPRESSLY FORBIDDING THE SCATTERING OF ASHES.
ALONG WITH RITUALIZED ANIMAL SLAUGHTER. THEY PROBABLY CONSIDERED IT A LITTLE REDUNDANT TO MAKE UP A SIGN.
WOW. WOULD YOU LOOK AT THAT?
THOSE LITTLE OVERSEXED, BLACK SEA FUCKERS HAVE DESTROYED THE WATER FOUNTAIN.
IF A GODDAMN MALL FOUNTAIN'S CHOCK-FULL OF ZEBRA MUSSELS, THE CITY'S INFESTATION PROBLEM IS GETTING PRETTY BAD.
SHALL WE GET THIS OVER WITH?

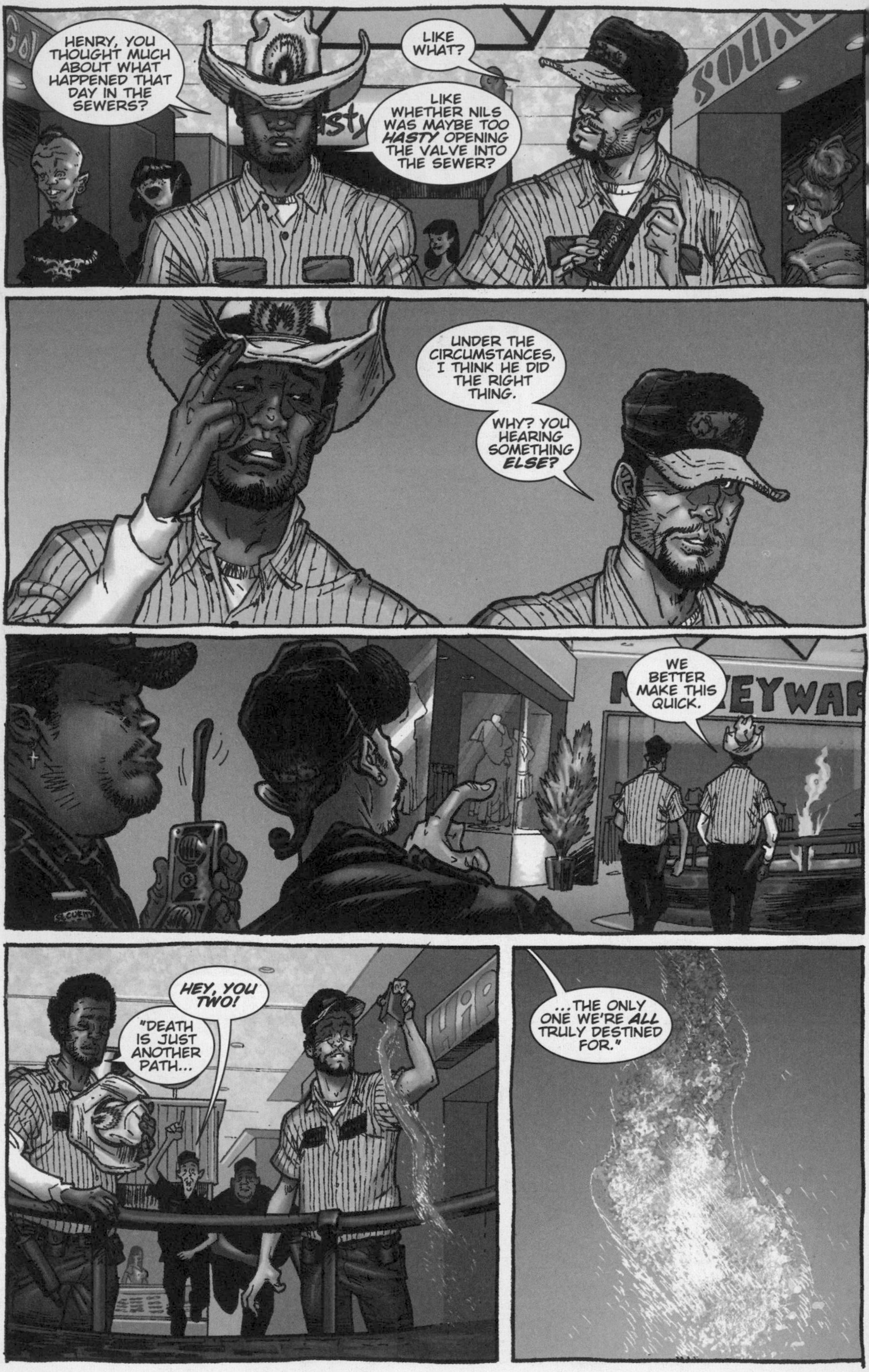
HENRY, YOU THOUGHT MUCH ABOUT WHAT HAPPENED THAT DAY IN THE SEWERS?
LIKE WHAT?
LIKE WHETHER NILS WAS MAYBE TOO *HASTY* OPENING THE VALVE INTO THE SEWER?
UNDER THE CIRCUMSTANCES, I THINK HE DID THE RIGHT THING.
WHY? YOU HEARING SOMETHING *ELSE?*
WE BETTER MAKE THIS QUICK.
HEY, YOU TWO!
"DEATH IS JUST ANOTHER PATH...
...THE ONLY ONE WE'RE *ALL* TRULY DESTINED FOR."

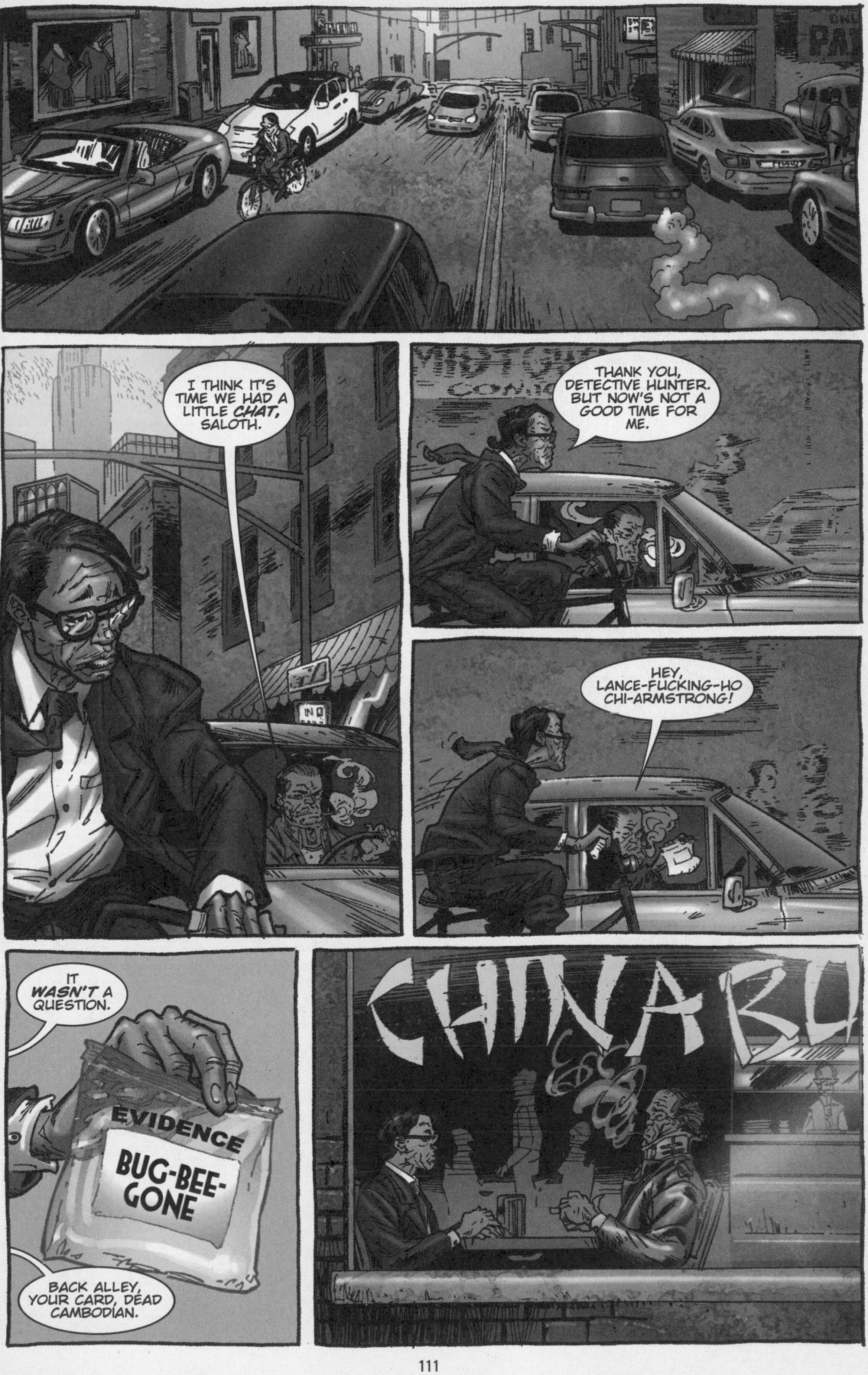
I THINK IT'S TIME WE HAD A LITTLE *CHAT,* SALOTH.
THANK YOU, DETECTIVE HUNTER. BUT NOW'S NOT A GOOD TIME FOR ME.
HEY, LANCE-FUCKING-HO CHI-ARMSTRONG!
IT *WASN'T* A QUESTION.
EVIDENCE
BUG-BEE-GONE
BACK ALLEY, YOUR CARD, DEAD CAMBODIAN.

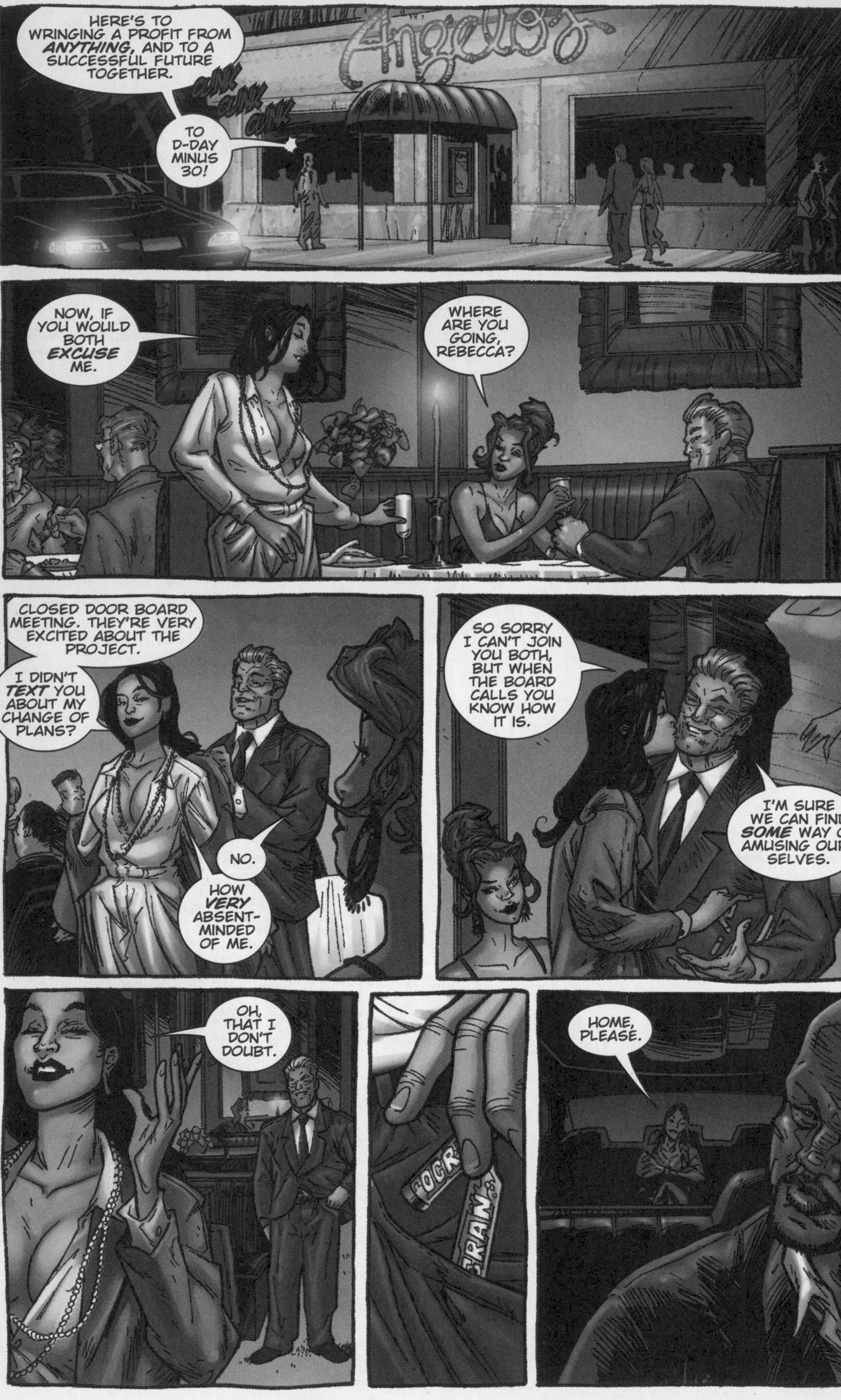
HERE'S TO WRINGING A PROFIT FROM ANYTHING, AND TO A SUCCESSFUL FUTURE TOGETHER.
Angelo's
CLINK CLINK CLINK
TO D-DAY MINUS 30!
NOW, IF YOU WOULD BOTH EXCUSE ME.
WHERE ARE YOU GOING, REBECCA?
CLOSED DOOR BOARD MEETING. THEY'RE VERY EXCITED ABOUT THE PROJECT.
I DIDN'T TEXT YOU ABOUT MY CHANGE OF PLANS?
NO.
HOW VERY ABSENT-MINDED OF ME.
SO SORRY I CAN'T JOIN YOU BOTH, BUT WHEN THE BOARD CALLS YOU KNOW HOW IT IS.
I'M SURE WE CAN FIND SOME WAY OF AMUSING OUR-SELVES.
OH, THAT I DON'T DOUBT.
HOME, PLEASE.

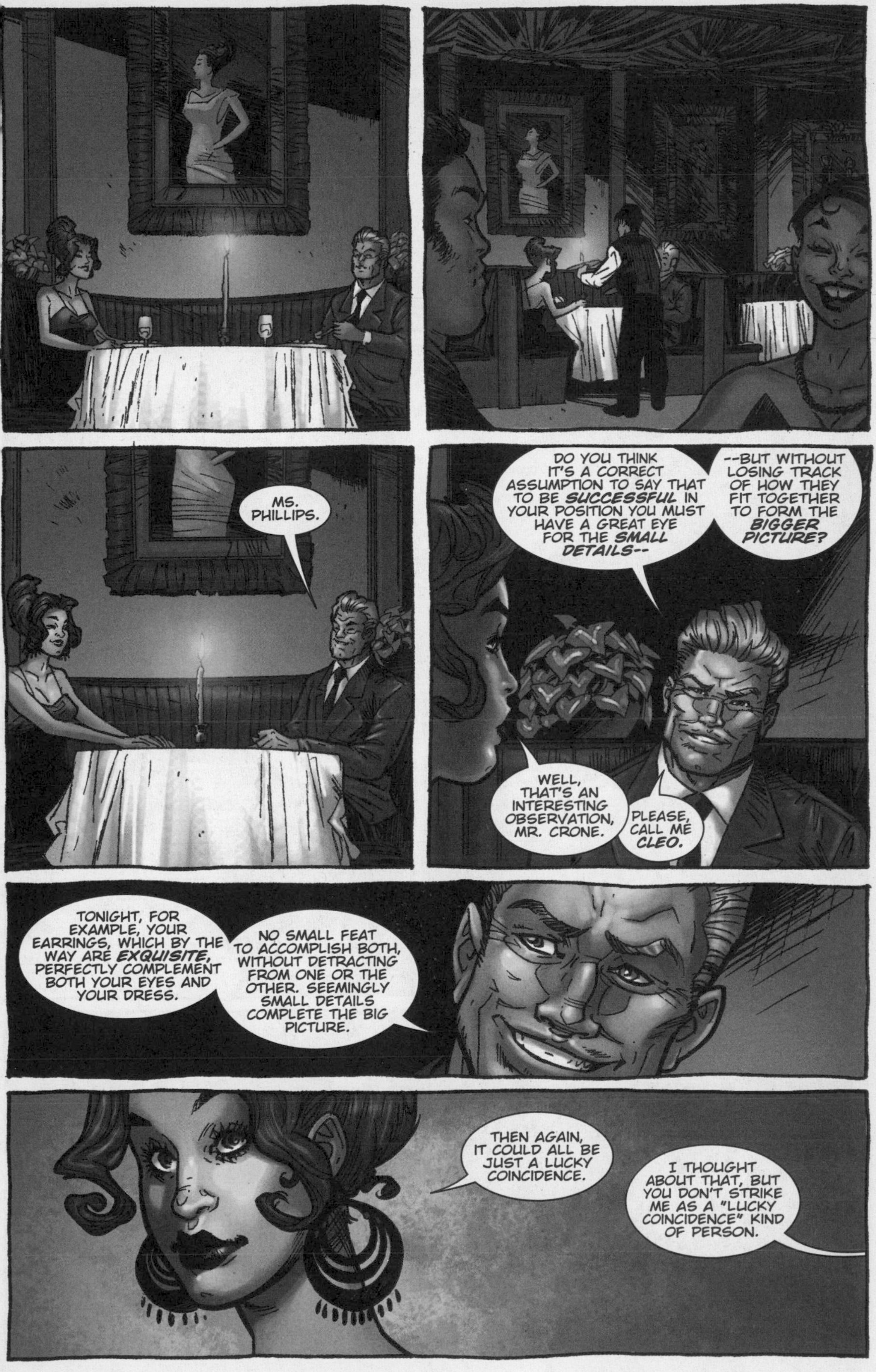
MS. PHILLIPS.
DO YOU THINK IT'S A CORRECT ASSUMPTION TO SAY THAT TO BE SUCCESSFUL IN YOUR POSITION YOU MUST HAVE A GREAT EYE FOR THE SMALL DETAILS--
--BUT WITHOUT LOSING TRACK OF HOW THEY FIT TOGETHER TO FORM THE BIGGER PICTURE?
WELL, THAT'S AN INTERESTING OBSERVATION, MR. CRONE.
PLEASE, CALL ME CLEO.
TONIGHT, FOR EXAMPLE, YOUR EARRINGS, WHICH BY THE WAY ARE EXQUISITE, PERFECTLY COMPLEMENT BOTH YOUR EYES AND YOUR DRESS.
NO SMALL FEAT TO ACCOMPLISH BOTH, WITHOUT DETRACTING FROM ONE OR THE OTHER. SEEMINGLY SMALL DETAILS COMPLETE THE BIG PICTURE.
THEN AGAIN, IT COULD ALL BE JUST A LUCKY COINCIDENCE.
I THOUGHT ABOUT THAT, BUT YOU DON'T STRIKE ME AS A "LUCKY COINCIDENCE" KIND OF PERSON.

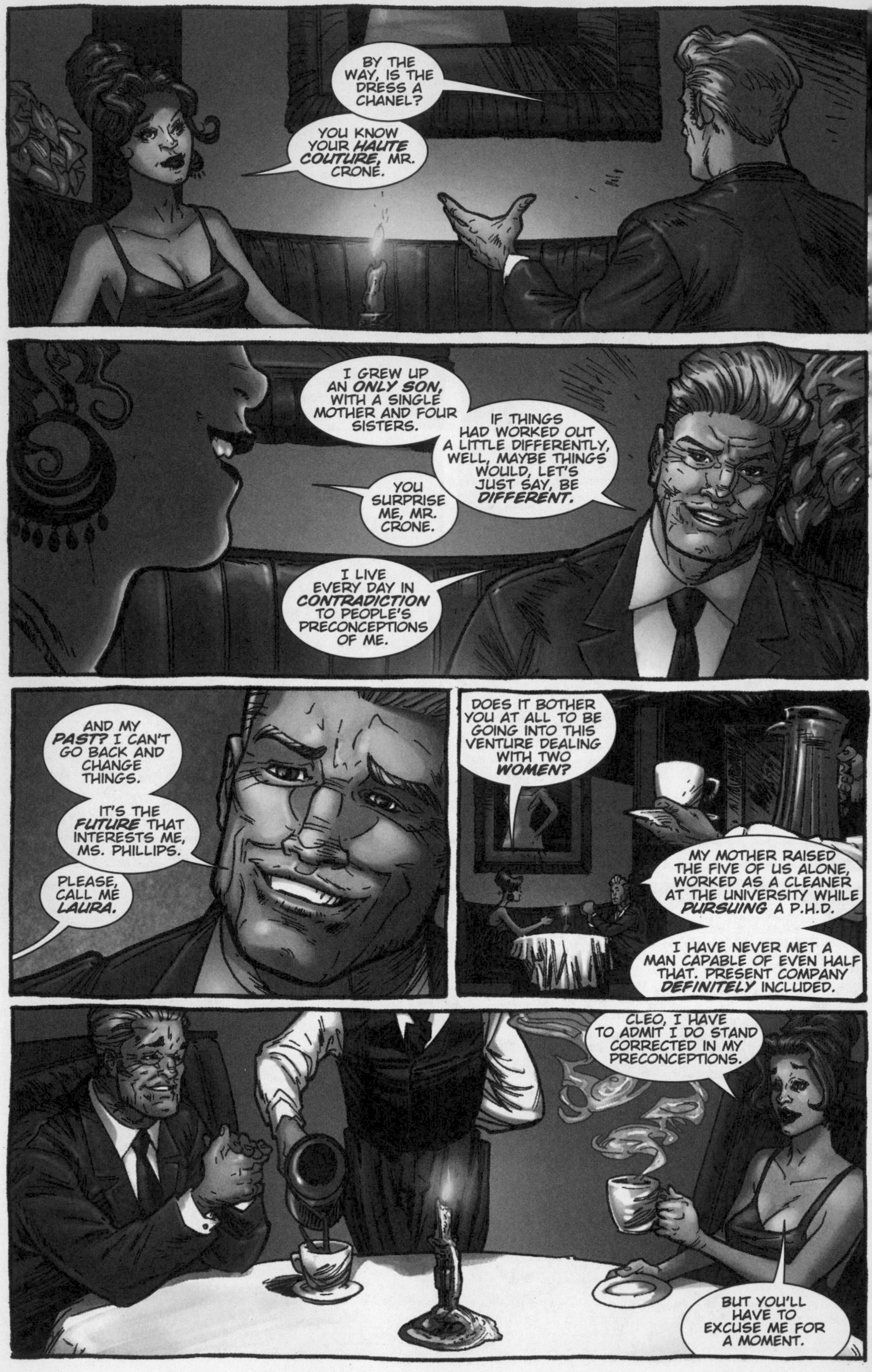

BY THE WAY, IS THE DRESS A CHANEL?
YOU KNOW YOUR HAUTE COUTURE, MR. CRONE.
I GREW UP AN ONLY SON, WITH A SINGLE MOTHER AND FOUR SISTERS.
IF THINGS HAD WORKED OUT A LITTLE DIFFERENTLY, WELL, MAYBE THINGS WOULD, LET'S JUST SAY, BE DIFFERENT.
YOU SURPRISE ME, MR. CRONE.
I LIVE EVERY DAY IN CONTRADICTION TO PEOPLE'S PRECONCEPTIONS OF ME.
AND MY PAST? I CAN'T GO BACK AND CHANGE THINGS.
IT'S THE FUTURE THAT INTERESTS ME, MS. PHILLIPS.
PLEASE, CALL ME LAURA.
DOES IT BOTHER YOU AT ALL TO BE GOING INTO THIS VENTURE DEALING WITH TWO WOMEN?
MY MOTHER RAISED THE FIVE OF US ALONE, WORKED AS A CLEANER AT THE UNIVERSITY WHILE PURSUING A P.H.D.
I HAVE NEVER MET A MAN CAPABLE OF EVEN HALF THAT. PRESENT COMPANY DEFINITELY INCLUDED.
CLEO, I HAVE TO ADMIT I DO STAND CORRECTED IN MY PRECONCEPTIONS.
BUT YOU'LL HAVE TO EXCUSE ME FOR A MOMENT.

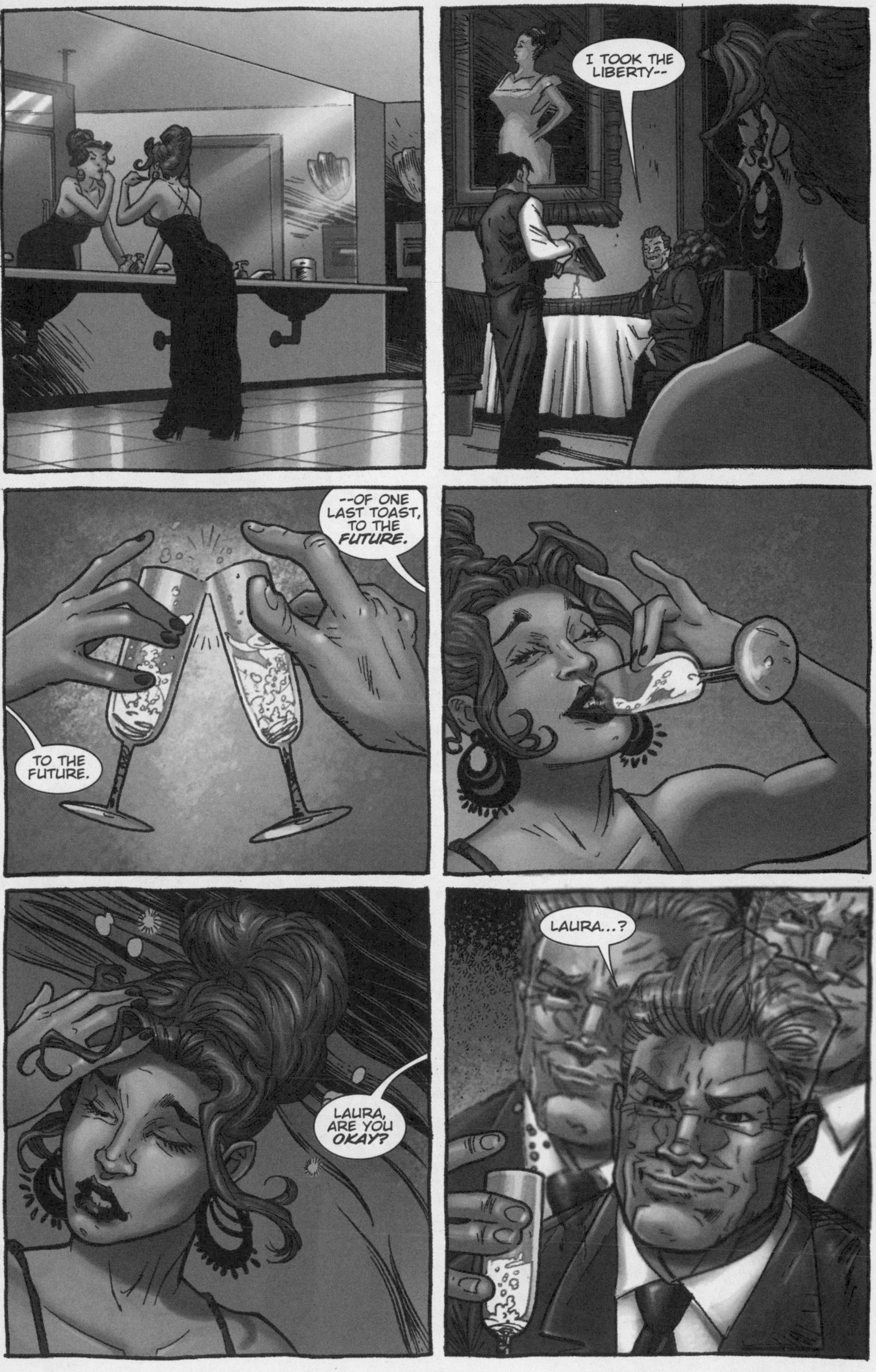
I TOOK THE LIBERTY--
--OF ONE LAST TOAST, TO THE FUTURE.
TO THE FUTURE.
LAURA, ARE YOU OKAY?
LAURA...?

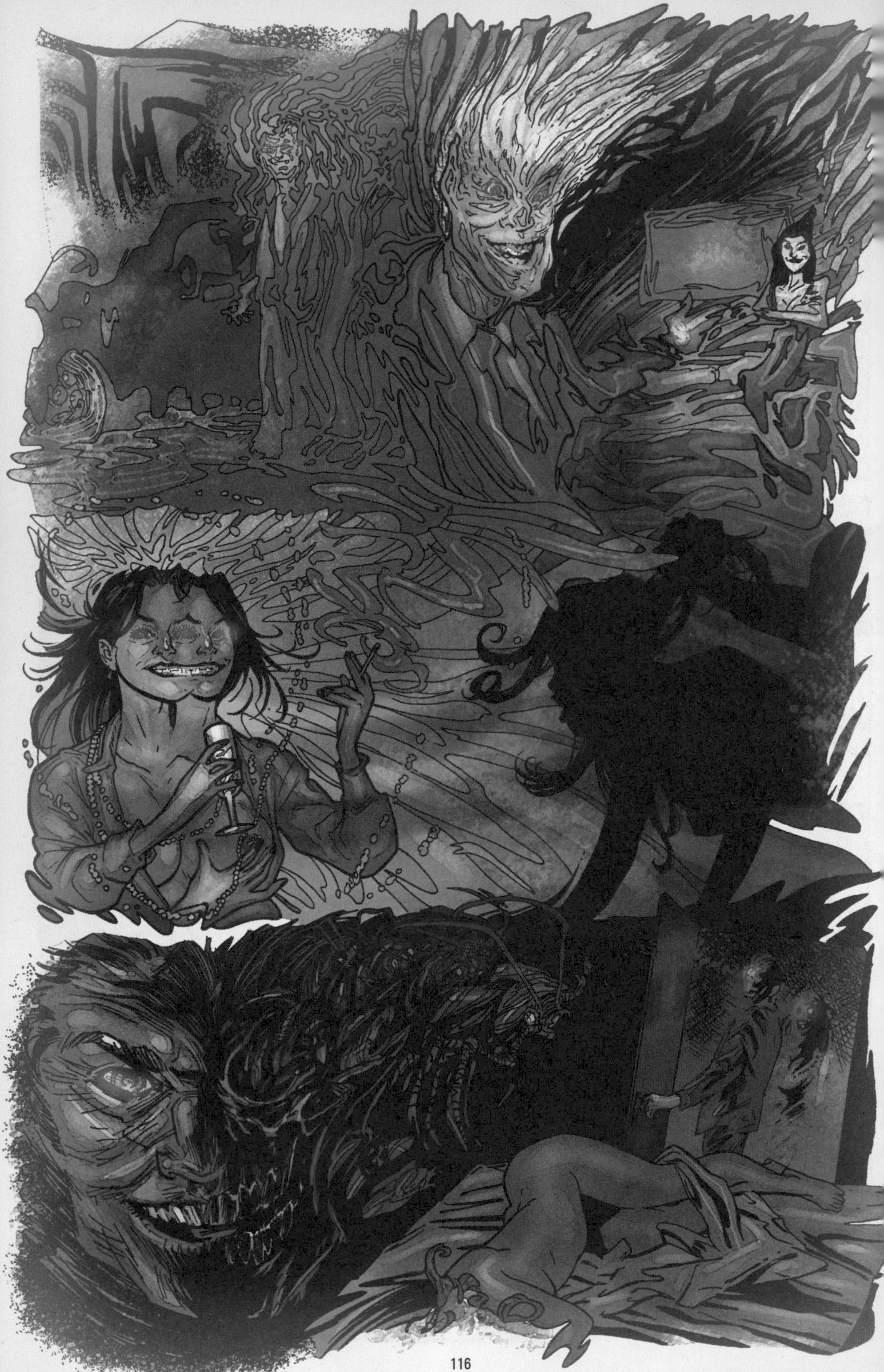

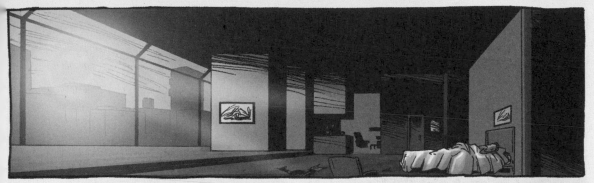

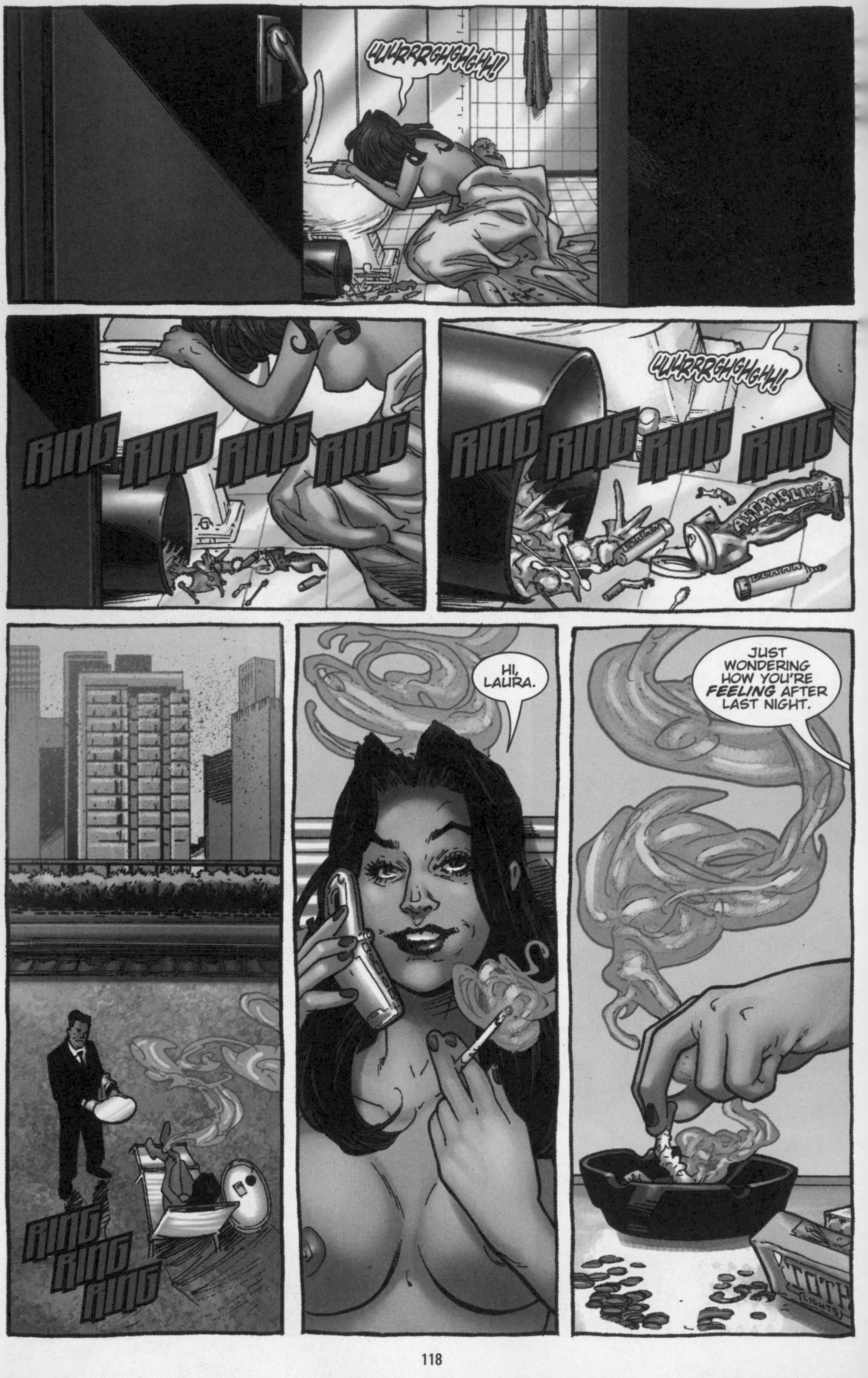
UUURRRGHGHGHH!!
RING RING RING RING
UUURRRGHGHGHH!!
RING RING RING RING
RING RING RING
HI, LAURA.
JUST WONDERING HOW YOU'RE FEELING AFTER LAST NIGHT.

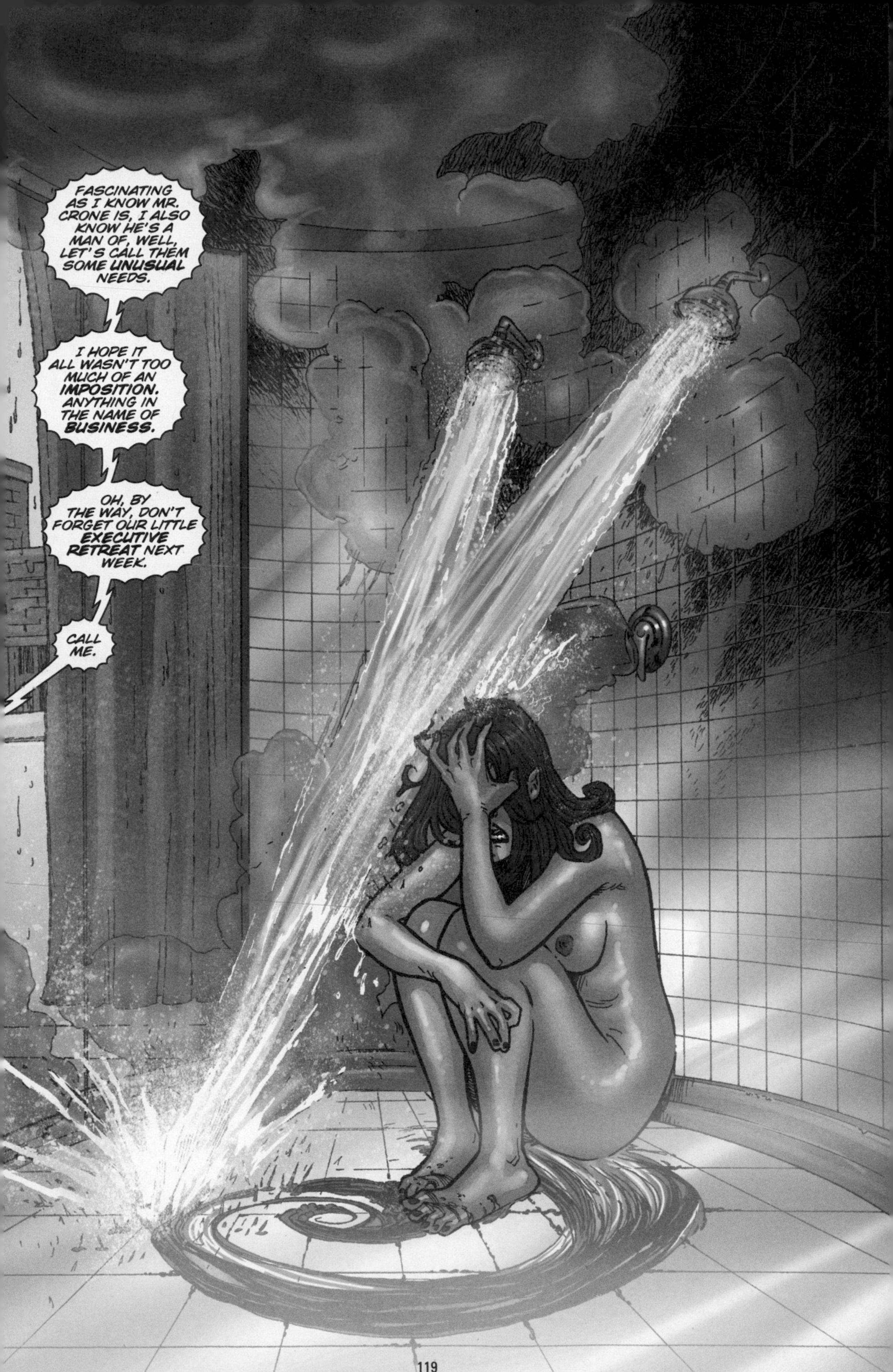
FASCINATING AS I KNOW MR. CRONE IS, I ALSO KNOW HE'S A MAN OF, WELL, LET'S CALL THEM SOME UNUSUAL NEEDS.
I HOPE IT ALL WASN'T TOO MUCH OF AN IMPOSITION. ANYTHING IN THE NAME OF BUSINESS.
OH, BY THE WAY, DON'T FORGET OUR LITTLE EXECUTIVE RETREAT NEXT WEEK.
CALL ME.

CHAPTER SIX

COVER ART BY **PHILIP BOND**
INTERIOR PENCILS BY **JOHN LUCAS**
INTERIOR INKS BY **DAN GREEN**

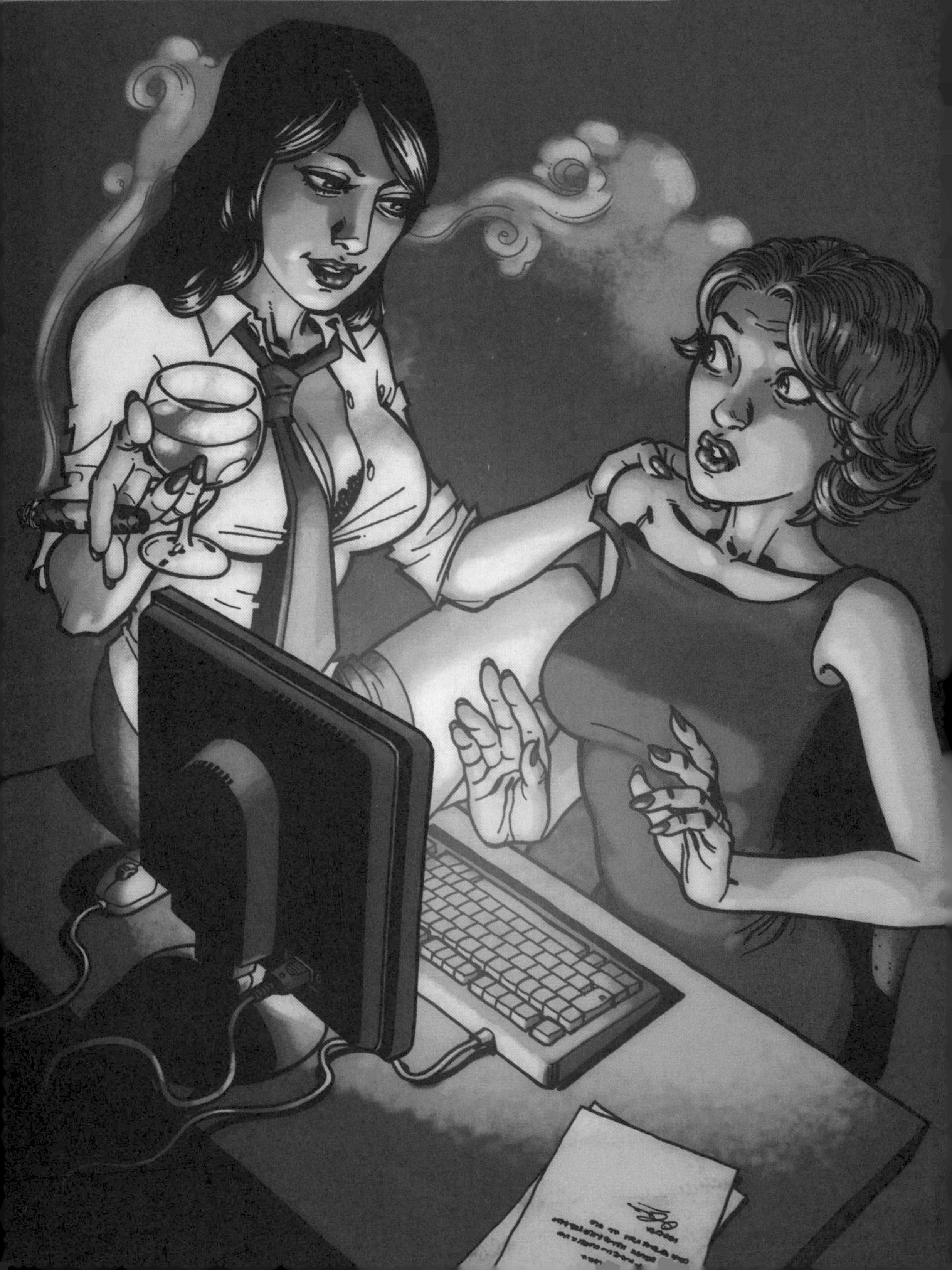

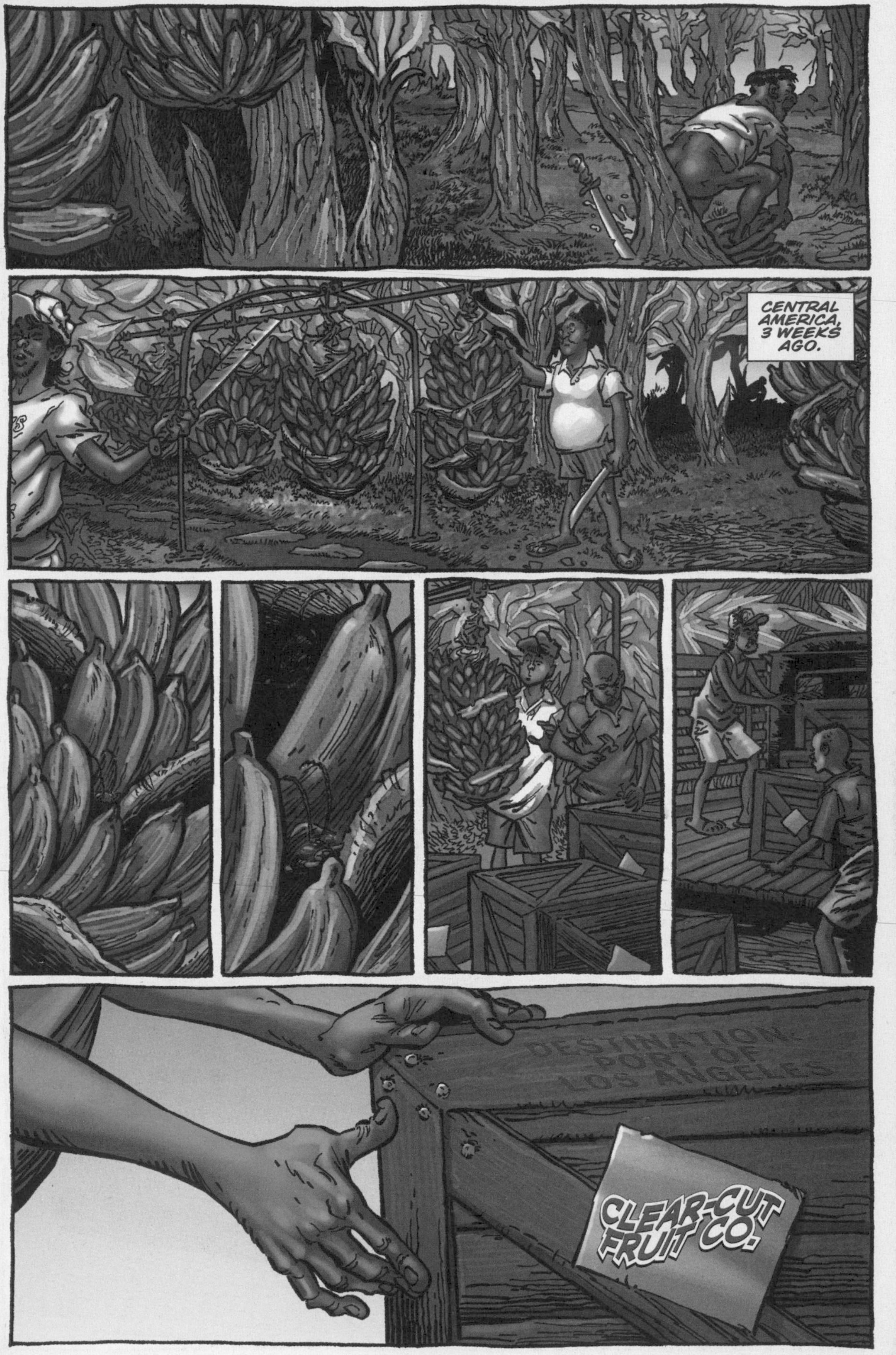
CENTRAL AMERICA, 3 WEEKS AGO.
DESTINATION: PORT OF LOS ANGELES
CLEAR-CUT FRUIT CO.

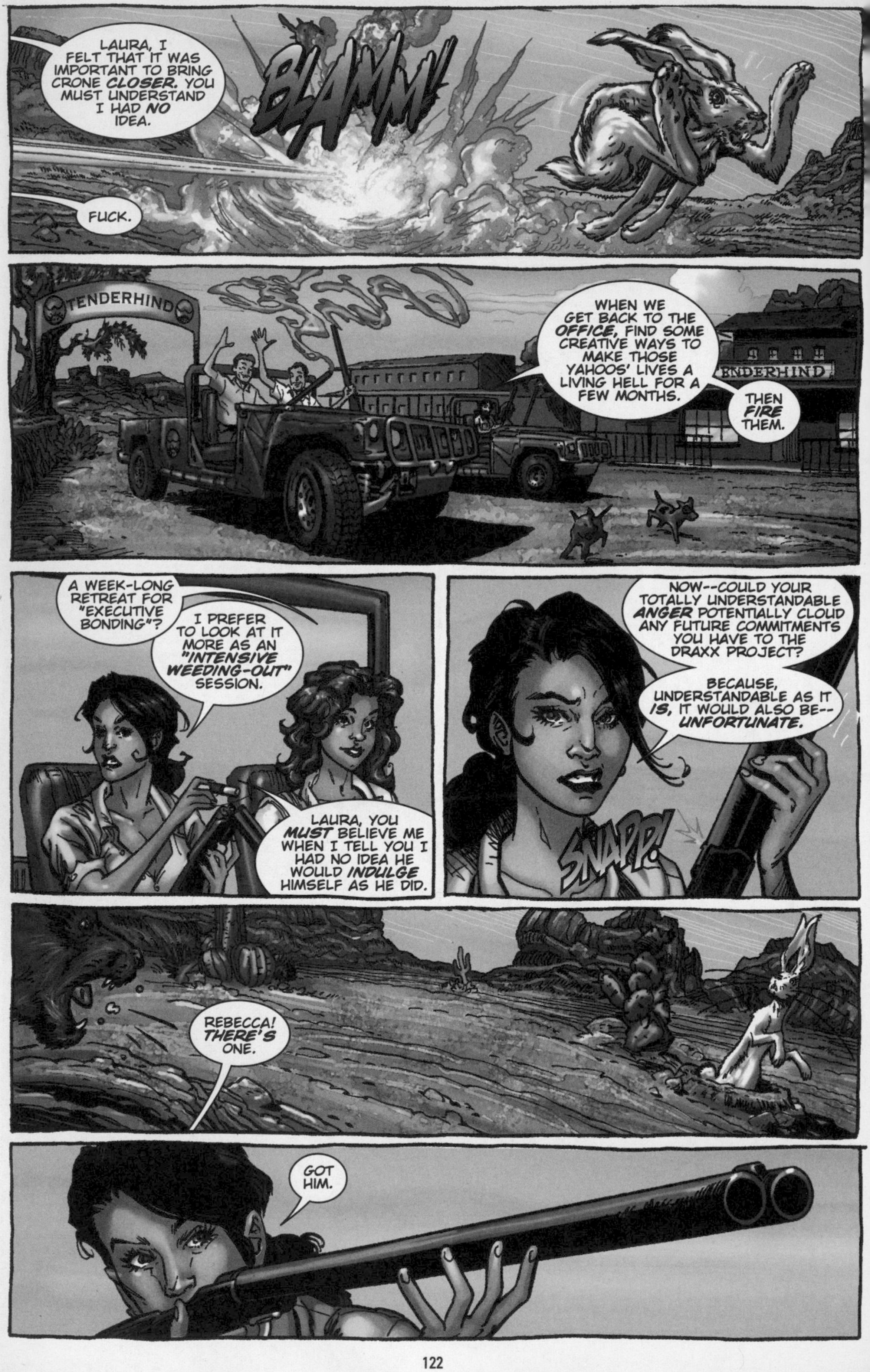
LAURA, I FELT THAT IT WAS IMPORTANT TO BRING CRONE CLOSER. YOU MUST UNDERSTAND I HAD NO IDEA.
BLAMM!
FUCK.
TENDERHIND
WHEN WE GET BACK TO THE OFFICE, FIND SOME CREATIVE WAYS TO MAKE THOSE YAHOOS' LIVES A LIVING HELL FOR A FEW MONTHS.
THEN FIRE THEM.
A WEEK-LONG RETREAT FOR "EXECUTIVE BONDING"?
I PREFER TO LOOK AT IT MORE AS AN "INTENSIVE WEEDING-OUT" SESSION.
LAURA, YOU MUST BELIEVE ME WHEN I TELL YOU I HAD NO IDEA HE WOULD INDULGE HIMSELF AS HE DID.
NOW--COULD YOUR TOTALLY UNDERSTANDABLE ANGER POTENTIALLY CLOUD ANY FUTURE COMMITMENTS YOU HAVE TO THE DRAXX PROJECT?
BECAUSE, UNDERSTANDABLE AS IT IS, IT WOULD ALSO BE-- UNFORTUNATE.
SNAPP!
REBECCA! THERE'S ONE.
GOT HIM.

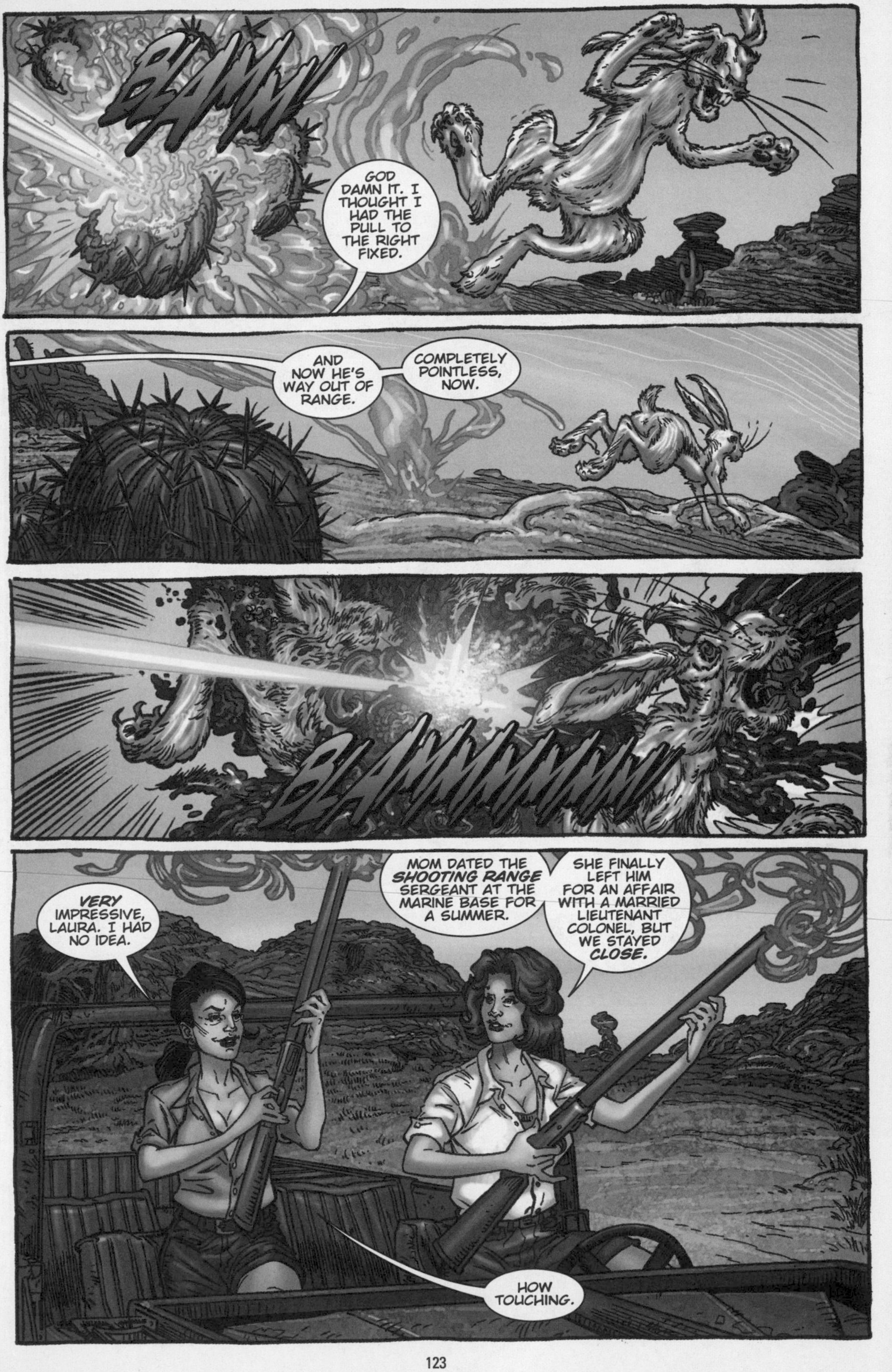
BLAMMM!
GOD DAMN IT. I THOUGHT I HAD THE PULL TO THE RIGHT FIXED.
AND NOW HE'S WAY OUT OF RANGE.
COMPLETELY POINTLESS, NOW.
BLAMMMMMMM!
VERY IMPRESSIVE, LAURA. I HAD NO IDEA.
MOM DATED THE SHOOTING RANGE SERGEANT AT THE MARINE BASE FOR A SUMMER.
SHE FINALLY LEFT HIM FOR AN AFFAIR WITH A MARRIED LIEUTENANT COLONEL, BUT WE STAYED CLOSE.
HOW TOUCHING.

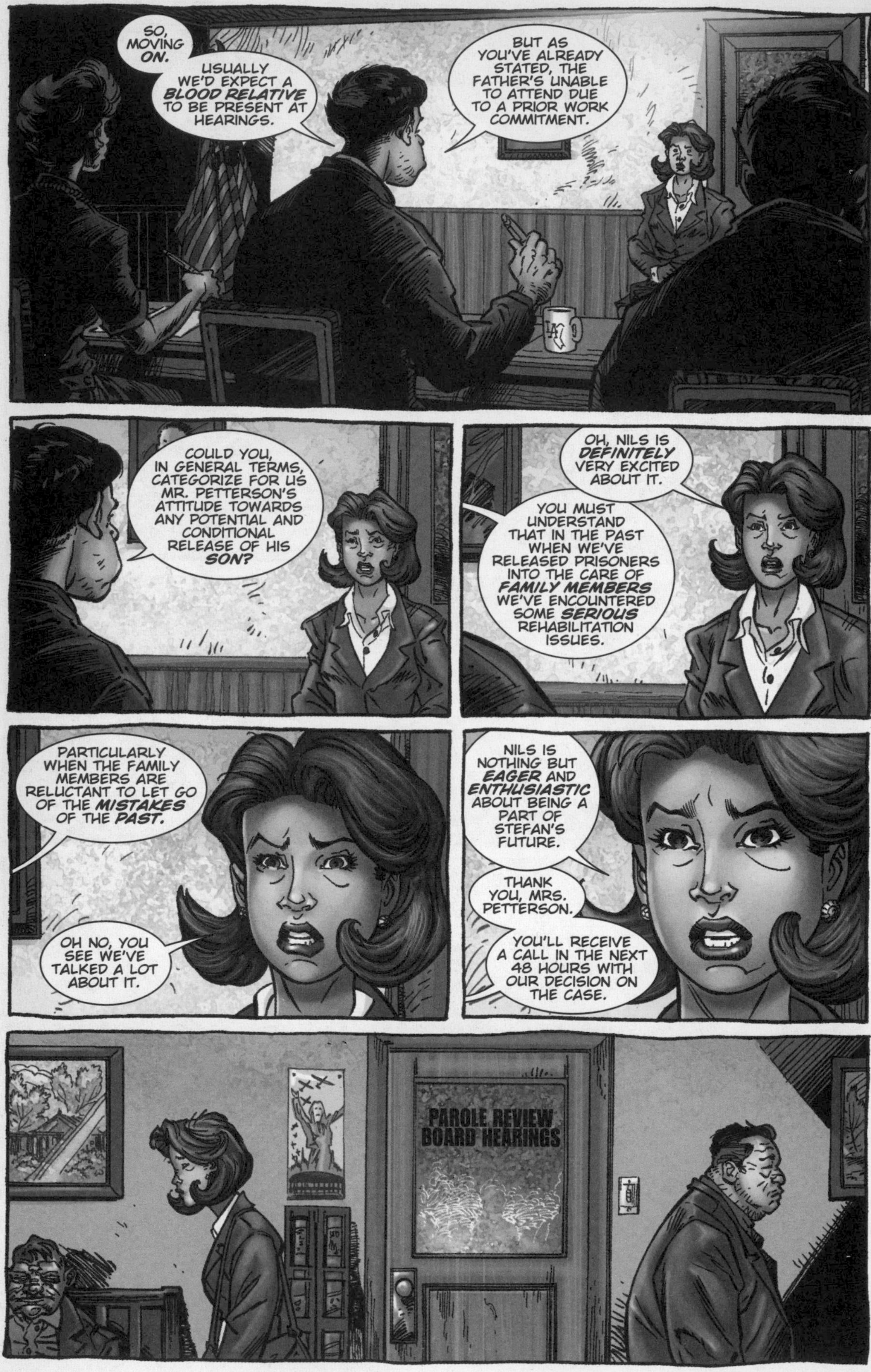

SO, MOVING ON.
USUALLY WE'D EXPECT A BLOOD RELATIVE TO BE PRESENT AT HEARINGS.
BUT AS YOU'VE ALREADY STATED, THE FATHER'S UNABLE TO ATTEND DUE TO A PRIOR WORK COMMITMENT.
COULD YOU, IN GENERAL TERMS, CATEGORIZE FOR US MR. PETTERSON'S ATTITUDE TOWARDS ANY POTENTIAL AND CONDITIONAL RELEASE OF HIS SON?
OH, NILS IS DEFINITELY VERY EXCITED ABOUT IT.
YOU MUST UNDERSTAND THAT IN THE PAST WHEN WE'VE RELEASED PRISONERS INTO THE CARE OF FAMILY MEMBERS WE'VE ENCOUNTERED SOME SERIOUS REHABILITATION ISSUES.
PARTICULARLY WHEN THE FAMILY MEMBERS ARE RELUCTANT TO LET GO OF THE MISTAKES OF THE PAST.
OH NO, YOU SEE WE'VE TALKED A LOT ABOUT IT.
NILS IS NOTHING BUT EAGER AND ENTHUSIASTIC ABOUT BEING A PART OF STEFAN'S FUTURE.
THANK YOU, MRS. PETTERSON.
YOU'LL RECEIVE A CALL IN THE NEXT 48 HOURS WITH OUR DECISION ON THE CASE.
PAROLE REVIEW BOARD HEARINGS

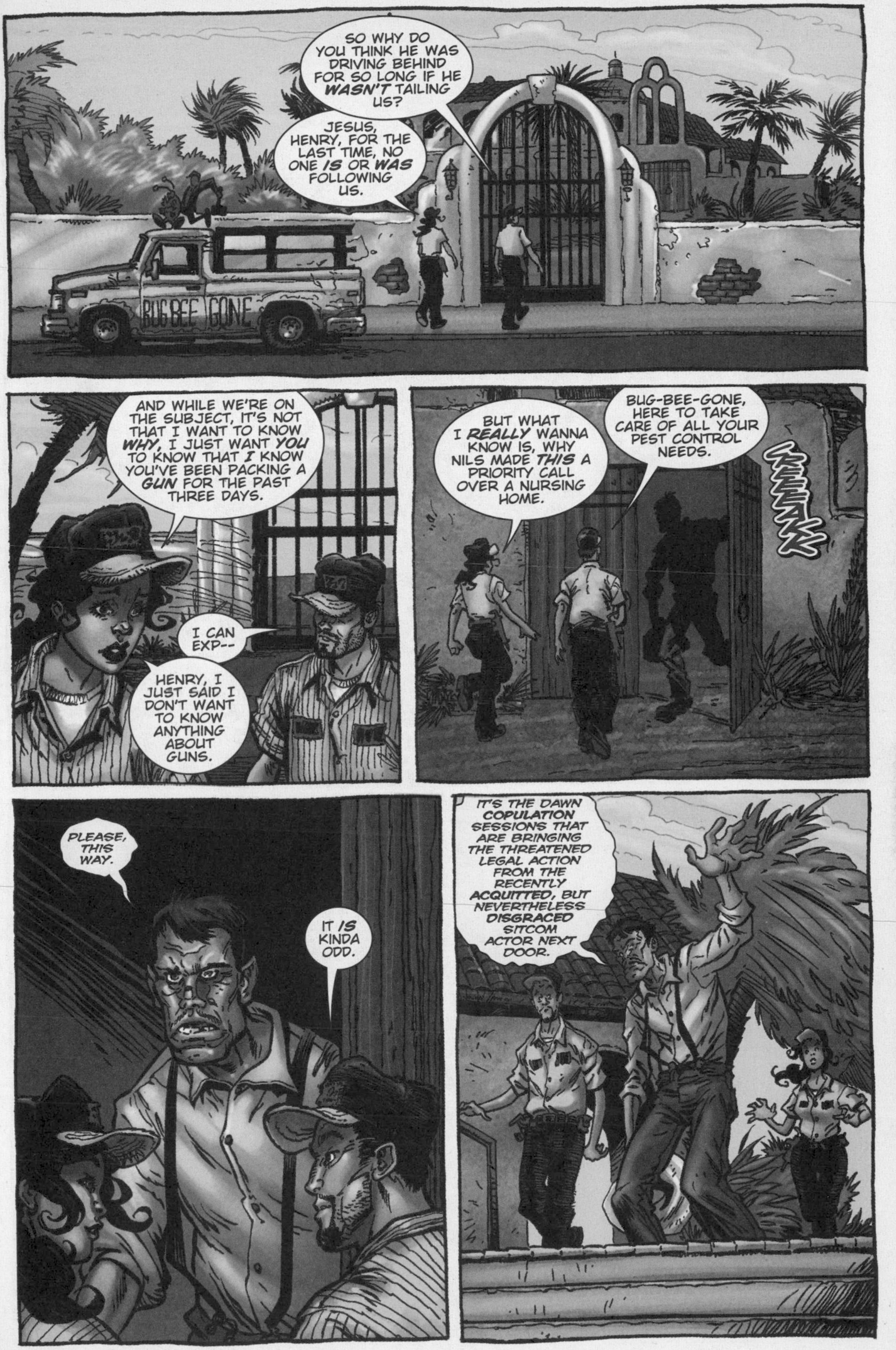
SO WHY DO YOU THINK HE WAS DRIVING BEHIND FOR SO LONG IF HE WASN'T TAILING US?
JESUS, HENRY, FOR THE LAST TIME, NO ONE IS OR WAS FOLLOWING US.
BUG BEE GONE
AND WHILE WE'RE ON THE SUBJECT, IT'S NOT THAT I WANT TO KNOW WHY, I JUST WANT YOU TO KNOW THAT I KNOW YOU'VE BEEN PACKING A GUN FOR THE PAST THREE DAYS.
I CAN EXP--
HENRY, I JUST SAID I DON'T WANT TO KNOW ANYTHING ABOUT GUNS.
BUT WHAT I REALLY WANNA KNOW IS, WHY NILS MADE THIS A PRIORITY CALL OVER A NURSING HOME.
BUG-BEE-GONE, HERE TO TAKE CARE OF ALL YOUR PEST CONTROL NEEDS.
CREEEAKK
PLEASE, THIS WAY.
IT IS KINDA ODD.
IT'S THE DAWN COPULATION SESSIONS THAT ARE BRINGING THE THREATENED LEGAL ACTION FROM THE RECENTLY ACQUITTED, BUT NEVERTHELESS DISGRACED SITCOM ACTOR NEXT DOOR.

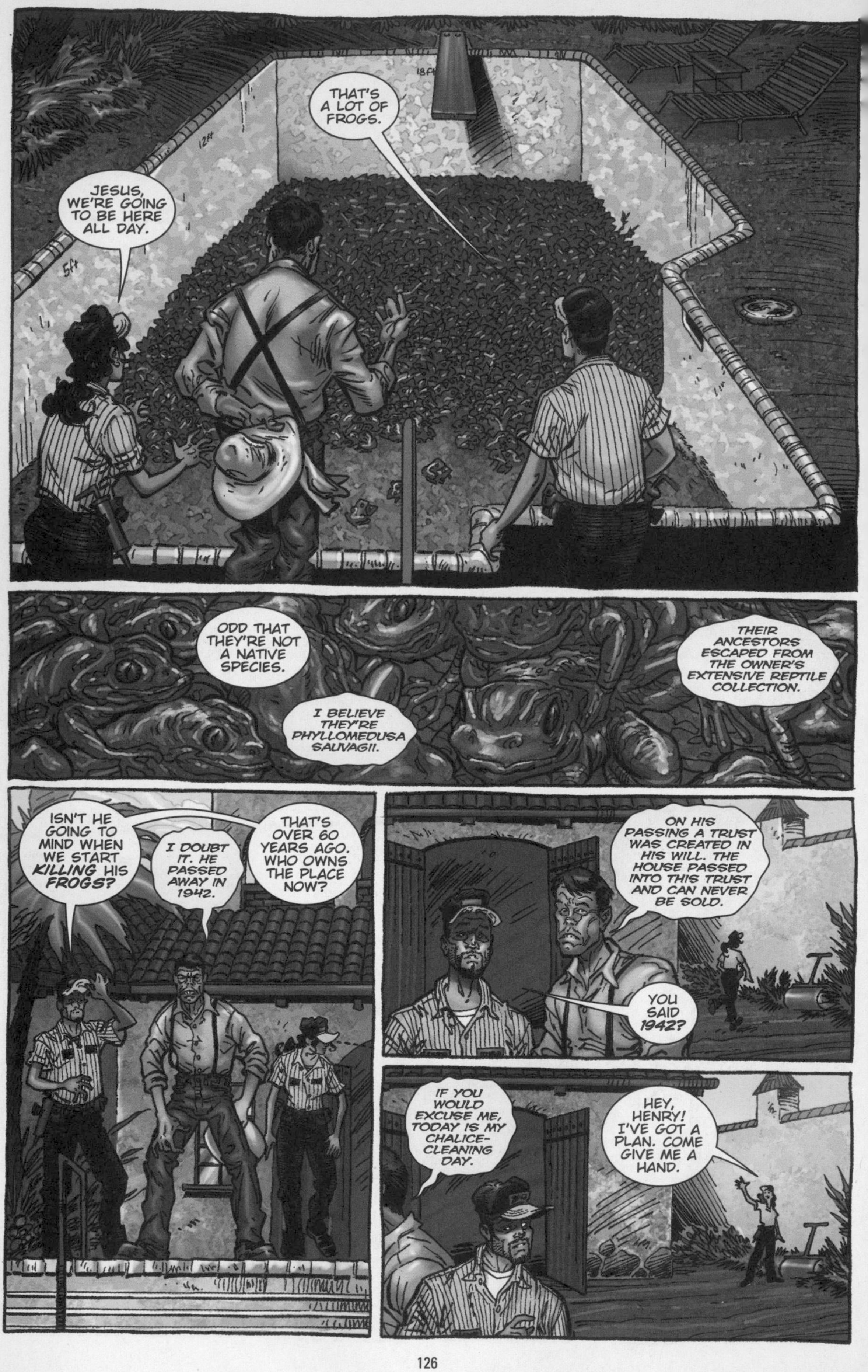
18ft
12ft
5ft
JESUS, WE'RE GOING TO BE HERE ALL DAY.
THAT'S A LOT OF FROGS.
ODD THAT THEY'RE NOT A NATIVE SPECIES.
I BELIEVE THEY'RE PHYLLOMEDUSA SAUVAGII.
THEIR ANCESTORS ESCAPED FROM THE OWNER'S EXTENSIVE REPTILE COLLECTION.
ISN'T HE GOING TO MIND WHEN WE START KILLING HIS FROGS?
I DOUBT IT. HE PASSED AWAY IN 1942.
THAT'S OVER 60 YEARS AGO. WHO OWNS THE PLACE NOW?
ON HIS PASSING A TRUST WAS CREATED IN HIS WILL. THE HOUSE PASSED INTO THIS TRUST AND CAN NEVER BE SOLD.
YOU SAID 1942?
IF YOU WOULD EXCUSE ME, TODAY IS MY CHALICE-CLEANING DAY.
HEY, HENRY! I'VE GOT A PLAN. COME GIVE ME A HAND.

SO WHADDA YOU RECKON, HENRY?

I'LL GET US OUT OF THIS CREEPY JOINT AND BACK OUT ON THE ROAD IN NO TIME.

5ft.

SPLORSH

I'VE BEEN MEANING TO ASK YOU SOMETHING, HENRY.

SQUISH

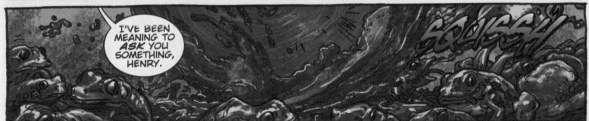

YOU GOT ANY SINGLE MALE FRIENDS? YOU KNOW, WHO MAYBE AREN'T TOO WEIRD?

WHAT THE FUCK--?

SORRY, JUST THOUGHT I'D ASK.

--IS THAT?

IT CAN'T BE.

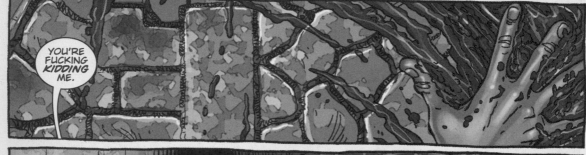

YOU'RE FUCKING KIDDING ME.

WHAT *IS* THAT?

WHAT BOX?

IT'S THE KEY-- THE KEY FROM THE BOX.

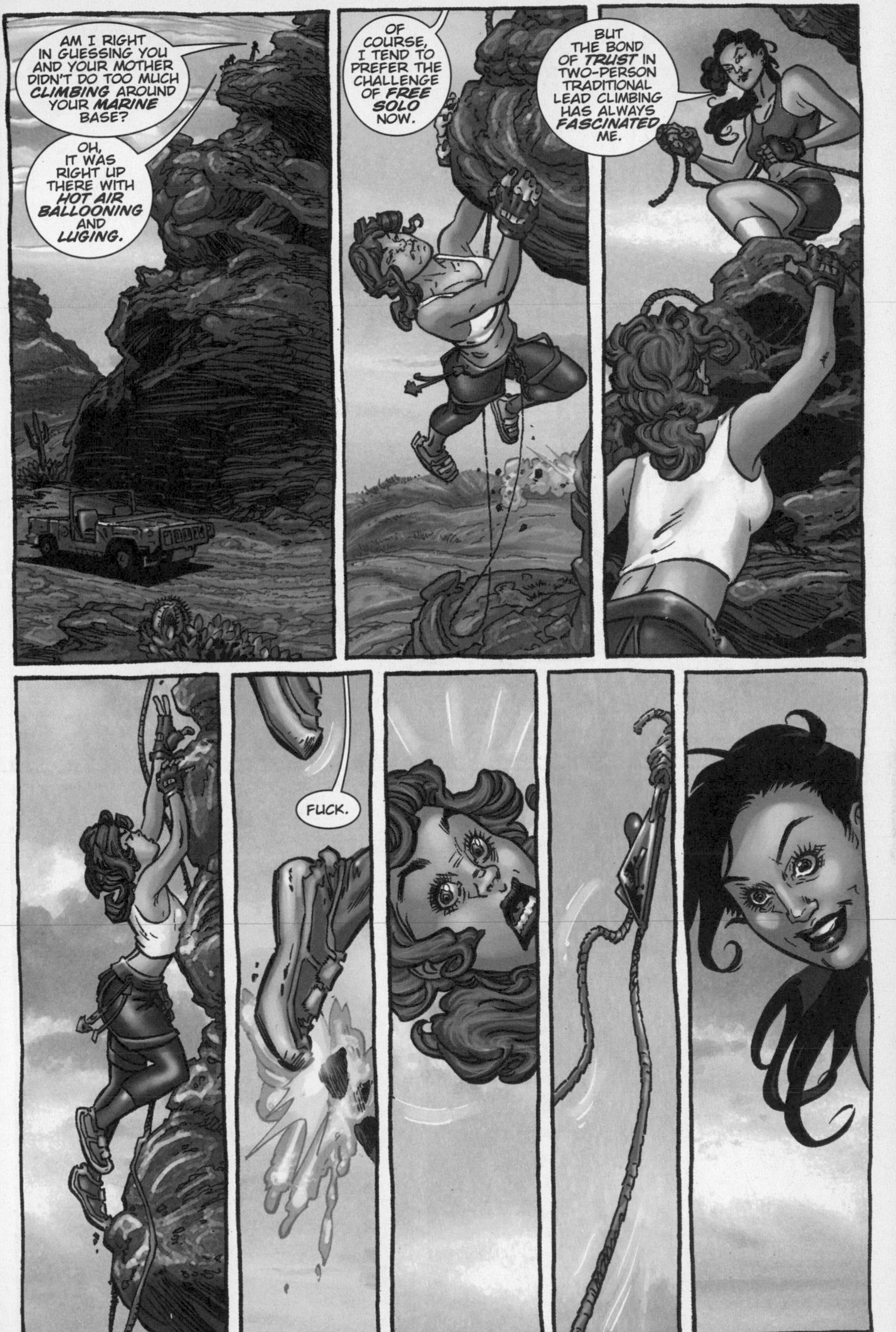
AM I RIGHT IN GUESSING YOU AND YOUR MOTHER DIDN'T DO TOO MUCH CLIMBING AROUND YOUR MARINE BASE?
OH, IT WAS RIGHT UP THERE WITH HOT AIR BALLOONING AND LUGING.
OF COURSE, I TEND TO PREFER THE CHALLENGE OF FREE SOLO NOW.
BUT THE BOND OF TRUST IN TWO-PERSON TRADITIONAL LEAD CLIMBING HAS ALWAYS FASCINATED ME.
FUCK.

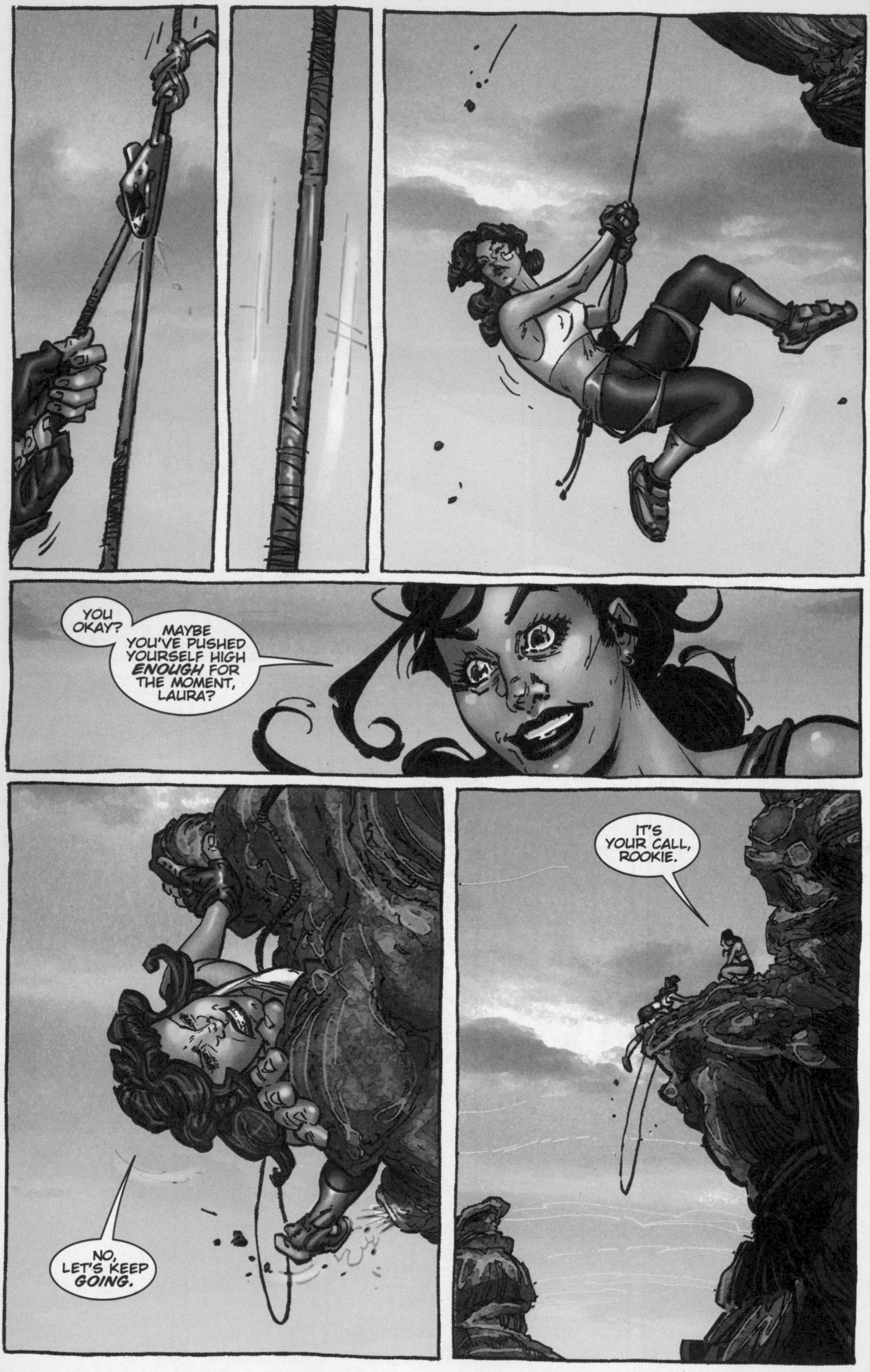
YOU OKAY?
MAYBE YOU'VE PUSHED YOURSELF HIGH ENOUGH FOR THE MOMENT, LAURA?
NO, LET'S KEEP GOING.
IT'S YOUR CALL, ROOKIE.

YOU DIDN'T *DOUBT* I'D STOP YOUR FALL BACK THERE, DID YOU?

WHY, SHOULD I HAVE?

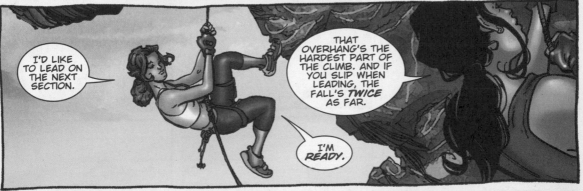

I'D LIKE TO LEAD ON THE NEXT SECTION.

THAT OVERHANG'S THE HARDEST PART OF THE CLIMB. AND IF YOU SLIP WHEN LEADING, THE FALL'S *TWICE* AS FAR.

I'M *READY*.

SECURE. WHENEVER YOU'RE READY, REBECCA.

ON MY WAY.

SHLLP

FIPT

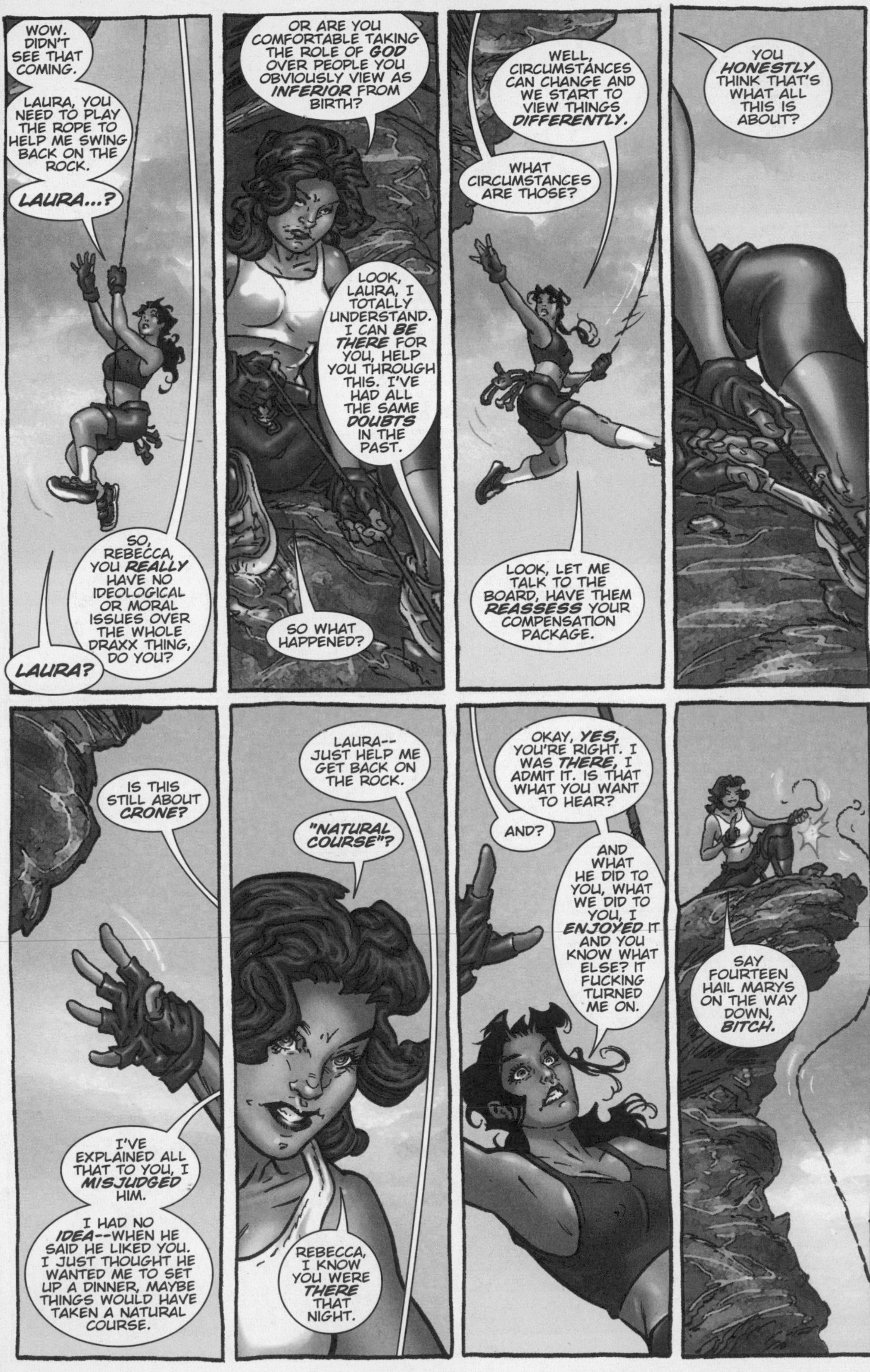
WOW. DIDN'T SEE THAT COMING.
LAURA, YOU NEED TO PLAY THE ROPE TO HELP ME SWING BACK ON THE ROCK.
LAURA...?
SO, REBECCA, YOU REALLY HAVE NO IDEOLOGICAL OR MORAL ISSUES OVER THE WHOLE DRAXX THING, DO YOU?
LAURA?
OR ARE YOU COMFORTABLE TAKING THE ROLE OF GOD OVER PEOPLE YOU OBVIOUSLY VIEW AS INFERIOR FROM BIRTH?
LOOK, LAURA, I TOTALLY UNDERSTAND. I CAN BE THERE FOR YOU, HELP YOU THROUGH THIS. I'VE HAD ALL THE SAME DOUBTS IN THE PAST.
SO WHAT HAPPENED?
WELL, CIRCUMSTANCES CAN CHANGE AND WE START TO VIEW THINGS DIFFERENTLY.
WHAT CIRCUMSTANCES ARE THOSE?
LOOK, LET ME TALK TO THE BOARD, HAVE THEM REASSESS YOUR COMPENSATION PACKAGE.
YOU HONESTLY THINK THAT'S WHAT ALL THIS IS ABOUT?
IS THIS STILL ABOUT CRONE?
I'VE EXPLAINED ALL THAT TO YOU, I MISJUDGED HIM.
I HAD NO IDEA--WHEN HE SAID HE LIKED YOU. I JUST THOUGHT HE WANTED ME TO SET UP A DINNER, MAYBE THINGS WOULD HAVE TAKEN A NATURAL COURSE.
LAURA-- JUST HELP ME GET BACK ON THE ROCK.
"NATURAL COURSE"?
REBECCA, I KNOW YOU WERE THERE THAT NIGHT.
OKAY, YES, YOU'RE RIGHT. I WAS THERE, I ADMIT IT. IS THAT WHAT YOU WANT TO HEAR?
AND?
AND WHAT HE DID TO YOU, WHAT WE DID TO YOU, I ENJOYED IT AND YOU KNOW WHAT ELSE? IT FUCKING TURNED ME ON.
SAY FOURTEEN HAIL MARYS ON THE WAY DOWN, BITCH.

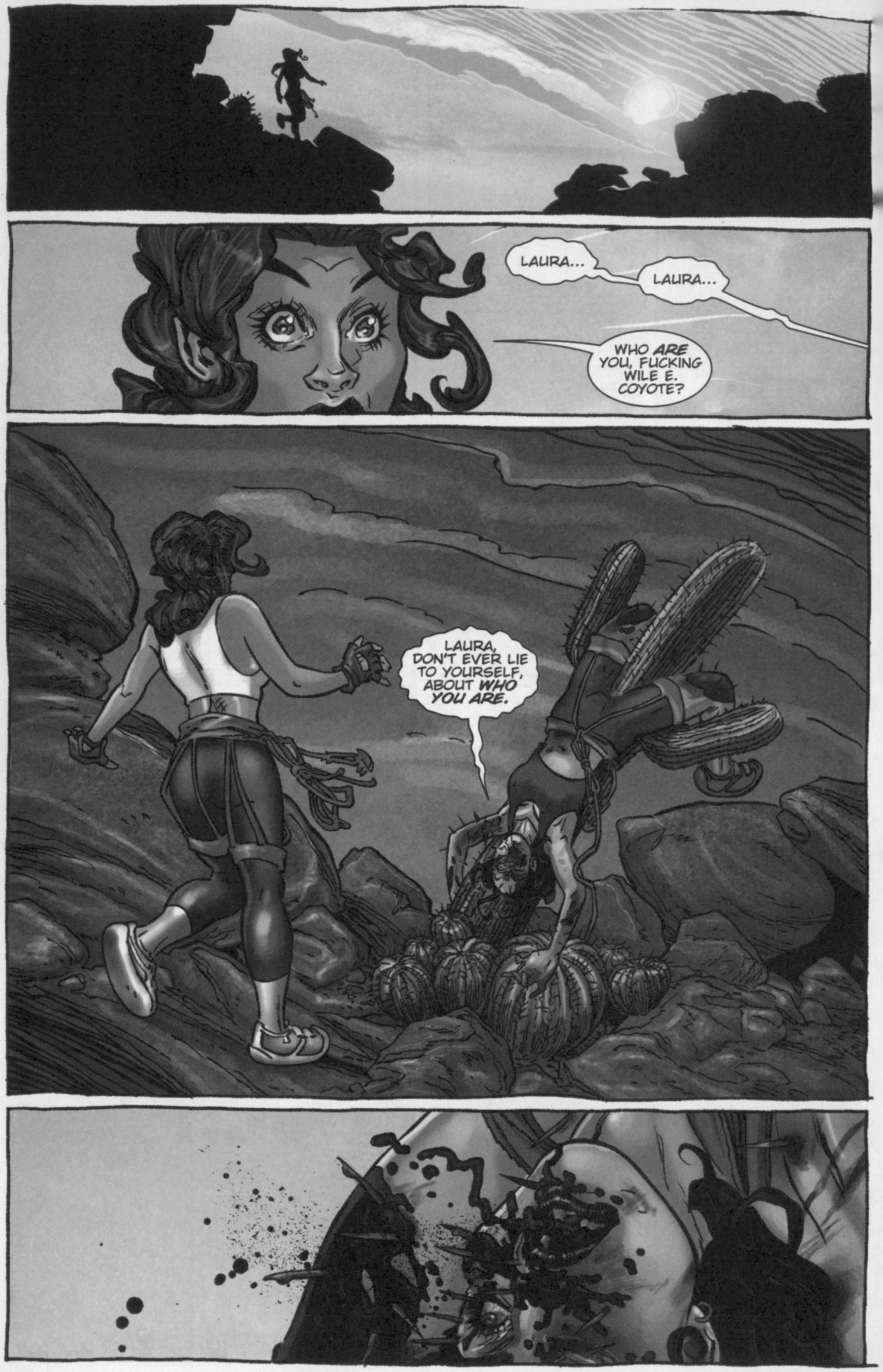
LAURA...
LAURA...
WHO ARE YOU, FUCKING WILE E. COYOTE?
LAURA, DON'T EVER LIE TO YOURSELF, ABOUT WHO YOU ARE.

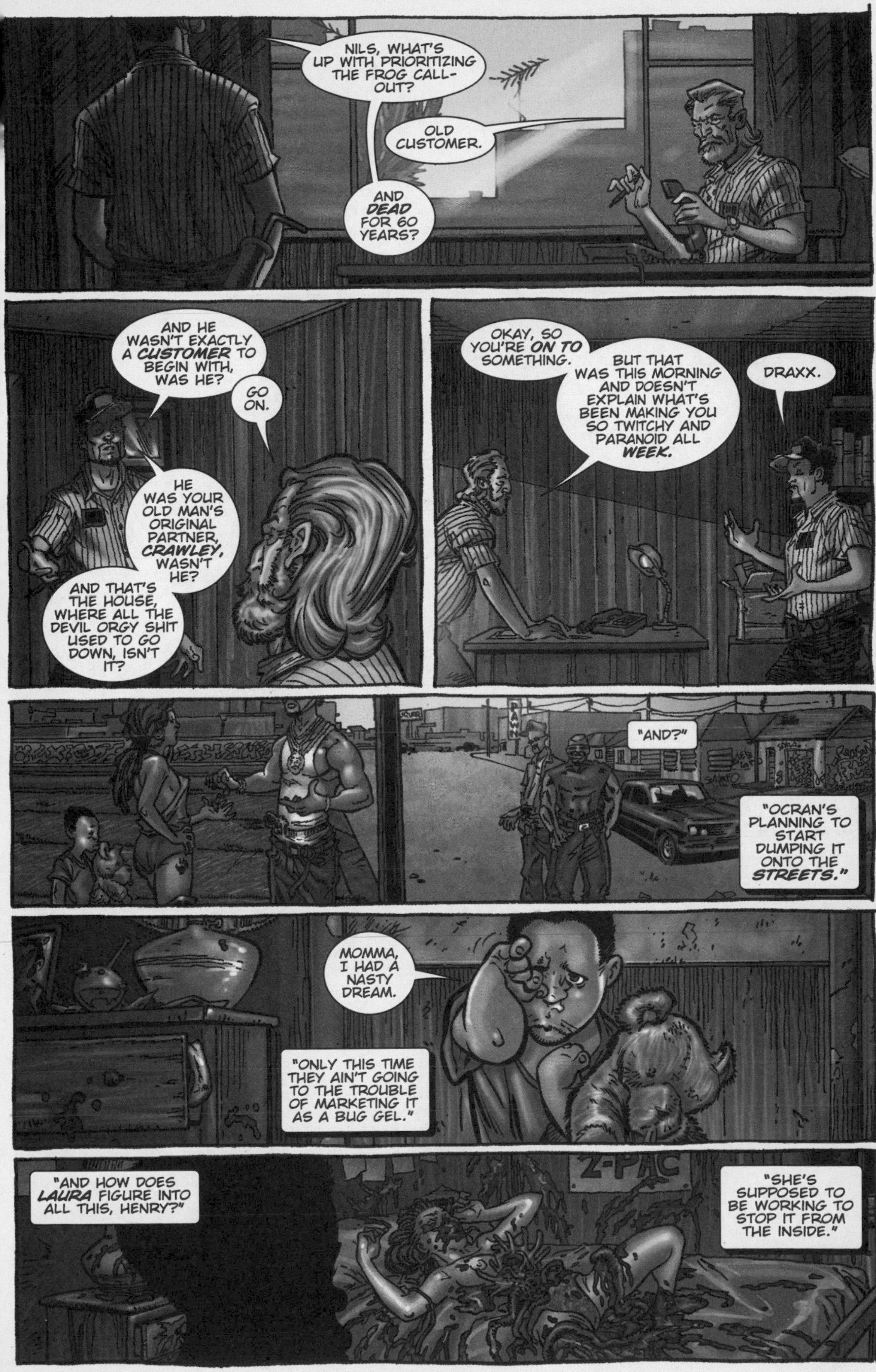
NILS, WHAT'S UP WITH PRIORITIZING THE FROG CALL-OUT?
OLD CUSTOMER.
AND DEAD FOR 60 YEARS?
AND HE WASN'T EXACTLY A CUSTOMER TO BEGIN WITH, WAS HE?
GO ON.
HE WAS YOUR OLD MAN'S ORIGINAL PARTNER, CRAWLEY, WASN'T HE?
AND THAT'S THE HOUSE, WHERE ALL THE DEVIL ORGY SHIT USED TO GO DOWN, ISN'T IT?
OKAY, SO YOU'RE ON TO SOMETHING.
BUT THAT WAS THIS MORNING AND DOESN'T EXPLAIN WHAT'S BEEN MAKING YOU SO TWITCHY AND PARANOID ALL WEEK.
DRAXX.
"AND?"
"OCRAN'S PLANNING TO START DUMPING IT ONTO THE STREETS."
MOMMA, I HAD A NASTY DREAM.
"ONLY THIS TIME THEY AIN'T GOING TO THE TROUBLE OF MARKETING IT AS A BUG GEL."
"AND HOW DOES LAURA FIGURE INTO ALL THIS, HENRY?"
2-PAC
"SHE'S SUPPOSED TO BE WORKING TO STOP IT FROM THE INSIDE."

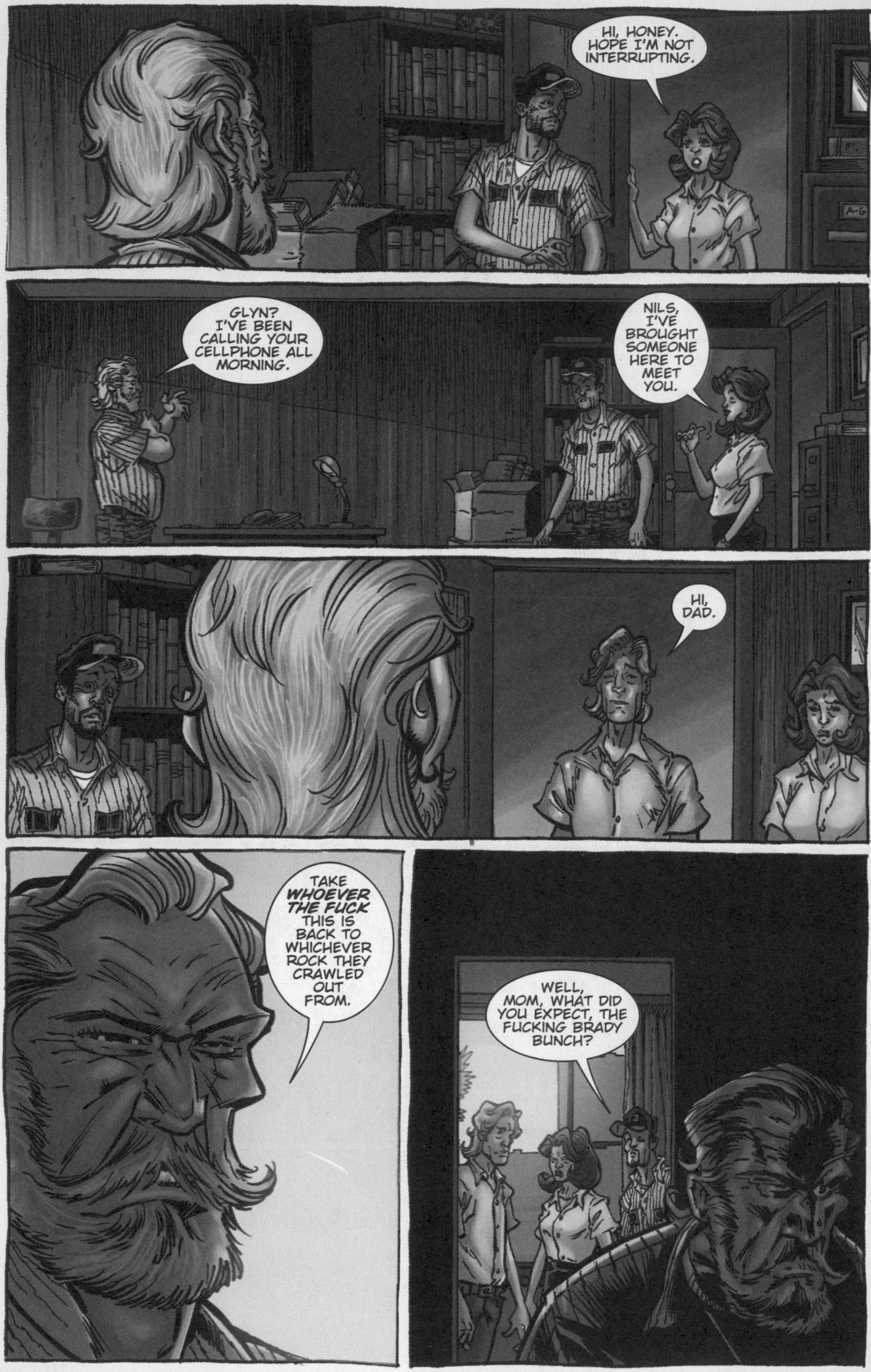
HI, HONEY. HOPE I'M NOT INTERRUPTING.
GLYN? I'VE BEEN CALLING YOUR CELLPHONE ALL MORNING.
NILS, I'VE BROUGHT SOMEONE HERE TO MEET YOU.
HI, DAD.
TAKE ***WHOEVER THE FUCK*** THIS IS BACK TO WHICHEVER ROCK THEY CRAWLED OUT FROM.
WELL, MOM, WHAT DID YOU EXPECT, THE FUCKING BRADY BUNCH?

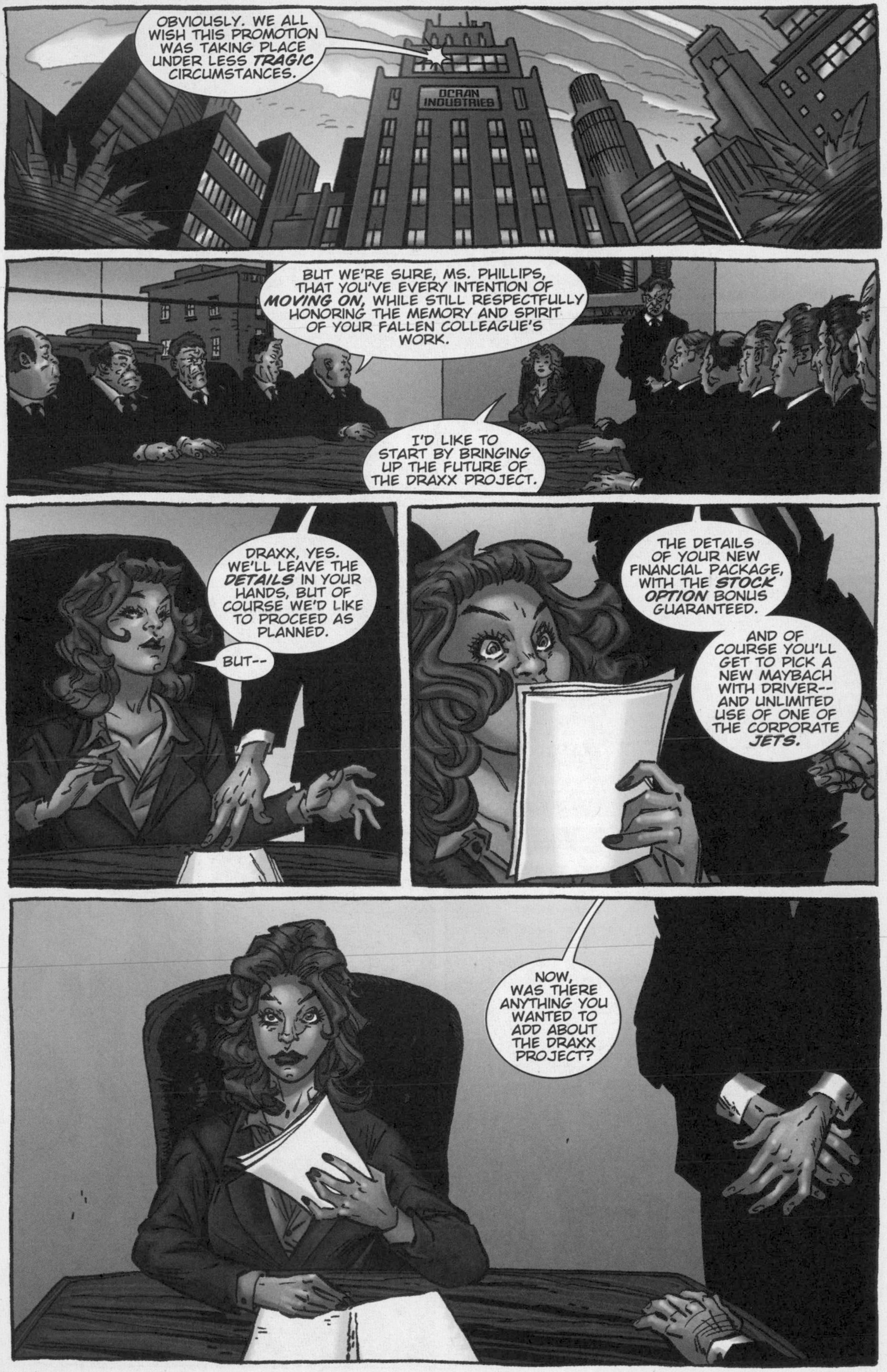
OBVIOUSLY. WE ALL WISH THIS PROMOTION WAS TAKING PLACE UNDER LESS TRAGIC CIRCUMSTANCES.
OCRAN INDUSTRIES
BUT WE'RE SURE, MS. PHILLIPS, THAT YOU'VE EVERY INTENTION OF MOVING ON, WHILE STILL RESPECTFULLY HONORING THE MEMORY AND SPIRIT OF YOUR FALLEN COLLEAGUE'S WORK.
I'D LIKE TO START BY BRINGING UP THE FUTURE OF THE DRAXX PROJECT.
DRAXX, YES. WE'LL LEAVE THE DETAILS IN YOUR HANDS, BUT OF COURSE WE'D LIKE TO PROCEED AS PLANNED.
BUT--
THE DETAILS OF YOUR NEW FINANCIAL PACKAGE, WITH THE STOCK OPTION BONUS GUARANTEED.
AND OF COURSE YOU'LL GET TO PICK A NEW MAYBACH WITH DRIVER-- AND UNLIMITED USE OF ONE OF THE CORPORATE JETS.
NOW, WAS THERE ANYTHING YOU WANTED TO ADD ABOUT THE DRAXX PROJECT?

MS. PHILLIPS, I HAVE A CALL FROM *MR. CRONE.*

HE'D LIKE TO KNOW IF WE INTEND TO PROCEED AS PLANNED TONIGHT.

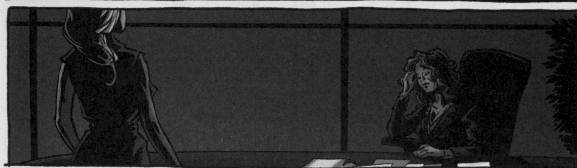

GET ME OUR PORT STORAGE FACILITY ON THE PHONE.

AND I HAVE A LITTLE JOB FOR THE *BLACK OPS* DEPARTMENT.

WE CAN DROP ALL THE PRETENSE OVER ITS *EXISTENCE.*

THERE'S AN *ADDRESS BOOK* I NEED RETRIEVED.

OH, AND HAVE THE *JET* PUT ON STANDBY.

DESTINATION?

NO, I JUST WANT TO TAKE IT UP FOR A RIDE.

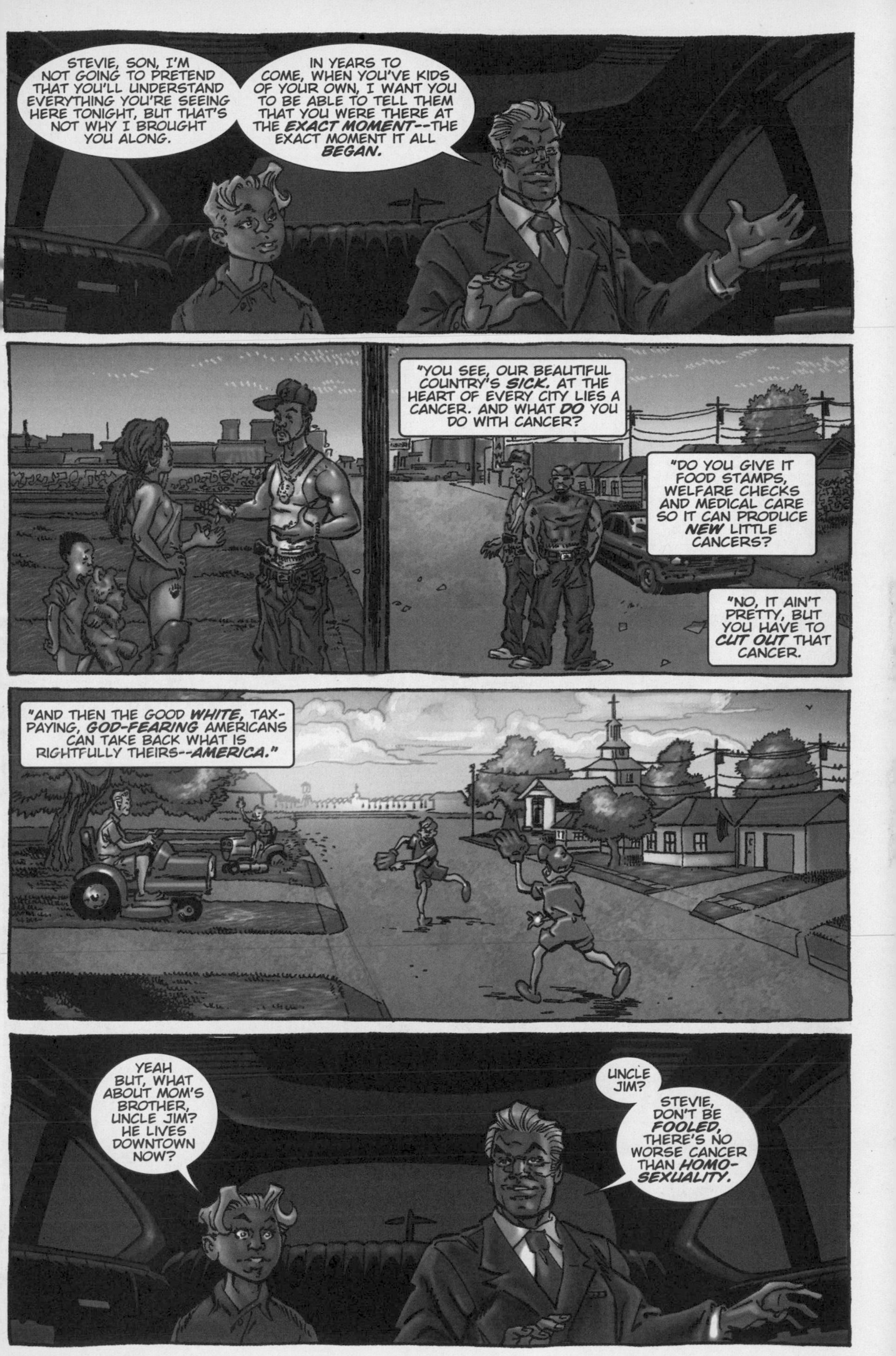
STEVIE, SON, I'M NOT GOING TO PRETEND THAT YOU'LL UNDERSTAND EVERYTHING YOU'RE SEEING HERE TONIGHT, BUT THAT'S NOT WHY I BROUGHT YOU ALONG.
IN YEARS TO COME, WHEN YOU'VE KIDS OF YOUR OWN, I WANT YOU TO BE ABLE TO TELL THEM THAT YOU WERE THERE AT THE EXACT MOMENT--THE EXACT MOMENT IT ALL BEGAN.
"YOU SEE, OUR BEAUTIFUL COUNTRY'S SICK. AT THE HEART OF EVERY CITY LIES A CANCER. AND WHAT DO YOU DO WITH CANCER?
"DO YOU GIVE IT FOOD STAMPS, WELFARE CHECKS AND MEDICAL CARE SO IT CAN PRODUCE NEW LITTLE CANCERS?
"NO, IT AIN'T PRETTY, BUT YOU HAVE TO CUT OUT THAT CANCER.
"AND THEN THE GOOD WHITE, TAX-PAYING, GOD-FEARING AMERICANS CAN TAKE BACK WHAT IS RIGHTFULLY THEIRS--AMERICA."
YEAH BUT, WHAT ABOUT MOM'S BROTHER, UNCLE JIM? HE LIVES DOWNTOWN NOW?
UNCLE JIM?
STEVIE, DON'T BE FOOLED, THERE'S NO WORSE CANCER THAN HOMO-SEXUALITY.

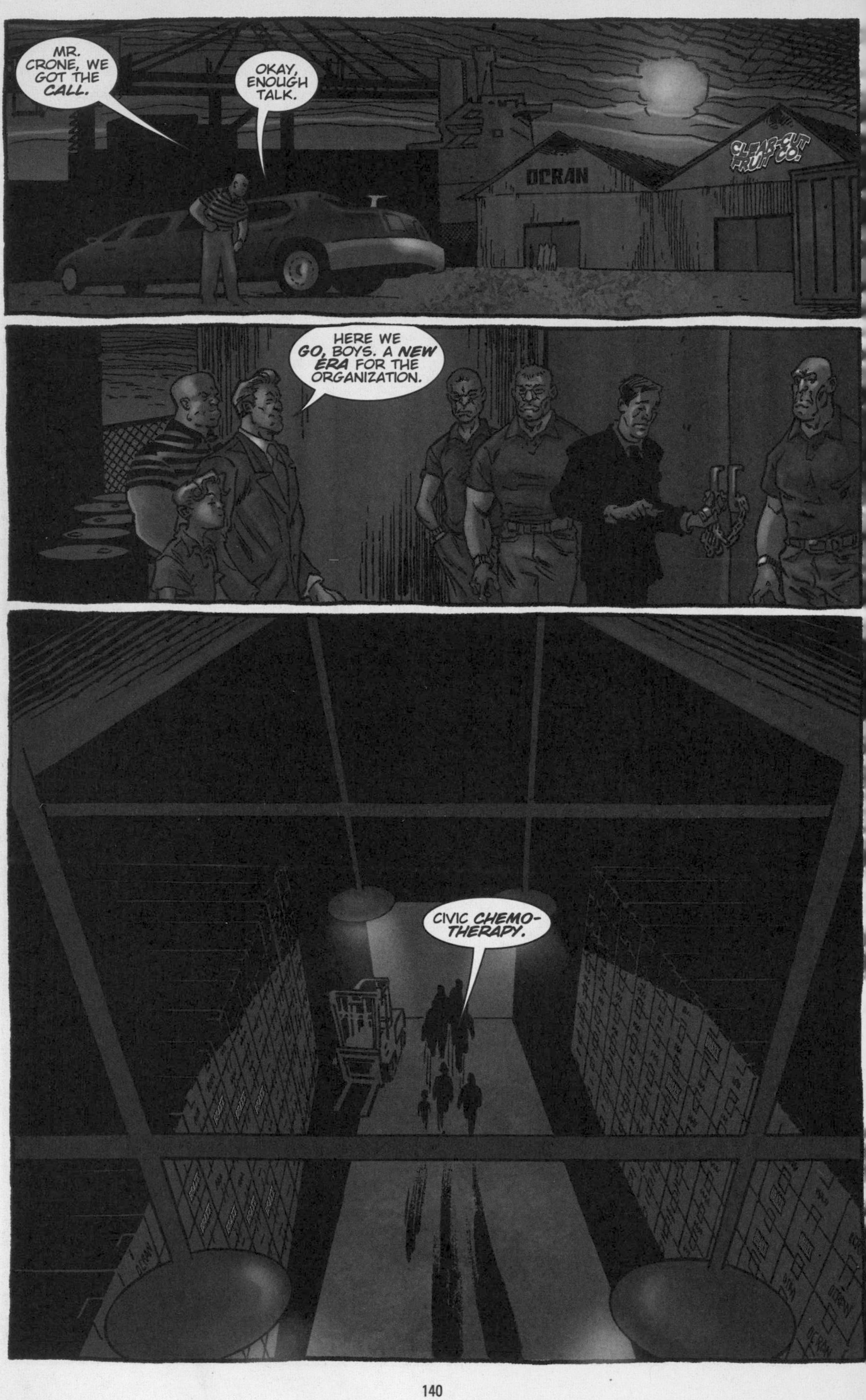
MR. CRONE, WE GOT THE CALL.
OKAY, ENOUGH TALK.
OCRAN
CLEAR-CUT FRUIT CO.
HERE WE GO, BOYS. A NEW ERA FOR THE ORGANIZATION.
CIVIC CHEMO-THERAPY.

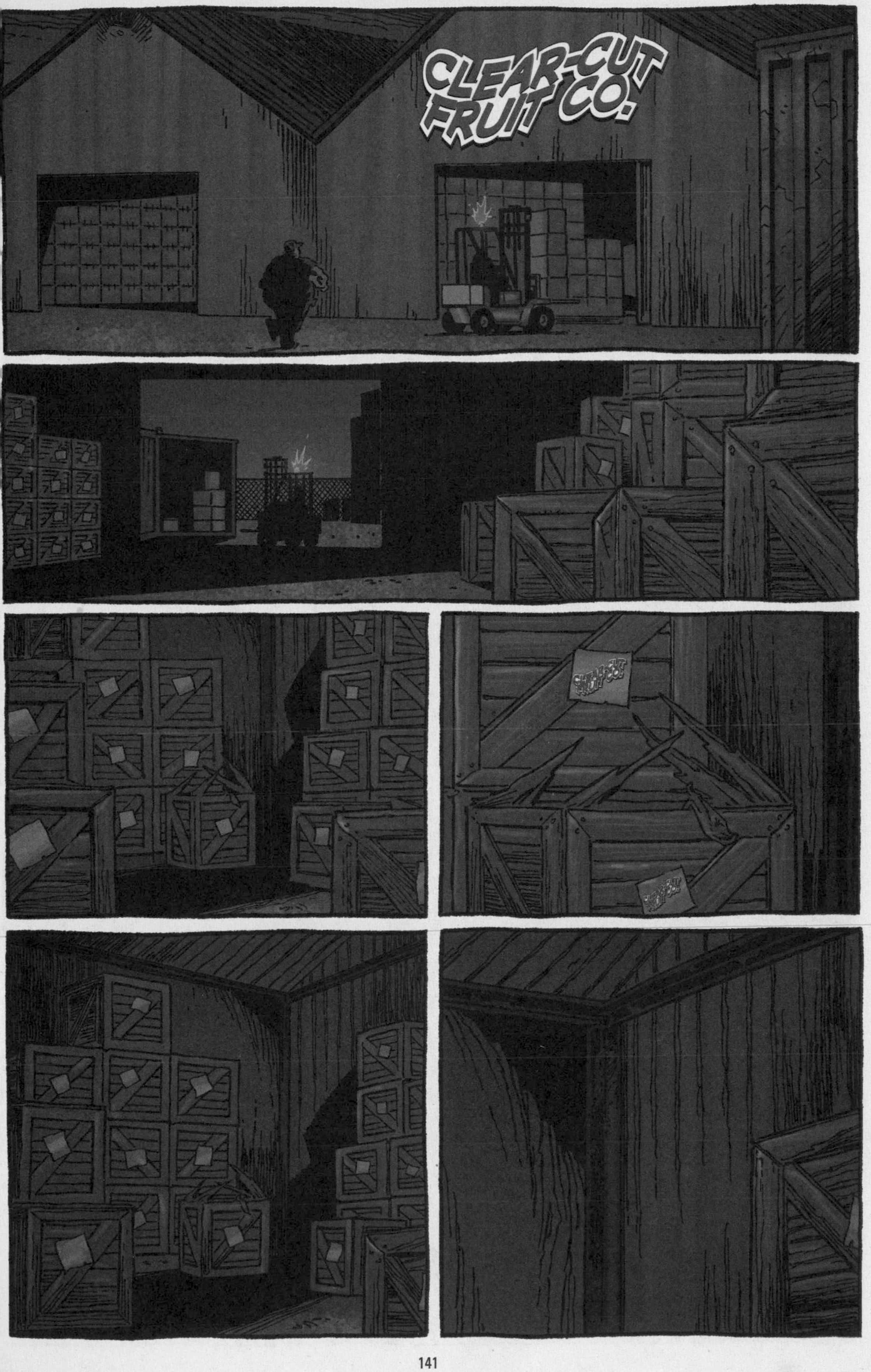
CLEAR-CUT FRUIT CO.

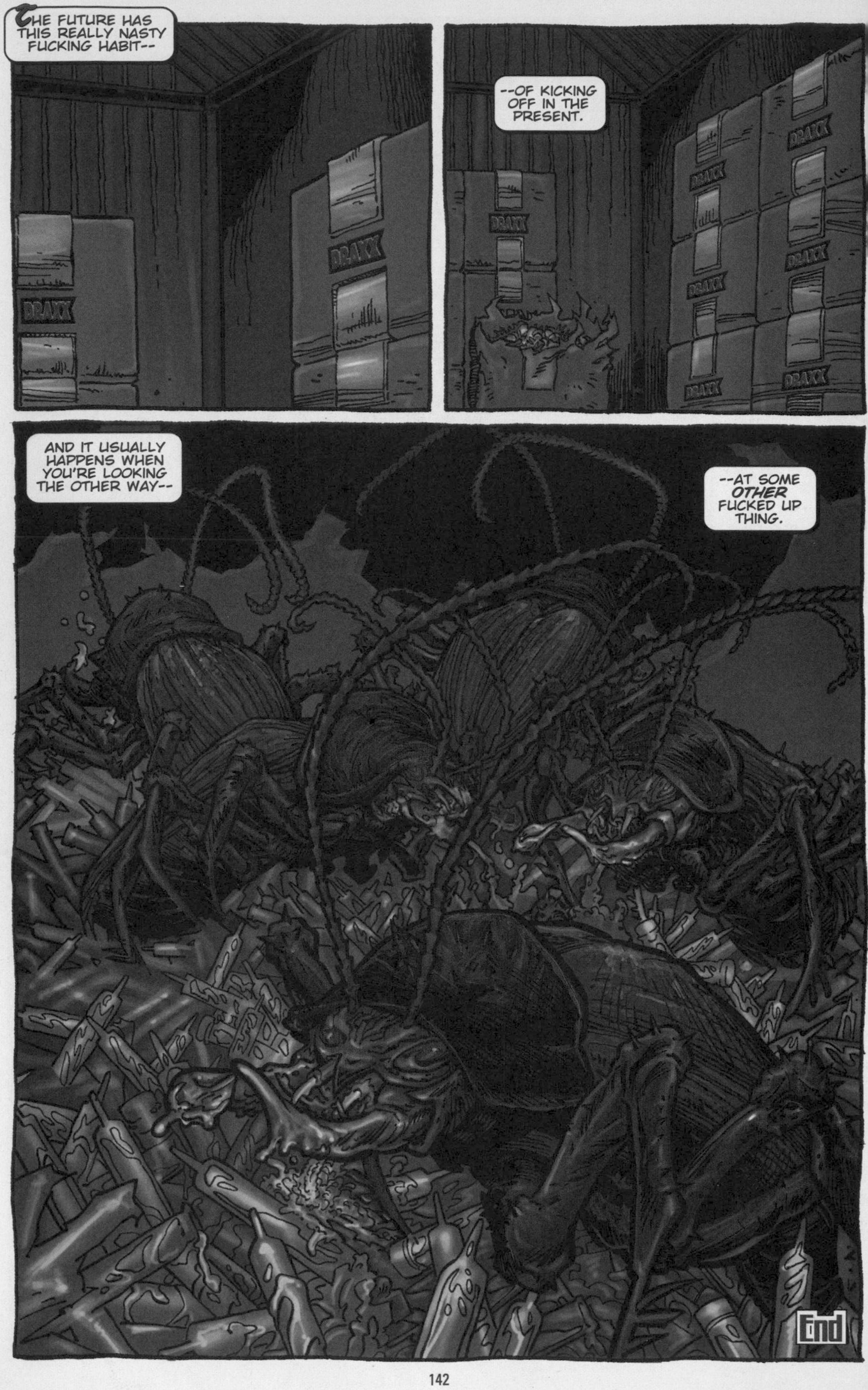
THE FUTURE HAS THIS REALLY NASTY FUCKING HABIT--
--OF KICKING OFF IN THE PRESENT.
DRAXX
AND IT USUALLY HAPPENS WHEN YOU'RE LOOKING THE OTHER WAY--
--AT SOME *OTHER* FUCKED UP THING.
End

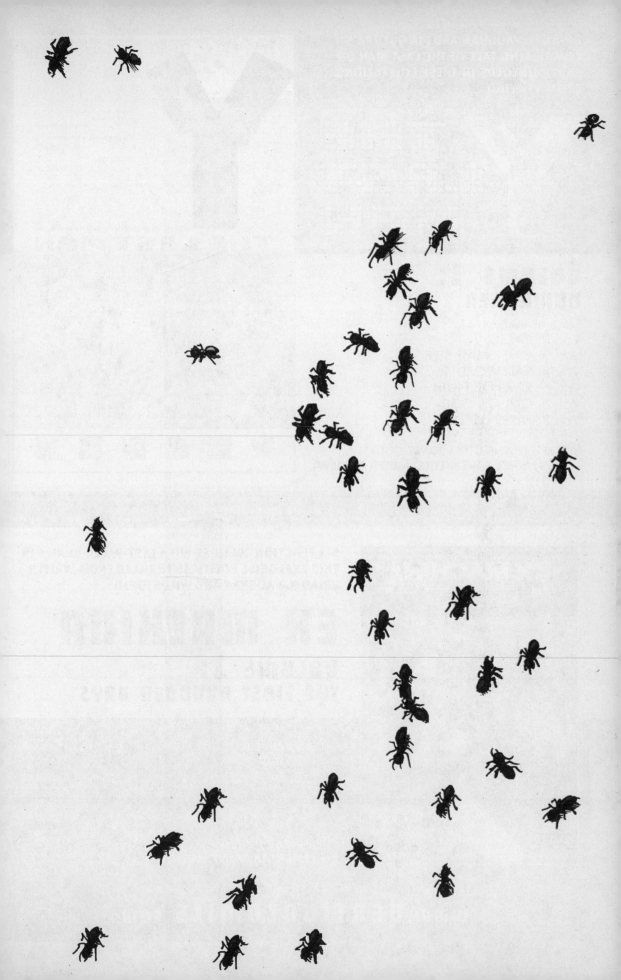

BRIAN K. V
COMPELLI
EARTH UN
FROM VER

Y THE LAST MAN

VERTIGO
BOOK 1
"This is why God created comic books."
— RevolutionSF.com
"This book blew us away."
— WIZARD
Brian K. Vaughan Pia Guerra José Marzán, Jr.
THE LAST MAN
Unmanned

VOLUME 1: UNMANNED

ALSO AVAILABLE:

VOL. 2: CYCLES
VOL. 3: ONE SMALL STEP
VOL. 4: SAFEWORD
VOL. 5: RING OF TRUTH
VOL. 6: GIRL ON GIRL
VOL. 7: PAPER DOLLS

"COMPLETE AND UTTER COMIC GOLD."
— *PUBLISHERS WEEKLY* (STARRED REVIEW)

EX MACHINA
THE FIRST HUNDRED DAYS
BRIAN K. VAUGHAN TONY HARRIS TOM FEISTER

SCI-FI ACTION COLLIDES WITH FAST-PACED DRAMA IN THIS EXPLOSIVE POLITICAL THRILLER FROM WRITER BRIAN K. VAUGHAN AND WILDSTORM:

EX MACHINA

VOLUME 1: THE FIRST HUNDRED DAYS

ALSO AVAILABLE:

VOL. 2: TAG
VOL. 3: FACT V. FICTION

"TERRIFICALLY INTRIGUING."
— *ENTERTAINMENT WEEKLY*

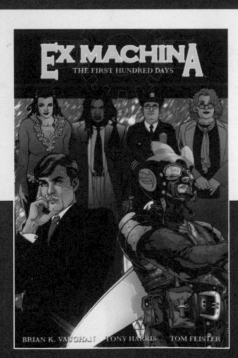